If It's A Choice, My Zygote Chose Balls

Making sense of senseless controversy

JEREMY HOOPER

ISBN: 0615574548
ISBN-13: 9780615574547
Library of Congress Control Number: 2011944625
Good As You, New York, NY

For peace, for love,
for Andrew

CONTENTS

INTRODUCTION

Oh hey, what's up? I'm Jeremy, and this is my book, which I'm totally psyched that you're reading. Or skimming. Or sacrificing to the gods of antiquity. *Whatever*. But before I send you off into the sometimes wild, occasionally blue, always determined yonder that I've managed to peck out onto paper before the publishing industry collapses in on itself, let me first give you an idea of what this here literary endeavor thingamadoodle is all about.

First thing to know is that this is not so much a *gay* book. Not in the traditional sense, at least. Sure, the tales are those of a same-sex-loving person learning and living within America's most recent decades. And yes, the narrative is designed to advance understanding about the unnecessary trials and tribulations that lesbian, gay, bisexual, and transgender (LGBT) people still face every day. But the goal here is not limited to "gay rights," and the victims are not just those who are directly maligned. This mission is more human than the scope some have placed on the struggle for equality and more humane than the limits others have put on the same.

As a gay man, I know what it's like to feel alone, as if nobody could possibly understand what you're going through. I've experienced firsthand the confusion and the fear. I've seen how a lack of role models and negligently recited urban legends can lead scared youth to accept society's often demonized picture of those who are placed in the "other" box. I've walked in these shoes and now look back as a slightly older, hopefully wiser brother who wants to use his place of self-acceptance to provide hope for those who may be struggling. I also aim to repudiate the insanely insensitive claims that far-right social conservatives have affixed onto LGBT life, ultimately leading us all out of this overwrought age of decrial and into one of unending enlightenment. Ya know, simple goals.

The main reason I don't want to write a typical gay rights book is because even though I'm as out and proud as they come, I know that being gay, in and of itself, is one of the least interesting things about me (or anyone else). That's a potentially damning admission, considering I'm asking you to read twenty-five chapters all focused on themes with homosexual tendencies. It also happens to be true. If I had my way, I'd likely never utter the words gay, homosexual, queer, LGBT, or any of the assorted and sundry names that have been applied to my life and love. In fact, I don't use the labels, most of the time. When not fighting the good fight, you'll rarely hear me putting my sexuality front and center. I lead with my mind, not with my crotch. That mind is human, not just *homosexual* human.

But I also like to think that my mind is peaceful and decent, which is why I see a need to step up and fight the wanton bias that's made so many generations of LGBT people wretch. There came a point in my mid-twenties when taking on an activist role no longer felt like a choice. With a president on national TV telling millions of my compatriots that families like mine are "lesser than" (at best), how could I not give back a big Dubya.T.F? With state after state going to the polls to cast harsh votes against my ring finger, how could I not raise an eyebrow? With firsthand knowledge of the unnecessary familial strife that well-meaning but shortsighted parents are imposing on their kids for supposedly making "lifestyle choices," how could I stay quiet? How could I choose to sit this one out?

It wasn't only, or even primarily, because I was gay that I felt this need—it was because I didn't want to suck at being a conscious being! Apathy no longer made me feel benignly guilty, the way that extra scoop of ice cream, the three-hundred-dollar sweater, or reality shows about child beauty pageants did/do. At some point, passivity began to seem both negligent and dangerous. I started envisioning future generations asking me what I had done to beat back bias and "rooted for the lesbian contestant on *America's Next Top Model*" no longer felt like a suitable answer.

So all of a sudden I became a professional activist, something I never expected to be. Hell, something I had probably even mocked in my younger days—though something that suddenly felt like duty-bound kismet. For many of my predecessors in inactivity, the light bulb moment came through the unimaginably devastating plague of AIDS. For me, it was the closed mindsets that once turned a disease into a pandemic and that continue to reduce a rich, vibrant population of human beings down to a disposable band of "militants" with an "agenda-driven" "lifestyle." Once my fog was lifted, there was no turning back. One question: how to move forward?

When thinking of the skills that I could bring to a fight, I knew that personality was going to be key. I have a theatrical background, both by nature and by training, which means that I sacrifice few opportunities to punctuate even the most depressing of life moments with a touch of flair. I was convinced that the LGBT world could use a little bit of this style. Why should clenching my fist out of frustration mean that I had to remove the tongue from my cheek? The anti-gay side calls us "angry" because we take to the street in protest? Okay, so what will they say when I instead take to the written word with heart and wit?

I also knew I wanted to directly challenge the lies. Conservative groups write gay people off as "sex-crazed" because our movement is bound in part by sexuality? Alright, well then I'm going to show them that our far bigger hard-on is directed towards love, with our most toe-curling orgasm coming from their side's theoretical cease fire. Or if they say that we who fight for basic fairness are anti-family and anti-values? Fine, then I'll force them to answer why they are the ones whose "values" leave empty chairs at countless family holidays. Wherever the misrepresentation, I was determined to serve as the accountability agent.

My first step was to launch a website called Good As You (www. GoodAsYou.org), where I could take on the daily slate of anti-gay, anti-equality nonsense. My "agenda" was a simple one: to demand respect, teach peace, make a few jokes, hold any and everyone accountable if and when they create unsafe space for LGBT people or their S(traight) allies, and do it all in the most firm but fair way possible.

I continue this journey with the book that you're about to read. Through both the site and these physically- (or digitally-)bound pages you hold in your hand, I'm using my own life travels as a vehicle for the larger LGBT rights fight because I really do see my trek from scared, Southern gay boy to out, legally married, big-city activist as a fitting parallel for the larger rights picture. But navel gazing is not the goal. By sharing my story, I hope to:

- Clue potential allies in to how much homophobia/heterosexism can hurt, thereby cultivating a broad coalition of fair-minded LGBT and S individuals

- Inspire this fair-minded bloc to curb apathy and take charge of the conversation, reducing and ultimately extinguishing the arrogant "culture war" mentality that has hijacked American politics for the past several decades

- Get us past the point where anyone's basic civil rights or human worth are up for debate

- Drain and replace the organized anti-LGBT movement's snake oil, as if they are the out-of-town parents, and I the seventeen-year-old who discovered the keys to the liquor cabinet

Hopefully you, the reader, will be entertained. Maybe you'll laugh, maybe you'll cry, and maybe you'll do that laughter-thru-tears combo—emotions are a lovely thing. Most of all, I want you to get active, the same way that I did just a few years back. Regardless of your race, age, political affiliation, sexual orientation, or ear lobe status (free hanger here), I want you to see the crucial *need* to step up and give a damn. I want you to *want* to make a difference in this, one of the major (if not most major) civil rights battles of our time. Even if just in your own mind, I want you to engage in this important conversation. Even if you only rally Judy from Accounting, then that's one more Judy than we had before (and you *know* how fickle that one can be).

Because the thing is, not only *can* we tolerate and respect all of this world's inhabitants—we *need* to co-exist for society's sake. We must bridge the gaps that separate the LGBTSQ consonants, co-mingling between and within the clumsily constructed communities the false "culture war" script has demanded of us. Just as with any civil rights struggle, the fight for LGBT equality is one to which more than just the members of the community can and should relate. In a population where humanity is quickly being replaced with technology and discourse limited to that of liberal think tank versus conservative interest group, we must boil LGBT issues down to the far simpler principles of love, respect, and right versus wrong. We must start talking like human beings, not robotic talking point machines. We must be better as a people.

In some cases, I've changed the names. In all cases, I hope to change hearts and minds. Maybe even yours?

It begins subtly enough.

1) RAINBOW LACES

We'll call him Ethan, so as to protect his anonymity. We'll call him gorgeous, so as to protect my five-year-old self's taste in boys. Although we won't actually call him, since the two of us managed to drift in completely opposite directions during the twelve years of public schooling that followed our kindergarten graduation. But at age five, it was little Ethan who set your humble scribe's heart all a-flutter. Sweet, swoon-worthy Ethan.

Oh, but wait, I'm getting ahead of myself. First we need to set the scene. It's the mid-'80s, a few miles east of Nashville, Tennessee. A regular boy from a regular home attends his perfectly regular kindergarten graduation ceremony in a regular public school gym-atorium. It's astonishing, the clarity with which I remember this post-K pomp and/or circumstance. There was the white flat hat, which felt so awkward, yet amazing, on my head. It was hard to balance and even a little rough on my tiny little neck. But after a year where I'd mastered basic phonics, cut and pasted countless shapes, and boldly resisted the urge to test my child safety scissors' ability to cut the hair of the goldilocks who sat in front of me, no heavy hat was going to bring down my chin on this day. Head high, future bright.

It was also the day I put on my first pair of dress shoes. They were nothing more than cheap Payless and couldn't have been anything close to comfortable, but these faux suede kicks were as magnificent as any that I could imagine. Not Velcro, like my tennis shoes. No crass character images on the sides to tell the community my sole priorities belonged with He-Man or Voltron. These were big boy shoes, the kind I imagined one of my then-heroes, President Reagan, would wear. What can I say? Both my liberalism and my shoe fetishism were nascent at age five.

Beyond the costuming, I can also vividly recall questioning the whole commencement procedure that we kids were being asked to follow. The plan was for us to walk across the stage, grab a rolled-up piece of paper from the principal, and then get our *real* diplomas later that day. It's a perfectly common exercise, one that's likely used at the majority of school commencements. To me, though, this whole song and dance made absolutely no sense. First and foremost, it just seemed plain inefficient to have us go through the motions twice, when as best I could tell, all of my classmates had learned enough in the past year to master the simple concept of diploma distribution. But beyond just efficiency, the request also made me feel like I was participating in a charade. It was like we were putting one over on all the Polaroid-happy loved ones in the bleachers. They were expecting the gymnasium processional to be the bona fide thing, when in actuality it was all a ceremonial sham. I just wasn't comfortable with the ruse.

All of these memories and more are still quite present in my attic of recollection. My mother has always told me that I have a memory like a steel trap, and nowhere is the ironclad nature of my mind's recall ability more fully on display than in its capacity to look back upon this particular 1985 event with such astonishing lucidity. Of course, the fact that it's the first time I remember having a same-sex attraction might have a little something to do with why this pre-first grade ceremony has stuck on my mind for the past couple of decades.

Now, obviously kindergarten me didn't *fully* know what I was feeling; I just knew that I needed multicolor laces on my high-tops RIGHT NOW because Ethan had them on his shoes and Ethan was the coolest human being at Lakeview Elementary, if not on the planet. His hair, meticulously styled into an oh-so-'80's "rat tail." His parachute pants, just like the cool kids on MTV wore. The subtle strut in his step as he walked down that white carpet wearing his cheap flat hat and carrying his sham diploma. Ethan was the jam, and I, on the cusp of first grade and all the real world issues that come with it, wanted to know more.

It's admittedly easy for a writer to look back on a situation twenty-five years later and slightly revise the details to serve his or her own interests. This is even true for someone with as much of a mama-approved memory bank as myself. In fact, some scholars suggest that no one possesses the ability to accurately recall events exactly as they were since the human mind, by design, will inject subsequent life situations and acquired biases into the prior experiences, therefore skewing the recollection. It's a particularly annoying theory for a memoirist who wants to wring every last ounce of truth out of his journey for the purposes of collective understanding.

There are also, again admittedly, some flat-out gaps in my ability to conjure up this kindergarten rite of passage. For instance, can I tell you one thing my then–best friend Nicole did, said, or wore on that May 1985 day? *Absolutely not.* Or do I remember where my family went to celebrate the fact that my educational progression would now be measured in numbers rather than letters? *Um, maybe Shoney's, though it very well could've been Bonanza or Cracker Barrel.* Due to lack of interest, these ancillary details have made my time-lapsed mind go, "meh, whatever."

But if I put the shoe on the other foot, do I recall what color laces were on Ethan's high-tops? Well hmm, let's see. *Yellow on left, green on right. The shoes had a Velcro strap on top and were not exactly white. They may have once been white, but childhood wear and tear had rendered them less than ivory. They were now grayed, dingy, and much less appropriate for such a hallowed occasion than were my dressy cheapies, but neither the quality nor the suitability deterred me. I wanted nothing more than a pair in that exact same state as Ethan's!* Or something like that.

The image is too full and real to be an imaginative figment. It goes well beyond shoes, too. His eyes (brown), his delicate features (slightly rosy), which side of the gym he entered on (right versus my left)—all of these details are fully present. The reason, I suspect, that this particular scene is so colorful and detailed is because it's one that played out in my mind throughout the days, weeks, months, and years that followed. The memory didn't lapse because I didn't *want* it to. I kept reliving it throughout elementary school and beyond because I was attracted to Ethan, plain and simple.

And there are many, many Ethans that hold a prominent place in ye olde time capsule. There was the boy we'll call Josh, who in sixth grade Math class smelled like "clean" in the most tantalizing of ways. I suspect it was just his soap or whatever, but the smell was so, so vibrant. As an evening bather myself, Josh's luxe morning fragrance felt gloriously indulgent. His blonde curls were pretty sweet as well. Or "rad," as vintage parlance would have dictated.

Let's see, there was also the basketball star—let's call him Stephen—who made my seventh grade year by suggesting we work together on a class project. This guy was the beyond-cool kid, the one that everyone, even in the higher grades, knew by name since his height, skills, and charming personality transcended the usual pre-teen confines. For my starstruck self, he was the twelve-year-old equivalent of "husband material." Now here he was announcing me as his intended, if not in life, then at least in planetary diorama-dom? Okay, hey—ya gotta start somewhere.

There was also the crazy-hot guy with black hair who asked me—ASKED *ME*!—to be his junior high locker partner. Or what about my buddy M.M, who, when I caught him kissing my girlfriend (we'll get to that later) in our junior year of high school, thought my anger was due to the lip-locked pair's indiscretions. In truth, it was due to my desire to see more of *his* side of the tonsil hockey. Oh, and these last two were post-pubescent, when both my hormones and the horniness were at whorish levels, so by this point, the ideas in my head were nothing close to vague. By the time I got to these adolescent crushes, I wanted to go to at least third base, if not hit a bona fide homo run.

These were boys to whom I was attracted, the same way that all the peers around me had their own puppy passions. Sadly, all of my crushes would have to exist only within my young head if I wanted to continue existing. There were no hands to be held in the hallway and certainly no sweet smooches. All because I was born the kind of human who is widely considered to be different, no matter how standard to the societal template my sexual drive was and is.

My earliest memories are those of a gay person. Does this mean I was the so-called "sissy kid" who talked with a sibilant "s" and eschewed stereotypical boy culture for a childhood filled with dolls and tutus, as prevailing notions may lead one believe? No it does not, as neither my nor anyone else's sexual orientation means any one concrete thing in regards to carriage or manner or interests. Being a gay Jeremy Scott Hooper simply means that in my experience as a human being, in terms of crush, attraction, and biological responses to fellow human beings, it has been and always will be the male of the species who captures my attention. While this natural attraction has ultimately led me to a life I optimistically predict will be lived happily ever after, such same-sex yearnings have unfortunately brought great strife and pure anguish to many a male and female. Memories that should be benignly joyous are instead, for loads of the world's LGBT people, major issues. Milestones with which hetero-sexuals' lives are often measured are routinely denied to those of the queer persuasion. Or if not denied, then qualified in some way.

And love? Love is put on pause until one's mind and situational reali-ties afford something of a sense of comfort. Most people get there eventu-ally, and many at earlier ages now than even seemed possible in the past. In some tragic cases, though, this pause can last a lifetime. There are also cases even more tragic, namely the far too many who are told that, because of their burning love, there is an even worse pain that will last for all eternity.

To be LGB or T is to be part of a ragtag crew whose members fully know what it means to feel different—all of us, to a person. The degrees to which gays, lesbians, bisexuals, and transgender individuals experi-ence these divergent feelings of course varies, but at some point, those whose realities have been historically branded with "dare not speak its name" status have all undoubtedly felt segregated from society in some way, shape, or bias, whether it comes from family, friends, or faceless foes in Op-Ed pages. Butch or femme, conservative or liberal, black or white, rich or poor, hip or geeky, Neil or Patrick Harris—it doesn't matter. To be LGBT is to know what it means to feel queer in some very real sense of the word. Still. Now. In the twenty-first century, throughout the entire developed world.

Right, so this may lead you to say, "Oh wow, wise prophet— gays face discrimination. *Shocking.* Can't wait for your startling 'sky is blue' revelation!" But after cutting you a salty look, I'd tell you that very few of us—not even you, Mr. or Ms. Catty—are looking at and/or processing the problem of anti-LGBT bias as thoroughly and aggressively as we should be. We've all grown up in a society wherein that bias has been far too tolerated, which has made us, as a col-lective, far too complacent—or in some cases, downright complicit. Even those of us who think we deplore homo-hostility as a rule aren't always focused enough on the little bits of nonsense that keep 'mosex-uals from freely enjoying the same banalities of life as their 'rosexual counterparts. We don't always counter the everyday absurdities that enforce separation because so many of us have casually swallowed the idea that life's progression is innately meant to be different for LGBT people. Not even pejoratively different, necessarily. Just an agreed-upon "otherness."

Think about it for a second, heterosexual pals. You know that Valentine you so sweetly sent your crush in third grade? Everyone around you thought it was just *so adorable* that your interest had turned towards the opposite sex. The adults were simply gushing. *"Oh, he's got a little crush—CUUUTE!!!"*

Or maybe it was the seventh-grade dance, when you spent the whole night with your latest locker-leasing love, swaying to the cheesy music in some really awful clothing. Remember those simple memories of horrible dresses, stale cookies, and even worse power ballads? Do you smile when you think of the innocence that comes with those recollections? The non-event of the occasion?

Well, now imagine those things for me and anyone else who might be reading this while gay, would ya? Those scenes simply don't exist in my and many other gay people's memory banks. Sure, I sent some Valentines and attended my share of dances; I just did these things without any true emotional connection. These kinds of memories are not cute little points of nostalgia for me, but rather awkward remembrances of merely going through the foreign-feeling motions because I had no other viable option. Most every page of my scrapbook has an added layer of gawkiness that goes beyond bad hair and tight rolled jeans. It may sound silly, but it's like this void in my life that can never be completely filled, only patched over. Many should-be casual tales come with an ancillary subplot pertaining to my sexuality and the limitations it afforded a small town kid in the late twentieth century. It doesn't even make me sad or mad, really, because it's the only life I've ever known. It does, however, make me conscious of the asterisk that's widely placed on my existence.

To me, it's this "different" feeling that most ably binds LGBT people into a community. Sure, gaydar, the ability to pick a sweet lez out of a gay stack, gets lots of press, though it turns out that LGBT people's super-hero powers are not limited to just identification. We can also look at one another and know—wordlessly, upon meeting, without prior research—that at some point in our newfound acquaintance's life, he or she too has most surely felt some degree of purposelessly hostile heartache. It may have been from internal struggle, or it may have been from all-too-real bullies. The other person's may have been harsher than our own, or it may have been more benign. Whatever the case, it's fairly reliable to assume that some degree of square peg-iness was most certainly there.

It is certainly not sex practice or gender identity/expression that provides the glue, as that gamut is as widespread and varying within the LGBT community as it is in the population as a whole. Politics certainly don't offer nearly as common a bond as the uninitiated might imagine; faith views vary wildly; "gay culture" itself is largely a construct, with any trend hitting the market sure to make just as many LGBT scenesters gag as it will make others go Gaga. No, no—the LGBT community's truest connective thread involves the collective knowledge that a sizable portion of the population either did, does, or eventually will see us as disconnected from the larger societal picture because of no virtue greater than our attractions or expressions. I'm sure of it. This is a truism that connects the dots from well before Oscar Wilde and one threatening to extend way past Oscar from *The Office*.

Breaking it down, we can start at the physical component. LGB people have impulses that no part of the known world greets with anything close to full and unqualified acceptability. "T" humans feel trapped in the wrong bodies in ways that even less of the known world cares to understand. Hormones rage, because they're gonna. But for LGBTs, far too much messaging reduces those natural impulses into unnatural misfires. Puberty and its associated explorations are tough enough already. When that given awkwardness plays out in a closet, the experience tends to darken.

There's also the mental difference, with strife brought on in a myriad of ways. For instance, there's the internalization of others' reactions to the aforementioned physical realities. A growing mind is quite a perceptive trap. When a trusted love one makes an anti-gay comment or takes caution to shield a child's eyes from some positive LGBT portrayal, that moment, even if seemingly small, can jar someone who is coming into an understanding of his or her truth. This can lead to the feeling of dread of being "found out" by friends or family. Not fun.

Similarly, there's the still-subpar parity in terms of media portrayals, which only reinforces the idea that basic human worth is a two-sided, "agree to disagree" issue. For many LGBTs, this messaging is coupled with the inability to find anyone in their immediate sphere who "gets it." Even in the most accepting areas of the world, Cinderella still always gets with the charming *male* shoe fetishist, toys are gender-marketed from birth, and news reports still give equal time to those who paint gays as marriage's evil stepsisters. All of this limited/negative messaging becomes internalized. Developing brains understandably get scathed.

Of course, there's huge spiritual difference, too. When I was wee little, I had such awesome times sitting on my grandmother's knee, doing that "here is the church, here is the steeple" thing with our enjoined hands. Sometimes our fingers would remain inside, with "There are all the people!" proudly announced whenever we finally opened the doors (i.e., our thumbs). Other times, we'd leave our fingers on the outside so that the activity would culminate in a pensive "Where are all the people?" rumination. Never then would I have thought the people inside might have scattered because I brought some of my pesky gay cooties into the sanctuary. Considering that I grew up in a heavily Southern Baptist city, and considering that this same denomination still refuses LGBT members and literally kicks out churches that are said to be too lenient on the same, it very well might have been my little 'mo ass that was emptying out the prayer hall! It didn't take me long to realize the unfortunate faith-based realities on which I would be forced to focus, regardless of wherever my own theological studies might lead me. It doesn't take *any* LGBT person long to feel the crossness of others' personal faith condemnations.

Then there's the social difference, which we've already touched on. The dates, the Valentines, the rainbow-laced Ethans: those add up. The denials carry emotional weight. For some, this weight merely presses down on the pause button, and for others it becomes an insurmountable obstacle. The funks can range from petty to scary or somewhere in between. The torment might be internal, or it might be a constant struggle to escape the school day without working a fresh, newly-footprinted-ass look (rarely in style in any season). Few on Team LGBT play the game in the ballpark of equal justice.

When thinking about what causes such needless differentiation, most people immediately jump to homophobia. Fair enough. Even though that word, which carries the implication of fear, is technically a very limited term, it is, undeniably, the one that we've come to adopt in culture as a catchall for any and all anti-LGBT sentiment. So going along with the culture, let's be clear that, yes, homophobia hurts us. Schoolyard "smear the queer" games can start almost as soon as the alphabet lessons do, and the teasing can turn deadly serious. Anti-LGBT hiring and firing practices still happen every day, putting one's bedroom privacy over his or her boardroom proficiency. Gay-targeted beatings and even murders are all very real and obviously just as frightening. Far too many ring fingers are still far too naked. Homophobia plays a role in all.

Yet the adoption of that particular term has somewhat limited our discussions, allowing an arguably more pervasive problem to go largely unchecked. That problem? Well, it would fall under the heading of heterosexism, if we were to give it a specific label. Simply put, it's the idea that heterosexuality is preferred and/or superior, with any variation on that supposed male/female norm falling somewhere along the "abnormal" spectrum. It's that casual sort of mindset, based largely on stereotypes and continued misrepresentations, that keeps people voting against LGBT rights and then justifying it by saying, "oh, but some of my best friends are gay." It's that view that keeps civil unions on the table as an acceptable alternative to full marriage equality. By and large, it is what keeps many would-be allies apathetic to the pro-equality fight because they see gays as that aforementioned "other." It's also the idea that leads even some LGBT supporters to see heterosexuality as a gold ring and homosexuality as a shortened stick. Plus it's a notion that places an unfair burden not only on gays, who supposedly have to prove themselves as worthy, but also on heterosexuals, who earn heightened scrutiny of their own imperfections and relational foibles.

Considering the broadly generalized way we as a society have defined homophobia, there are certainly elements of heterosexism that do get addressed through the word's blanket usage. In fact, it would be hard to look at almost any situation in which an LGBT person is being wronged in some way and not instinctually realize that the aggressor sees his or her target's orientation, identity, or expression as inferior. Oftentimes, the superiority complex is unaddressed because it's so damn obvious.

But think about what we hear so often from someone who has been accused of doing/saying/writing/singing/miming something anti-gay. What is that person's reliable line of defense? More often than not, it's that old nugget: "I'm not homophobic—I'm not scared of gays." Then in some more benign situations where the bigotry or bias is more nuanced (e.g., anti-gay legislation or votes), the aggressor will parlay this straw man line into a denial that hate or bigotry could've ever been a motivator for his or her actions. People handily use the personally defined term of homophobia as an escape. A way to shed onus.

The setback here? This "I'm not homophobic" emergency chute is an easy out that often sidesteps the actual wrongdoing, therefore stopping us from having the more valid, more needed conversations that we should be having. Because the obvious truth is that it doesn't take outright fear to say something offensive. It also doesn't take myopia that's reached the level of hate or bigotry to lead someone down a biased path. It only takes the general idea that to be gay is to be "lesser than." By lumping everything together under the umbrella term homophobia, we are in many ways dancing around the more fundamental root of every single anti-gay everything. That basic root: the assumption that heterosexuality is the one true norm, and that anyone who falls out of a certain orientation or gender identity is somewhat junky by design. That aggressively short-sighted view of the demonstrable, undeniably natural realm has pervaded our thoughts and minds for far too long.

To get somewhere true and productive, we who want to make Earth less "humanphobic" must take this fairness and equality conversation back to a more basic level. Just as the LGBT population is bound by feelings of differentiation, we who counter anti-LGBT sentiment—which is to say all of us who are aligned for a transcendent goal—must focus our refutations on challenging that same basic concept. Labels like homophobia or even heterosexism? To be honest, they're *all* kind of like, whatever. All of them are somewhat limited. Because at the end of the day, who the hell cares about *any* of the terms? Rather than focus on labels, we must instead take on the forcibly different playing fields on which all games of discrimination, from minor ("*waah, I didn't get to send a boy a message heart*") to major ("*I pay the same taxes yet don't receive thousands of the same rights*"), are contested. For whatever the reason.

Homo-hostile intent can vary, but words and actions are concrete. As long as those words and actions put heterosexuality on an unfairly sanctified pedestal to which millions of non-heteros can only hope to aspire, we are going to have a problem. It's a problem for which there's no acceptable solution but peace and acceptance—a complete and utter paradigm shift from what we've previously known.

Popular culture often cites Stonewall as being the defining moment of the modern rights movement. It's the well documented time when gay, lesbian, bisexual, and transgender beings stepped out onto the Greenwich

Village streets and began to forcibly claim their piece of the humanity pie—the force, of course, being a requisite only because the pie had been denied.

But for a colossal majority of heterosexuals, the ability to live and love is nothing close to a stone wall. Instead, it's a pretty little stone path. Perfectly landscaped and beautifully paved, with even some of those nice running lights on the sides to help guide the way. Maybe even a friendly little garden gnome being all cute and crap. Certainly no extra steps requiring extra force. The journey from kid crush to wedding aisle is not only easy and unadulterated; it's subsidized by society in most every way.

Why wasn't I or most any other LGBT person given the same respect? Why shouldn't my crush on Ethan be a cute little story my mother now shares at family functions? Why can't we live in a world where folks are free to live their truths? When will withdrawals from the gay memory bank be freed of additional fees? When will we get past our addiction to hetero-normative commonality, and when will love—true, heartfelt love—be greeted with the same open arms?

The answers are simple to come by, and we can get there with joint effort. For those adults who didn't have the luxury of enlightenment and for whom anti-LGBT misinformation has been as common as a Bush or Clinton in high office, the educational challenge is, admittedly, more difficult. It's nowhere close to impossible, for those who want to rise to it.

First and foremost, potential straight allies must remove the blinders. Before you get up from your chair, I should say that I'm not talking about those outdated venetians that make your home look more '80s than a New Coke shrouded in a commemorative Worlds Fair '82 legwarmer. No, I'm referring to the figurative blocks that keep folks uncommitted to progress on these issues. Before any movement is possible, these blinders must be removed from the eyes, allowing the light to finally come in. Then and only then can equality be fully perceived, as only through heightened perception can we first detect the stains or bias that we need to scrub away. It could and should be so simple for potential straight allies to do this, since all it takes is accurate perception of the known world and a willingness to stop acting like you who smooch another gender's lips and/or were born into traditional gender roles are the deciders of everyone's destinies. It's the deluge of deliberately cultivated discontent that makes this so challenging. But again, challenging does not equal impossible.

HOW TO BE AN EFFECTIVE ALLY IN TEN EASY STEPS

Step 1: Agree that heterosexuals do not own normalcy. Unless one gets one's definitions from Pat Robertson's Dictionary of Convenience, one knows that the standard patterns of LGBT existence have more than exceeded the "normal" bar.

Step 2: Return to the Golden Rule. The whole *"do unto others…"* notion is so cliché, it's easy to dismiss. That's a shame, as it's a pretty powerful life tool.

Step 3: Consider that you yourself have an LGBT family member. Because you might. Or do now. You don't get to control this reality.

Step 4: Vow to think beyond contrivance. If confronted with a political talking point or cherry-picked biblical interpretation, have enough self-respect to do the research rather than just parrot what you've been told. In a world where knowledge quests required you to thumb through an index book and then locate the actual encyclopedia volume containing your limited answer, your excuses earned a little more sympathy. This does not hold true in a day where getting to the Internet via one's contact lens seems just around the corner. Put forth an effort.

Step 5: Go gay for a day. Or an hour. Or a minute. Not in the sexual way, mind you—just in mind and spirit. It's not hard, since all you really have to do is imagine yourself born with the same sense of love and desire, just geared differently. Just give a strong, considered thought to the idea that your most basic of truths would ever be a topic of cable television debate.

Step 6: Form a staunch opinion. Don't just say you "get it" and become an armchair ally. The anti-LGBT opposition is almost exclusively filled with straight-identified people who've formed *intensely* strong opinions. LGBT people deserve the same from their allies.

Step 7: Have the uncomfortable conversations. When someone tells that hostile joke, don't give a courtesy laugh. Say something. I'm not asking you to be a frontline activist person, placard in hand and chant in mouth; just don't be an idle enabler. Be real.

Step 8: Make smart choices. Learn what a particular candidate, company, elected official, movie star, or any other public entity has done to either shun or accept, then put your support where your values are. Be it a candy bar, a White House hopeful, or a local news station whose tagline is "First on the scene, except the few times that nasty lesbian from Channel 6 got there first"—your consumer choice matters.

Step 9: Vote. Vote. Vote! Apathy is why equality loses at the polls. Your vote matters in every single election. Sometimes you even get a sticker or some other parting gift—and that's fun, right? Vote. LGBT opponents do, by the literal busload.

Step 10: Join us at the victory party. With the $$$ we've been forced to throw at LGBT activism, we could instead throw one hell of a bash. Dress code is lax. Humanity code never again will be.

And with that you're cured, hetero friend. So now let's talk about the children. Gays are coming for 'em. Didn't you hear? Lock the doors. Seal your windows. Hide your pets, liquor, and DVRed *Golden Girls* reruns. Operation Gay Recruitment is in full force.

Except not. At all. In truth, LGBT adults want what everyone should want: for the next generation to be better off than we were. It's just that those who do not care for the 'mosexuals have taken this basic, should-be-shared want and exploited it for their own gain. So fine, let them. We cannot and should not apologize for talking to even the youngest of children because the lessons of equity *must be taught from birth*. Anti-gay hostility is a fungus, a virus. It's a parasite that will suck all of the impurities from the larger host before then infecting a younger vehicle with the tainted ooze. We must protect our children from top to bottom, head to toe, heart to mind.

If you have kids and are shielding them from LGBT people or accurate information about the same, then that's problem number one. Stop it. Now. Seriously. Go right this very second and tell your little one about Heather and her two wonderful mommies. I'll wait.

{Writer goes to the couch and puts on a "Real Housewives of (does it really matter what city?)" marathon so that both he and his readers can be focused on the kind of people who are inclined to throw tantrums}

Done with that? Okay, good. Keep it up on the daily.

Finally, let's talk a little about LGBT people. It might sound weird that those who have personally endured the slings and arrows would need to address our own disservices, but I'm not gonna lie—we totally do.

For one, there's the tendency of les-bi-gay-trans folks, whether it be born out of ease and/or safety, to sometimes retreat to our supportive communities and neglect the work that so desperately needs to be done in regards to the moveable middle or even the stubborn far-right. When it comes to the latter, there's an understandable inclination to see the far-right as fringe and therefore unengageable, which only allows them to put more and more unchallenged talking points into the ether. We need to realize that by taking on the "fringe," our goal is not necessarily to change one of their seemingly committed minds. Would be nice, but it doesn't have to be the goal. We need to work with the understanding that many, many fence-sitters are eavesdropping on the conversation, weighing the anti-LGBT set's slightings against the pro-equality movement's pushback. This means that we must take on the "culture war" challenges laid before us just as aggressively as the other side fires them, so that when the scared mother in Kansas goes to find out about something like the "ex-gay" movement to see if it's right for her son, the Google Gods don't just give her rhetoric from a conservative think tank. It's the same approach I'm using for this book. I'm talking to many groups, yet also to none at all. Some points geared toward a gay person have intended takeaways for the straight crowd, with that cross-pollination extended for every possible combo. That's what we on the frontlines must be better about doing.

Another LGBT tendency is to accept less-than-equal bones from politicians because they feel and sound like progress rather than pressing forward for that which truly constitutes advancement. There's pragmatism that must be understood and respected, absolutely. But it's one thing to look at the big picture and work smartly towards it. Allowing oneself to be cropped out of said picture for the sake of political expediency? Well that's quite another. Demand better of your electeds. Demand better of yourself.

Moving more intra-community, there's also a problem with how some lesbian and gay people, specifically, question the sincerity of our bisexual friends. I don't get this. If you are going to question someone else's sexual identity, then what's to stop someone else from questioning your own? Plus why would you, someone who should understand what it means to have a sense of self that some work to deny or discredit, force others to explain their own uniqueness? Why do you have to personally "get it" in order to make it real?

Others fail to see how gender identity and expression have anything to do with sexuality. Again, why? If you think that gender identity/expression have nothing to do with LGB rights and protections, then ask yourself why most people get gay bashed. Rarely has the perpetrator witnessed any actual gay sex, only the person's appearance, which told the thug something was "funny" about his or her victim. Not that the harsh reality of identity/expression targeting need be the reason why one should stand with one's transgender brothers and sisters. However, if you as a lesbian or gay person *do* need a reason, then there's one.

Then there are our passions. Because of them, we tend to in-fight too much over petty things, sometimes letting ego get in the way of forward movement. This makes sense because LGBT people are not talking point machines. This fight is not purely political on our side, nor is it a get-rich-quick scheme (trust me). For LGBTs, the fight is intensely personal. Emotions can't help but be involved. Sometimes these flare-ups turn inward on our own movement, and sometimes that's actually a good thing that breeds accountability and transparency. Other times, the sniping is nothing but wasted steam—steam that should be directed towards common advancement.

We LGBT people want to and should be our own best friends, but we can and often do fall short. We can't pin all shortcomings on everyone else. We too must be better.

The reality is that we've *all* had a hand in fostering the kind of society that forces people like me to feel a need to pause life and write a book like this. The far more beautiful reality is that we can triumph over anti-gay bias in fairly short order if we only vow to make some very obtainable commitments. It's unlikely that we're ever going to find a total inoculation in any of our lifetimes, as strains of all past prejudices still exist among us well beyond the "official" civil rights struggles ended. Complete freedom should not be the goal, as it is decidedly unobtainable. But we *can* all strive to be as better as humanly possible. ALL and HUMANLY are the operative words there.

One day not too long ago, Ethan randomly friended me on Facebook. Who knows why? Perhaps my laces were pretty memorable too?

Or better yet, maybe he's ready to use those rainbow laces to bind together the kind of broad coalition that will make a future Ethan the subject of benign family dinner table conversation, not the setup of a future Jeremy's bias-battling book? That would be a nice graduation!

2) EZ-BAKED BOYHOOD

No, they didn't realize they were aiding, abetting, consorting with, and sometimes even harboring a known homosexual. But we've already established how I knew from a very young age that something within me was gloriously guy-crushed. Yet still, my childhood male-on-male friendships were pretty much like those of other boys my age. Differences in burgeoning hormones were not enough to divide us, and rarely did my internal figuring-it-out-iness elicit outward taunts or teasing.

We were Little League teammates. An able athlete, I was known as someone who was a consistent hitter and a "good glove." Beyond basic ball prowess, I was also an indefatigable rally crier, there to melodically carry the tenor part in the "We need a pitcher, not a belly itcher" chant whenever my services were called upon. Plus, I could pull off the cheap hat look well before Ashton Kutcher made it an early twenty-first-century trend. Oh, and every game came with a free soda from the concession stand, which for some reason tasted about ten times better than any Coke ever did or has since. So yeah, baseball and me were, for the most part, fast, easy friends.

My skills were also vital in the backyard. If one of my neighborhood boy friends needed help churning out a mud pie, I'd muck through the mire and whip up a baker's dozen of the sludge-based delicacies in the time it took others to lay their grass crusts. Cleanliness was never Godliness in young Jeremy's eyes. Fingernail dirt was thousands of times more favorable to me than polish.

I was also quite skilled at taking on a video game's Player 2 spot, with many an afternoon spent saving various princesses at my dude friends' houses. Would some of these boys grow up to be the same kind of citizen who'd vote against my adult self's life? Perhaps. In the '80s and '90s, the only buttons they were pushing involved an elaborate "Up-Up-Down-Down-Left-Right-Left-Right-B-A-Select-Start" combo in order to get thirty extra lives in the Nintendo game *Contra*. The only issues we needed to settle were those that came between us and the 8-bit digitized baddy who happened to be messing with our virtual day.

Oh, and don't even get me bragging about my achievements in the field of fort architecture. Hell, I could crank out a multi-level mini-condo with nothing but cardboard, mud, and ingenuity. Me being me, I would go the step further than the other neighborhood boys, turning the makeshift house into a home, perfectly appointing the scrappy play-cottage with PVC pipe chairs, milk crate coffee tables, and bubble wrap rugs. The aesthetic was straight out of *Better Homes That Live In Or Around The Gardens.* If my parents had taken me to Europe around the time the Griswolds went, I probably would've turned my attention towards fashioning a bidet out of the garden hose! Yet despite my decorative diligence, the finished product, like my aesthetic in general, was sleek, not frilly, and therefore safe for even the most macho of the neighborhood tough guys. And the other boys sure appreciated our fort's retractable skylight (yes, it had one), even if they themselves might not have taken the time to create it.

So sure, while I definitely had my own quirks and flair (some internal and some expressed), I shared the same sort of camaraderie with my buddies that is typically found in pre-pubescent boys, genuinely enjoying all the scrapes, snakes, and lakes that came with the territory. I was not, as many might assume of an adult LGBT activist who now seeks to combat bullying, spending my recesses getting sand kicked in my face. You'd far more readily find me out on the playing field getting muddied and bruised with careless delight, the first to suggest "touch" football was too tame and that we should opt for the more aggressive, full tackle version of the game.

Maybe it was my having a traditionally masculine older brother and uber-masculine father that led me to follow certain gender roles, or maybe I just genuinely enjoyed getting dirty and participating in competitive sports. No matter the reason, much of my '80s and early '90s existence was almost disgustingly that of a boy who could've fit into both the traditional and all-American boxes. My immediate surroundings certainly impressed upon me the supposed need to be that way. However, few of these "boy" activities felt forced upon me. They basically felt organic. If I had any objections, they were largely due to a myriad of other reasons (shitty coaches, lack of desire to give up a Saturday, the other kid smelled, etc.) and not the idea that I was being pushed into butchiness.

That being said, there were a few differences I clearly felt in terms of my relationships with my fellow lil' dudes. First and foremost were my attractions to them. As my earliest memory of same-sex magnetism dates back to kindergarten, the little fact that I found several of my friends hot was often on my mind. Of course I wasn't thinking that I wanted to snuggle with or smooch them in those early years, as the concept was not one my young brain even knew to be a human possibility. I did, however, know that many of them looked mighty fine in their Air Jordans and Hypercolor shirts. Also, I knew that whenever my mother would say that Nicole, Amy, or Tonya were "*soooo* cute," I'd be all like, "Yeah? Really? They *are*? SERIOUSLY? From *my* class you mean? Hmm…I never noticed." So there was that.

Another difference was that I, unlike many of my guy friends, had very well developed friendships with females from pretty much the get-go. In fact, at Lakeview Elementary circa 1986, I was bestowed the rare honor of being named the only male member of my first grade class' "Girls' Kissing Club," a playground-based organization that some of the little lasses had formed to taunt the boys. As you might remember, the XX and XY chromosomal sets tend to be warring factions in the land of elementary education, with very little diplomacy existing between the two. You might also remember that smooches are like weapons to those opposite-sex sects. This particular girl group was designed to codify that outlook into policy, with a mission statement saying that if boys came anywhere near their headquarters (i.e., the swing set), the girls would act as if they were trying to kiss them, thus threatening the offending boy with their lady cooties. Yet despite the girl troops' sole purpose of boy-ridding via puckered lips, I was told *I* could hang out with them if I wanted, because I wasn't like the other boys.

The true irony in this kissing club invite is that the reality of me not being like the other boys would be the reason I'd later in life run from those same girls when those same boys were now eagerly kissing *them*. But back in the day, I was proud to be the boy's ambassador to Girlville. I still suspected they might have cooties and, never one to take my health for granted, was always sure to get the required Circle-Circle-Dot-Dot shot combination before venturing into their frilly lands. The risk, however, seemed worth it. These young women were clearly much more in touch with their emotions, which was something I liked. After a few rounds of kick ball and discussions featuring such butch lines as, "Nu uh, He-Man could beat up G.I. Joe any day, you stupid face!" it was always nice to skip across the playground and agree with Tracy that "yes, this lip gloss does, in fact, taste like bubble gum."

Oh, and stickers. Loved. Me. Some. Stickers! Not sure why adhesive shapes were such a female-centered thing in my school, but they most definitely were. I didn't care. At least one day of the recess week you could find me on the sidelines, adhering away with garish delight. And if one of my lil' lady friends had a scratch-and-sniff set, then forget about it! Darkness could fall around me, and I'd still be marveling at the bold pizza flavoring that the decal manufacturer managed to cram on the representative slice.

So yeah, there was a definite duality working within me, one that fully embraced both what my known world considered to be tough and what that same world deemed as soft. I just never bought into the belief that the "sugar, spice, and everything nice" camp and the "snakes, snails, and puppy dog tails" contingent couldn't share in the joys that the other brought to the table. I liked them both.

In fact, looking back on my memories from the playground microcosm, I've realized I was never okay with anyone maligning another on the basis of any physical or biological state. This thought transcended boy/girl relations. Throughout my childhood, whenever the juvenile behavior and humor turned crass in terms of someone who was in some way segregated as inferior or odd, I felt weirded out. Be it directed at kid or adult, I was always bothered by the idea that someone could somehow be flawed or not as good as me because he or she was in some way different, and I felt a great sense of shame whenever one would let out *any* sort of prejudice.

For example, because of a particular firework's ability to quickly sail down the street once it was lit, some in my life's circle had given it the nickname "N*gger Chaser." I knew this to be fucked up. Another common one was a crude alternate regional term for the Brazil nut, which also drew on the N word for its equally syllabic and therefore even more pointless nickname. Racial inequality was the most apparent form of bias around me, and not just against African-Americans, either. Other words I sometimes heard, like "ch*nk" and "sp*ck," felt somehow wrong as well, even if nobody had ever told me they *were* slurs or even clued me in to what communities those labels were intended to decry.

Then as we grew older, talking about girls as if they were nothing but holes in which we boys should struggle to place various parts of our body made my heart (among other things) go limp—especially when the bathroom talk would turn aggressive, making it sound as if the female half had no choice but to give in to whatever never-gonna-happen-anyway fantasy a certain boy might have. I didn't want any part of it, independent of even my own lack of personal sexual interest. I was something of a feminist long before I was any other sort of activist.

And on an obviously more personal front, the all-too-prevalent "fag jokes" in the baseball dugout made me incredibly uneasy. These began relatively early, well before the pre-pubescent hack comedians could possibly have any contextual awareness of the Andrew Dice Clay joke they'd lifted. Still, there was a certain malice in their telling that struck me. Hard.

In calling up these memories, I certainly don't mean to paint my childhood friends and acquaintances as if they were sheet-wearing members of the "We Hate Any and Everything Squad." I definitely don't want to foster a crude Southern stereotype, and, in fact, want to reinforce that I'm deeply proud of my roots and the people who made me who I am. Obviously not everyone I knew embraced prejudice—not even close. And even the ones who *did* often didn't mean the words that were actually coming out of their mouths. Kids say all kinds of things. Few of us would want to be held accountable for every lapse in judgment.

Yet at the same time, it'd be highly disingenuous to ignore that discriminatory chitchat was a reality for me while growing up. It just *was*. Looking back on it through adult glasses, I question how so many fully-grown role models could have turned a blind eye to or even fostered it. I also wonder why I, despite being raised so fully in and around the thick of it, was somehow geared to find it all so faulty. I do genuinely believe it to be, in large part, hardwiring, since the easier choice would have often been to go against what felt like my natural grain. But why me? Did my mom overdose on "Kumbaya" when I was in utero? What made me have some semblance of an activist spirit even then?

Now, am I saying I've always conducted myself in a prejudice-free manner, that my feces smell like roses, and that one would look back on my life and find no derogatory comments? *Absolutely not.* Not being a smug machine built by ACLU lawyers in a daisy field in Berkeley, I certainly had my own human trappings. I, like the rest of my friends, spent my growing up time in a community with some obvious diversity lapses, so in some cases I had to first be put in my place to understand that what I had previously known as just part of my vernacular was, in actuality, a very hurtful comment.

For instance, you know that astoundingly racist firework label I mentioned a few graphs back? Well when I was five, I actually *used* that name. In a store. Loudly. In front of an African-American family. I didn't know what I was saying—it was, quite simply, the only name I knew for this particular money-burner. Hell, it's *still* the only name I know for it!

Oh, and those anti-gay jokes I talked about? I sometimes laughed. Partly out of protection and partly out of the comfort it gave me, at some lower points in my internal life, to not think of myself as one of "them." But I laughed, no matter the reason.

And while I truly was a bit of a Gloria Steinem before I could even spell *Ms.*, I never actually stood up and stopped any of the misogynistic shit that flew from various mouths. One particularly harsh line that sticks out in my mind: "Treat a whore like a whore; treat a lady like a whore." I said nothing in response. I guess you could say I was more of a –tivist in those early years, not yet embracing the "act" part.

The difference is that I can safely say that any and all of my discriminatory actions were out of uninformed innocence, never hurtful intent. That too may sound smug, but it's 100 percent true. Simply put, I've never, ever, *ever* wanted to cause pain to any living thing. I am the guy who literally cannot kill flies, instead ushering them and all other pests out the door. Giving every living being the fairest shake possible on this spinning orb is a bit of a passion. I never innately wanted to shun people for something they could not and *should not* change, and I have always been open to equality-encouraging education. I've never wanted to put folks on the defensive because of nothing more than who they are. It's one of my existence's most continued truisms: the desire to level the playing field, no matter how futile the effort may feel.

I think this is why I now dedicate the largest portion of my life to challenging bias, at least as it pertains to the LGBT community. I see too many sentient beings shunned in jarringly cruel ways because they act or sound or look or date or marry in a certain way, and I know that I have some sense of insight that can help to lessen this suffering. This book that you are reading isn't about vanity or money or rubbing shoulders with the New York literary or political sets. I work to stop others' pain. It is the one motivator that hasn't ever diminished and the one incentive I've never questioned.

I've always retained the optimistic belief that, at our human cores, very few of us *really* want to cause pain or anguish. In terms of LGBT people, I truly believe if all were educated on the actual nature of gays and homosexuality, most would stop acting in such hurtful ways and would start to instead see the LGBT community for what we are: just another part of the spectrum of normalcy. We might still disagree politically about things like how we teach about sexuality in the public school curricula, what religious exemptions we apply to certain legislation, or the stringency of hate crimes laws, as there are some differences in opinion that go beyond homo-hostility—but if we could at least get past the blanket stigmatization and multi-faceted demonization that keeps a certain population down in so many ways, we could trade the militant "culture war" battles for respectful discussions. We could embrace our collective humanity. We could stop fostering people, young and old alike, who are scared to be true to themselves. We could thrive.

Look, my passions run deep to the gut. If someone wants to think me unmanly for showing such a sensitive side—well go ahead, call me unmanly. I'll pity you for being so disconnected from your full range of emotions. Yes, I do get reliably misty when Shelby bites it at the end of *Steel Magnolias*—for that I'll never apologize. Yes, I get expressive when telling a funny story—it helps to accentuate. If you're telling me you're having another kid, straight male friends, be ready for some full body contact—I hug to congratulate. Emotional expression is a gift with which we've all been blessed; I, for one, refuse to withhold utilization of my full range simply because certain outbursts may be viewed as effeminate. From my experience, we men would be a better tuned pool of penises if we more fully embraced that which fearful society has told us is too feminine.

On that same token, I won't apologize for things that some might see as too gender conforming. I like to white water raft because I find it thrilling, not because I want to be stereotypically masculine. I've never gone out in a dress because my personal fashion sense has never skewed towards frilly, not because I'm scared of what others might think. Just as I'd hope that straight men wouldn't avoid tweezers or moisturizers if their faces needed a little TLC, I'd also hope LGBT people wouldn't avoid things to which they are naturally drawn simply because they think it'll weaken their queer street cred. The bottom line is for all of us to remove the barbed wire from our existences and start embracing the real. To live our lives, not someone else's preconceived script. "Masculine and "feminine" are just such ridiculous constructs—so ingrained yet so short-sighted.

The Girls' Kissing Club instilled within me a lifetime love for the smells of flavored Chapsticks. Backyard boy forts were where I first practiced my flair for design. Playing sports was a childhood pastime, but theater was a passion as well. All of these things were within, and tapping into them regardless of whatever social messaging was telling me to do is a big part of what shaped me into me. For that I am thankful. Now, as an adult, challenging myopic social messaging is how I hope to shape future generations into becoming more easily and fully realized versions of whomever they are meant to be.

Life's a playground. We all deserve to swing in peace.

3) CHEW MEAT

I never liked mom's pot roast. To my ten-year-old palate, which could've been seen as either refined or just plain picky depending on one's views, the meat always felt too tough while the vegetables surrounding the flesh seemed a touch too soft. Plus the gravy in which the whole concoction waded tasted kind of dirty. Grainy. Bland.

But as with so many other matters, some then known and others not yet realized, I was clearly in my family's minority when it came to affection for this dish. My other four immediates lapped it up as fully as I pushed it away. Requests for the brown chuck came often.

I also suspect the cost-per-size ratio had something to do with why the tough stuff was so regularly employed to feed our five hungry mouths. It's a testament to my parents' good sense that they shielded my two siblings and me from whatever economic realities they were facing, bad or otherwise. That said, I always knew we weren't rich, at least in the monetary sense. In fact, when looking back through adult eyes, I realize we were probably at times too far below the poverty line for the ends to even smell each other's desperation, much less meet. This mix of need and want meant my taste buds' pain was not infrequent.

So based upon my just-professed disdain for the dish, it'd be more than fair to assume that recollections of pot roast nights are among my childhood's worst. Moreover, if you were to factor in the adult vegetarianism that I'll reveal to you right now, it'd be understandable for you to think that I'm going to spend the next few pages decrying the taste bud masochism I was forced to suffer. But on the contrary, this roast is on the menu of some of my mind's fondest family table-based memories. That's because the nostalgia is not only that of a meal to which I brought a less-than-half-full glass of enthusiasm. Buried within the memories that disappeared in one intestinal pass are much deeper flashbacks, ones involving a father and son who were able to bridge the chasms that existed between them in order to casually chew the fat. Literally.

He called it "chew meat." That was the name for the excess blubber my mother would cut off the meat midway through the cooking process. Basically it was the by-product of culinary liposuction. Or to put it another way, if PETA was tasked with creating its vision of Satan's chewing gum, this beefy castoff would be it. White in color, borderline gelatinous in texture—just vile in almost every regard! Yet whether it was through nature or nurture, my father came to see this quarter-cooked cow fat as a fine appetizer. It was an uber-provincial forshpeis that, in pop's eyes, could rival the world's finest amuse-bouche.

Dirty from digging ditches and grouchy from 5:30 a.m. wakeup calls, majority shares of dad's post-work moods were forgivably lackluster. But when he smelled the braised aroma of mom's roast—the exact same smells I'd have been bemoaning ever since arriving home from school—his voice would gain a certain lilt. Dad's dark clouds would fall away almost as easily as the mud on his boots. He'd brighten up for the roast itself, yes—but also for the chew meat.

"Ooh, there's a lot of it on this one," he'd proudly declare as his calloused hand lifted the hot lid, a special something now detectable in his eye. It wasn't a twinkle, exactly—that would be both inaccurate and hackneyed. It was more like an ocular grin, his eye reminding the rest of his worn out body that life's not so bad.

Or then again, maybe it was just worksite saw dust that gave his eye that special quality. Either way, my own peepers saw it as comforting. I, the artistic son, was forever in search of those golden moments when I could bond with nothing-if-not-macho dad. If I was a composite portrait of interests that knew no prescribed gender lines, dad was a Polaroid of passions that had only developed its most red-blooded of tones—proudly so. It was sometimes a struggle to find my "ins."

The most obvious available options were tough for me. Fishing trips came with pre-dawn revelry, which put them on a bad foot with me from the get-go. There were parts of those trips I enjoyed, especially once we got a small boat and I could do some driving. I did love the outdoors. Plus there was something about red-and-white coolers that made anything in them taste infinitely more amazing, so lunch on the bank of Old Hickory Lake was a nice selling point. Although those positive feelings were overshadowed by the fact that I really didn't want to rock a fish from its aquatic home and *certainly* didn't want to see one being gutted. God I hated that.

Local Triple-A baseball games came with the plus that was ice cream in a helmet, the "yum" yin to pot roast's "yuck" yang. However, these outings also meant faking enthusiasm for players I cared nothing about in a way that felt somewhat odd to me. I was always good at baseball, and I genuinely loved playing the game. I've also always loved the atmosphere of a ballpark. That aside, I've never been a reliable spectator of *any* sport, not to a point where I actually care to follow stats. Those just aren't my chosen soap operas. Plus, when asked to concentrate on in-person games, I have a bit of MTV generation ADD for them, my mind always waiting for some jump cut editing or pyrotechnic flashes that never come. So while just sitting relatively still for nine innings and rooting for faceless players was one of dad's great happy spots, it was something I could do only so often.

Then there was dad's fondness for working on cars, which, to me, seemed as dangerous as it did unappealing. I think it was the jack that scared me most. How could that piece of rickety-looking metal hold up a two-ton Ford? Didn't this hobby allow a demonstrably wide entrance for cranium-crushing human error? And seriously, was the risk really worth it when there was an auto shop literally at the foot of the hill? No, no—that one was a complete and utter non-starter.

Oh, and when it came to films, well, I was much more willing to pretend that my mother was dragging me to *Terms of Endearment* against my own protestations than I was to play-act enjoyment at one of dad's *Rocky* and *Jaws* screenings. It's not that I didn't like stereotypically tough guy flicks on the whole. Sure, on cable I'd stay on one for a whole afternoon, mind on soft cycle and hand in chip bag. But when committing to two hours in the theater, I most always sought dialogue and plot more than action; dad sought the inverse.

The answer to our disconnects? Broiled animal fat, natch. I could, with minimal effort, meet dad at this table of queasy cuisine. If worms in my stomach meant no worms on the end of a fishing hook, then my young self was willing to make that tradeoff.

"It's the best part," declared dad's reliable mid-chew refrain.

But it wasn't. It so, so, *soooo* wasn't. Even though I loathed the "good" part of the roast, I could still detect the comparably subpar status of the semi-cooked sinew. I had to fake it when I nodded in agreement, lending my affirmation to our shared time in the kitchen rather than to the meat itself.

"Be careful not to swallow it whole," was mom's only warning. "You could choke."

She, of course, knew I didn't really like it. Mothers always know. Though seeing as how she wasn't going to be the one to pull me out of any kind of closet, mom supported this manly whole cow consumption whole hog.

My two siblings were mostly unaware of the ritual. Brother was also 100 percent boy, as the gender was defined to me at the time, and therefore in need of no extra effort in the area of father-son relations. *Married with Children* reruns were his foretelling pre-dinner custom, and whatever sporting event was in season was his and dad's shared post-meal entertainment. Dad time was as involuntary to him as breathing.

Sister was daddy's one and only little girl, with a similar lack of struggle in finding her niche in the traditional family model. For her brand of pretty Southern belle, it was cute to be disgusted at the grit and grime of guys, and chewing on bovine brawn squarely fell on that side of boydom. If she even caught wind of what dad and I were doing, she'd accurately assess the grossness before immediately returning to her scintillating *Teen* magazine debating the hotness levels of Cruises and Depps and Lowes. God, I was jealous of her!

"Here, you take this piece," said dad. "It's bigger."

He was always so generous, which was a big reason why I struggled so much with my inability to connect with him. I recognized his kind heart for exactly what it was and knew that as long as either of us was alive, he'd have my back. I saw that he was a man of pure and deep emotions. Within myself, even at that young age, I felt so many of these same qualities. What I didn't feel was the freedom to express them. I didn't have dad's beard and ruggedness to handicap my sensitive side. To show myself would have made me vulnerable. Whether accurately or insecurely, I felt constant pressure to ratchet up my macho dial when dealing with him.

"Thanks, dad," I said, my voice dropping an octave. "Wow, it's really tough tonight."

Dad's mold came from a burly workshop; mom's lived in a dainty kitchen. I was an amalgamation. With this roasty ritual, we found the odd opportunity to combine the two.

So I chewed. And he chewed. With our mouths overfull, neither of us had the opportunity to hit a verbal third rail. It was an odd heart-to-heart delivered through the vehicle of beef. The cow may not have been sacred to the industry that took its life, but dad and I were determined to see that its sacrifice was not in vain.

Two decades, 886 miles, and seismically disruptive disagreements later, there are many things I couldn't possibly tell you about my childhood. More positive food memories have long disappeared down my mind's disposal, composting alongside the clothes that tapered when they should've flared and the teenaged dates that packed female genitalia where the male bulges should've been. But just as reliably as certain memories have faded, overall appreciation for my father has increased exponentially. I find myself humbled by how hard he worked to provide for his family. I am impressed with his ability to meet the physical exertion that his job took on his body, and I'm eternally thankful he had the drive to keep it all together. But perhaps most of all, I'm regrettably embarrassed by how little I showed my appreciation back when a simple "thanks, pops!" might have made a nice difference on a particularly beleaguered day.

This mix of admiration and regret must be why my mind has vaulted this seemingly foul culinary memory to such a place of prominence. In my adult life, these memories are shorthand for the undercooked connective tissue that needed just a little more time and attention to fully flesh out. They remind me that while I was Nintendo and old *Mary Tyler Moore* reruns and he was putting greens and *SportsCenter*, for certain glorious moments we were both chew meat.

DESPITE WHAT YOU MIGHT'VE HEARD . . . #1

➢ Some stereotypical gay traits are quite lovely. Rather than panic that your son might be 'motastic, instead panic that he might be gay and *still* buy you an ugly scarf, three days after your birthday, in a cardboard box wrapped with a plastic grocery bag, which he hands to you over a frozen dinner served on mismatched souvenir plates from The Museum of Watching Paint Dry.

➢ Not all pre-pubescent lady lovers are butch tomboys. Some are what we call "Flavored Lipgloss Lesbians."

➢ A gay boy will probably not try to mess around with your straight son if you invite him to your kid's sleepover. However, I cannot promise the same for your brunch spread, should the juice be from concentrate.

➢ No, "throws like a girl" is not an accurate or even okay way to describe your son's lack of baseball proficiency. "Throws like a girl *who's really shitty at baseball*" might work.

➢ While little straight girls are busy planning their white weddings, little gay boys are actually *not* plotting ways their future selves can ruin the same. We save that for the future drunk uncles who, even at age six, are failing to hold their peace after going on a Capri-Sun bender.

➤ If your son wants to dress up as a girl for Halloween, it doesn't mean he's gay. Unless he's planning to go as Dolly Parton, Lady Gaga, Little Edie Beale, or political pioneer Tammy Baldwin, in which case, probably.

➤ Humpty Dumpty? We gays had nothing to do with it. You can't prove anything.

➤ While flattering that so many have been honored by being likened to the talented star of such films as *Carrie* and *Coal Miner's Daughter*, it's probably time we stop disparagingly referring to gender non-conforming boys as "sissies."

➤ The tooth fairy, Santa Claus, a stork, a moon-bounding cow, hetero-only society, the Easter bunny, gays that can and should "change," and a grandma-devouring wolf: all storybook fantasies.

➤ Some children were born in the wrong physical bodies. It's everyone else's job to embrace either an open mind or a shut mouth.

➤ Let's be honest: action figures and dolls are often just a few inches of plastic away from each other. So before we get all hung up about who's playing with what, let's acknowledge that *everyone*'s playing with over-priced synthetics rather than actual friends.

➤ Should your son express a concurrent interest in both popsicles and Eskimos, it doesn't necessarily mean anything.

➤ Jack and Jill do not provide the only, or even the best, model for child-hood coupling. Hell, they couldn't even get down a damn hill without busting their glutes!

➤ Okay, so it's not LGBT or equality-themed, but I do have to wonder: isn't it weird that we gladly give our kids Clue, a game that is 100 percent based around murder? Not knocking it—big Miss Scarlet fan here. But seriously, murder? What next, an aggravated kidnapping game? Maybe it'd go something like...

COMMERCIAL SCRIPT —"TIP"

Voice Over: For years you've loved playing Clue with your family. Now, in the storied tradition of turning major capital offenses into family board games suitable for ages eight and up, comes "**TIP: The Aggravated Kidnapping Game.**"

Young Girl: I get to be Miss Cherry this time!

Young Boy: Okay, but I go first. [*Rolls dice*]. Six. [*Moves token*] One, two, three, four, five, six. That puts me in the "Shady van with the blacked out windows"!

V.O.: With its classic Clue-style gameplay, kids will be able to jump into the action right away.

Young boy [*thinking, clearly trying to give his best guess*]: I suspect Chef Mango with the "Promise to take his victim to his house to play video games"!

Young girl [*shows Chef Mango card to boy*]: Okay, now it's my turn. I'm gonna take the secret passage from the "Cheap, rundown hotel room" to the "One-room meth lab in the middle of the desert." And I'm gonna suspect Dame Pomegranate with the "Sleeping pills hidden in a cookie."

V.O.: Plus, with a source material derived from real crime, adults will love to play along.

Mom [*entering room*]: Hey, room for one more?

V.O.: And there's no need for parents to feel like hypocrites letting their kids play. After all, the game has cartoony graphics and colorfully named suspects. The little ones will *never* make a connection between this zany cast of characters and the man they saw on the local news [*Crime report plays on TV in background*].

Young boy: I'm ready to accuse. I say Father Grape, with the "Big net on a long stick," in the "Unsupervised playground."

[*Boy pulls correct cards out of envelope*]

I WIN!

[*Young girl and mom show mix of "ah shucks" regret and reluctant congratulations*]

Mom: Okay, we're playing again. And this time, *I'm* gonna solve the crime, all the while never thinking about how crazy it is that we're all playing a game about such a heinous incident.

V.O.: "TIP." Figuring out who shattered another family's life has never been this much fun!

. . . .

It might sound messed up now, but is it really worse than bashing someone over the head with a candlestick? I'm thinking not.

Okay, back to the other stuff . . .

➢ Gender need not determine the color of a child's outfit. If blue brings out your girl's eyes and pink looks nice with your boy's rosy cheeks, then embrace it. We're talking about sartorial covers, not genetic makeup.

➢ Kids are brutally honest. Adults can be brutally dishonest. Who could stand to learn something here?

➢ If it's a choice, my zygote chose balls.

4) I'M GOING NUTTY HERE

She was always popular and pretty, my seven-and-a-half-year-older sister. As anyone who's paid attention to teen culture in the past millennia might expect, this was a combo that filled her adolescent world with equally statused young men. And not just any guys, either. I'm talking about the brooding guys. The hot ones. The ones who you could be sure excelled in at least one sport and who would also be the hit of the postgame party to follow.

You know the kind of teen boy who'd probably get beaten out by the loveable dork in a John Hughes film but who seemed to always win out in the home movie version? With the good hair and the golden tan and the strategically popped polo collars? These were sis' prototypical suitors. They were always around our house, either struggling to capture or maintain her heart. To me she was like a crisp-haired, blue eye-shadowed, '80s version of Snow White, and the boys were her fluttering birds.

Yes, sis' was a nice teenage fate, for sure, and I, no dummy, was determined to involve myself in her good fortune. Not a difficult or surprising thing to do, since sis and I were always very close. Not sure why; we just kind of clicked. Whereas my brother and I were sibling rivals through and through, my sister and I were more like friends. I valued the opinion of the oh-so-'80s cool girl with the requisite wardrobe and soundtrack to match, and she was charmed by the wisecracking lil' dude who'd verbalize the things that were on everyone else's mind. We were family allies, protective of each other in different but equally important ways.

The guys in my sister's life usually caught on to our bond, and, in order to score points with her, they'd sometimes look for ways to incorporate me in their courtship practices. Typically this would involve an expressed interest in whatever video game I happened to be playing at the time or perhaps mitting up for some backyard baseball. Or when sis and dates reached the car years, it might be that they'd volunteer to take me to McDonald's for the limited edition orange sorbet milkshakes that became my H.W. Bush–era crack. At other times, the guys would even open up the dates in ways that brought me into the mix, taking me to see the Harlem Globetrotters at the local arena, or maybe to the zoo, in hopes that busying me with literal animalistic behavior might up their chances of satisfying their figurative urges. If they wanted to offer up whatever it took to get my pre-pubescent approval, who was I to deny myself the tangible rewards?

Though sometimes the benefits of having an older, date-worthy sister involved something far greater than box seats or fast food cuisine. In some cases it was nothing more than crucial insight into the male form, through the vehicle of another Hooper who was attracted to the same, that served me the most and provided me with the longest-lasting souvenirs.

It was a sticky hot summer day in 1989. That's when sis brought home two male friends, both of whom had just gone swimming. One of them was very attractive and one of them "holy crapballs!" hot, both at the apex of their ripened late-teen years. These two strappers came into our house adorned in a clothing style that I certainly had come to enjoy by that time: nothing but a swimsuit and a towel. There they were in our doorway, their nice toned upper parts with tantalizing happy trails on full display. Bulges constrained only by a tenuous drawstring. "Well, hello there," I said to both the boys and my suddenly rocked biology.

But while what was already exposed was nice and nipply, there was more on my mind than just midriff. Because I, a swimming trunk wearer myself, knew that one tends to "go commando" when wearing such an outfit. Plus I also knew that when sitting, the outer layer of trunk could leave an open exposure, while the inner layer, so snug while standing, could loosen just enough to free the family jewels. And while outline of anatomy through Lycra short was still a plenty interesting and welcome sight for my young eyes, the possibility of a certain set of objects falling from its tenuous home within the fabric intrigued me in the same way that I imagine Isaac Newton's gravity-bound apples inspired him. Maybe, just maybe, if I played my cards right, today would be the day I could see a little sumpin', sumpin' extra, thought nine-year-old me.

I was determined. Once Mark and Jared made it clear they'd be staying for a quick snack and a soda, I, with interest stiffly piqued, also decided to pop a squat and have a little something to munch on. I hastily grabbed some Funyons, and I'm sure we probably all had Cherry 7-Up. Taste buds, schmastebuds. The only treat I really wanted was eye candy.

The duo sat down in our den to talk about whatever bit of whatever was being discussed on this acid-washed summer afternoon. Maybe the Tiananmen Square protests, maybe *Honey, I Shrunk The Kids*—whatever was pressing on this particular day. All I know is that I made some sort of a logical entrance into the conversation before strategically choosing to plant my young bum in my father's favorite chair, since the sight lines afforded by the particularly uncomfortable seat just so happened to be the best for carrying out my plans. Had I given even half a crap about what they were saying, I would've been more focused on sound quality rather than vision and would have probably sat elsewhere. But I didn't, and I wasn't, so I didn't. At that precise moment, sight was the only sense on my mind, since I had one mission and one mission only: **to see balls.**

Now, I had certainly seen naked male anatomy before, though not nearly enough for my young liking. You must remember, access to such visuals were far more limited during those days, as the view-anything-anytime-you-like access that the Internet affords was still a reality known to only a select, geeky few. These were still encyclopedia times, and a cross section of a scrotum with the vas deferens clearly labeled, while educational, was not going to satisfy my youthful curiosity. Plus, nude dudes never got any below-the-belt attention in American cinema, and lingering at my local pool's shower too long to catch a peek was a sure-fire way for a young'un to get branded a "fruit." So for those of you under a certain age who won't understand why I'd go to any length to simply catch a gander of testes, just know that the ages pre-Internet left far more to the young boy's imagination. Figuring it out required more than a few keystrokes.

And balls were a particular curiosity. Both enjoined and separated from the more popular shaft, the testicles were a total oddity to me. I of course had them, but I wasn't sure what they did. I knew it hurt like, well, *balls* when the baseball would Sunday hop into the place where my pinstripes didn't shine. I didn't, however, know their true function, sexual or otherwise, or know whether they would make any more sense once I got older. These two dudes were to be my lab nads, like it or not. It seemed a victimless enough crime.

As Jared and Mark chatted up my mother, convincing her they were perfectly upstanding young men worthy of frolicking with her daughter, I seized the opportunity to begin my scrote-seeking endeavor. But how to do this? What's the plan here?

My first thought was to twist my body a bit, hoping I'd be able to see into either Jared's or Mark's baggy aquatic apparel. Alas, both sets of legs were too low and no amount of body contorting was going to help my cause. As "throw your leg up in the air so I can better see your scrotum" seemed unlikely to yield desirable results, I decided to come up with another strategy.

The next plan to come to mind involved a mirror, which I could cup in my hand and maneuver for the purposes of peeping. That sounded annoying from the get-go, since it would require me to leave the room, get an appropriately sized piece of reflective glass, and come back without anybody taking my perfect spot. Plus it was risky. What if the mirror accidentally caught a ray of sun and beamed it in my mother's eyes? Something told me that "Sorry, mom, I was performing a virtual castration" was unlikely to quell her likely suspicions. So that one was a non-starter.

Upon looking around and realizing where I was sitting, it only took a second for me to come up with what would be the third and final plan. You see, dad's chair, while the only place he ever sat and much beloved by him and his behind, was woefully uncomfortable and, frankly, poorly constructed. Remember, I chose it for its sight lines, not its opulence. Frankly, it was rock hard and musty. Plus when one sat in the ultra-hard throne, the two cushions that made up the backrest and seat would slide out from under the sitting person, forcing him or her to constantly pull the padding back into place. Everyone knew this happened, leading most to just avoid the chair altogether. While avoidance was my usual modus operandi as well, today would be the day I'd use the seat's annoyance to my benefit. For today my M.O. was 100 percent 'mo, and the incredible slipping chair was just the ride I needed to take me to Gonadville (population: a pair).

The plan went like this:

STEP 1: Wait for the optimal light to shine through the window. When aiming to see the place where the sun is said to not shine, one needs as cloudless of a setting as possible.

STEP 2: Lean back in the chair in the way I knew was guaranteed to yield the most cushion slippage. If my past experience was correct, the end result would leave me almost horizontal in the seat within the minute, as the padding slowly drifted down and outward.

STEP 3: Involve myself in the conversation in a way that made it seem as if I was so enthralled by the musings that I hadn't even noticed what was happening to my sitting status, and then wait for the line of sight between my eye and either Mark's or Jared's open short to align.

STEP 4: Keep the eyes moving. Fixating on one point might draw suspicions. The key was to dart my peepers from TV to mom to the window to my bag of Funyons to open dude short, and then I'd repeat the process. Like hot potato, yet with pairs of (eye)balls.

Okay, got that? Ready? On three! One, two . . .

The cushions slid, and I rode them down, all the while feigning interest in the conversation. Lower, lower, lower.

"Yes, I too think it's Rick Moranis' finest cinematic vehicle, Jared."

Lower still. Eyes in quick-yet-casual motion.

"Sure, I'd love to hear your Dana Carvey–as–George Bush impersonation, Mark. There's nothing I love more than an impression of an impression."

Almost there. Body nearly horizontal and family too impressed with Mr. Faux "no new taxes" to notice I'm ruining my dinner with processed onion rings and ruining my ocular virginity via a poorly constructed sit spot.

"Did anybody see *Roseanne* this week?" I threw in for extra measure.

Okay, position set. Eyes toward Speedo-branded nether regions.

Until lo and behold, I saw it: one hairy testicle and maybe even a slight peek of shaft. It was bigger than I had imagined; was also less of a circle and more of an oval than I had ever assumed. Flesh and fur in perfect balance.

CONCLUSIVE FINDING: Both were beautiful, the gonad and the strategy.

Okay, so why do I share this particular (and admittedly odd) story now? Well, because in a weird way, this attempt to size up the balls of my sis' friend does very much relate to the struggle to be gay in this world. Seriously. No, I'm not joking. Hear me out.

In my situation, I had analyzed what I could get away with, how best I could manipulate my given set of circumstances so that I could gain the most desirable result, and I'd kept my eye firmly on the prize, which in this case was a glimpse of nut. I'd focused my energies on one particular cause and convinced all those around me that I was merely a concerned participant in the conversation. I had used a tactic. Lo and behold, the nutty tactic actually paid off.

But the thing is, LGBT people are *always* having to use tactics to advance their knowledge or understanding. Developmental information is not always offered up to us the way it is to our straight and/or gender-conforming peers. Whereas heterosexual kids are subjected to the embarrassing "birds and the bees" speech, few parents address the kinds of relationships where beaks or stingers are doubled. Or in terms of gender, while the roles have certainly opened up over the years, a kid who doesn't fit in the pink/blue mold is still far more likely to face obstacles than are those who so easily address their genes with either jeans or a dress. Both sexual orientation and gender identity can be pretty formidable foes in the whole figuring-out-life process. Gambits are often in order.

Instincts are beautiful. The innate desires that define our characters should not be controversial. For far too many LGBT people, however, these perfectly normal, perfectly natural patterns of behavior *are* made contentious. On matters that really require no thought at all, we who fail to fit into certain relational or gender paradigms are forced to give a second consideration before acting. What is unthinkably easy for straights is a major source of difficulty for gays, for whom the normal questions of childhood take on a whole other level. All too often, the answer-gathering process becomes a dangerous spelunking mission when it should be a "take the good, take the bad" fact of life.

I think this is one reason why so many LGBT people are so attuned creatively: because we often *have* to be clever in order to figure it all out. Our curiosities, like all curiosities, are begging to come out and play.

However, our society is not always as welcoming to LGBT impulses as it is to straights' own instincts. What's that saying? Curiosity killed the cat and institutionalized his gay brother? Or something like that.

Just think about my previously relayed instance of testes rubbernecking. How many stories have been told about young boys hoping to sneak a peak of a topless female? It's a familiar clip in even wholesome movies. Yes, most adults would intervene, perhaps seeing it as their responsibility to preserve the kid's innocence/protect the unwilling model. That's fair enough. But for LGBT people, the matter becomes something else. The childhood inquisitiveness is often ripped from the realm of pre-adult rite of passage. The parents aren't as likely to take the dirty magazine into their bedrooms and laugh about it behind closed doors—they're far more likely to show some kind of dread. They are more likely to show a real fear. This can create a foreign, oddly uncomfortable land within the home that can be downright scary for those who are forced to travel within it.

Kids are "why?" machines. *"Why is the sky blue?"* *"Why is grass green?"* *"If we're Christians, then why does mommy always say she worships Xanax and white wine?"* Asking questions is what these little tykes do. And if kids are the workbooks, then parents are the teacher's editions. In a kid's mind, the grownups have all of the answers.

So what happens when the answers are repeatedly withheld? Well, a kid can start to pick up on the possibility that the reluctance is purposeful. When the answers don't jibe with the kid's own queries, the notable disconnect can be disquieting. The questions, previously geared toward outward exploration, can turn to an inward examination. The weirdness can become internalized, transferring into a general sense of foreboding about life's natural progression. I know I always felt this internal trepidation. It made me feel like I was completely alone in the figuring it out process, which is something that became increasingly scary when figuring it out went from explorations of why Fred Flintstone only has three toes to why I couldn't stop thinking about those two balls.

Even if I was, on balance, a happy and fairly adjusted kid, I certainly felt like a misfit in many ways. I was a misfit who didn't always get my desired answers from cheesy sitcoms or made-for-TV movies; a misfit who needed more places to turn than were available to me; a misfit who felt I had all of the pieces for a successful human puzzle, but a misfit who had an increasing realization that much of my surrounding world would rather solve than enjoy me.

Misfits have no choice but to get creative.

Years later, I'd adapt my clever strategies to size up and tackle the nutty words and actions of the professionally homo-hostile. But while marriage equality, inclusive hate crimes legislation, employment non-discrimination, HIV/AIDS awareness, and the whole equal rights plan might make up a far more principled slate of goals than does witnessing a post-pubescent testicle in its natural habitat, my commitment to the task at hand (or eye, as it were) was just as steadfast on that summer's day as it is during any current rights debate. That's because I know that while these simple matters of equality and fairness may be (ahem) meatier than my young eye's desire to see a real-life Almond Joy, the basic rights attached to them are just as natural as my childhood curiosities. And no one can neuter my passion to be myself—then, now, or ever!

5) YOU'RE GROSS, WORTHLESS, AND HELLBOUND (J/K)

Stop me if you've heard this one:

Two gay men were having sex. Ya know, the gay guy way? When all of a sudden, one of them stopped and said he had to go to the bathroom.

"No, don't," said one of the men. I'm enjoying it too much."

"I'll be quick," said the other

"Well whatever you do, don't jack off," said the first guy

A few minutes pass, and the guy who's still in bed wonders what's taking his lover so long. Both confused and concerned, he goes into the bathroom, only to find that there's fluid ALL OVER the walls. It's simply covered.

"I thought I told you not to jack off," screams the one, now-annoyed partner.

"I didn't," says the other. "I farted."

[*ba dum, dum*]

I was twelve when I first heard gay sex used as a punch line, coming (no pun intended) in the form of the above joke. I'll admit that I laughed at it. Heck, I chuckle a little even now because the imagery is ridiculous enough to elicit a smirk, independent of intended connotation. With my current level of exposure and understanding, I can laugh at the foolishness while remaining good-natured.

Unfortunately, "good-natured" isn't the way I'd classify the laughs that came from my classmates at the time. In fact, what I remember most about this crass joke is the thrill so many of my school chums got out of not only the visual image but also the mere possibility that two men could ever do it. It's hard to remember whether the anti-gay slurs outweighed the laughs, but it was definitely a close horserace.

Here's another one that sticks out in my mind's sludge bucket, circa eighth grade:

Q. "What'd the gay guy say when the butcher sliced up his salami?"

A. "What do you think my butt is, a slot machine?"

This exchange was followed by laughter, of course. Then I vividly remember one of my best female friends responding with the startling, "Eureka!"-like revelation that "fags must have big a-holes." The others concurred and added their own rectal assessments, taking the joke beyond the kicker and into the realm of kicking gays for the sole reason of being 'mo. The whole thing led to a conversation about who and how gays are, and what they supposedly do. Needless to say, "perfectly appoint the summer homes they share with their charming life partners" was not the consensus position.

That same year, a kid showed up at school wearing a shirt that had an admirable "Stop AIDS" message on the back. It would've been a great tee, perfectly tuned to the safe-sex '90s, if not for the front of the shirt. For the front consisted of two stick-figure men having anal sex, with a circle/slash *Ghostbusters*-like symbol over the act. Somehow its wearer had acquired, chosen, and left the house in this shirt!

Oh, and wait a minute, what's that over there? Why is that adult covering her face with the papers? Is she, a teacher, actually—no, seriously it can't be. She can't really be *laughing*, can she?! Cuing other kids to laugh? About AIDS? Really?

And we kids were still really young, too, just tweens who were slowly losing the "w," so it's not like my friends had formed their opinions based on careful analysis of the post-Stonewall gay rights movement or cogent considerations of the so-called "clobber passages" that are used to justify religious-based homo-hostility. This kind of detestation isn't instinctual—it is undeniably nurtured behavior. The revulsion was clearly cultivated at my friends' homes, fostered by parents who must not have accepted LGBT people as part of their own fabric. Weird, because these parents were always so nice to me, the good kid that many of them wanted their own children to be more like. Would they have felt the same way had they known my truth? Would they have let me drink from their cups if they'd known that I'd grow up to reject the anti-LGBT Kool-Aid?

By this time I had long been processing my same-sex attractions, even if I hadn't come close to fully accepting them. By now I took the point-edly targeted laughter to both heart and mind, the way a graphic artist might file away a particularly beautiful sunset until he or she has the proper tools and canvas to share the vision. Tools, like say, a publishing platform. A canvas, like say, this book.

So what, then, are the lessons I learned from these amateur comedy hours? Well, first and foremost, that anti-gay attitudes and platitudes are largely born out of the unknown. In my hometown, there were no openly LGBT people. I don't mean there were virtually none—I mean there *literally* weren't any. Chickens who crossed roads were in reasonable supply. I think I even saw a flying pig once. But as for out gays and lesbians? They were nowhere to be found.

To my peers and me, LGBT people could be turned into an easy bit of comedy because the very idea of an out person was so comically unrelat-able. In our community, one needn't be abjectly anti-gay to find humor in these jokes, since the mere idea of gays being gay was already so absurd to everyone around. To those who told them, a joke about gay men was like a joke about aliens. There was no human connection, so there was no need to be humane.

Another takeaway from the Junior High Ha Ha Hut was that it rein-forced within me the fact that humor holds great power. By then I was already a student of sketch comedy and knew from *Weekend Update* how slyly one could deliver a pointed, even serious, message if he kept his tongue planted in the cheek. Plus, through the pervasive stains imprinted on me by the other forms of targeted hostile humor that peppered my early childhood years, I got the first inklings of how destructive ideas could be solidified in the same way. Now here was a real world application, and I was starting to personally feel like the joke-butt. This continued exposure to homo-hostile "hilarity" was in many ways a reinforcement of lessons I'd already begun to learn. But whereas the jokes from my younger years felt like pick-ups and putdowns with no real moral instructions attached, the teen form felt more instructive (and destructive, as it were). These jokes felt more like declarations or even lessons—lessons I felt a growing responsibility to challenge.

This feeling did have one positive effect, in that it even more fully heightened my sensitivity to others' plights. As a Christian-identified, straight-as-far-as-anyone-knew, skinny kid in an environment that placed a premium on the same, I never experienced true discrimination in my formative years. Sure, my brother always made me the Luigi to his Mario. And yes, the neighbor's mom made us use the back entrance so we wouldn't track mud on her pristine floor. Those things hardly classify as hurtful bias. These jokes did. There was a palpable shift in my early teen years, where my mind went from being an apathetic ally on certain social justice causes to at least a lip service supporter. With less and less ability to fake my status as an "other," I started to more clearly see a whole host of other wrongs that were going on around me. Out and proud gay man was still not a role I could carry off in 1992, but I could at least ease into becoming a laidback liberal almost-ivist.

Mostly, these jokes, coupled with the previously inexperienced pain that comes with being cast aside as an outsider, just made me uneasy. With these kinds of supposed knee-slappers, I felt the first rumblings. [*rumble, rumble*] Of what it feels like to be a punch line, not because of something you said or did but just because of who you are. [*rumble, rumble*] Of how much of a thrill heterosexism can bring to some hearts. [*rumble, rumble*] Of how others' condemnations could lead one to question if maybe there was a reason to hate the people one had been taught to hate. [*rumble, rumble*]. Of fearing that by being myself, someone might want to take me in the back alley and . . . [*rumble, rumble*].

I was still a few years away from fully figuring out who I was/am/always will be, and I was a few more years away from admitting the same. But seeing who I *wasn't* and who I *didn't want to be* forced me to (a) admit that my sensitivity chip had been somewhat rocked and (b) look inward and ask why I, lifetime lover of a good laugh, had taken these particular kinds of jokes to heart. Perhaps most dishearteningly, they made me question if maybe I too were set up for a life in which my very existence would be seen as a joke.

It's not really gay jokes themselves that are even the worst part. There's actually something to be said for poking fun at every group of people equally, since we are a pretty ridiculous human collection that's more than ripe for chops busting. If LGBT people demand equality, then this must also pertain to a gentle ribbing every now and then. Jokes, even ones that exploit stereotypes, can absolutely pass over the bar of acceptability. Fair play.

The unfortunate truth is that the most common anti-gay jokes are *not* typically concerned with fair play. What I do and did find so startling about overheated anti-LGBT humor, then and now, is how jugular-ripping the comedy often is and how much pure satisfaction so many seem to get out of it. For some, it's as if the louder the cackle, the more they will distance themselves from any inkling they or others may have that they themselves might be gay. The jokes can operate as both shields and bombs, working in concurrence to build up by breaking down. Whereas one might follow up a run-of-the-mill joke with "no offense," the unspoken subtext that follows some of the worst anti-LGBT jokes is "Know offense and know it well, you f***ing queer." It's often easier to find the aggression than it is to find the kicker.

It's not my kind of humor, that aggressive stuff. I don't want to put anyone on the personal defensive, pretty much as a rule. That's why in my own work I always try to take the piss out of the message rather than messenger. You never know the life story that led one to embrace certain words, so gunning for a person on a character level can come across as misguided and counterproductive, and the choice can lead to an unbecoming bit of face-egg that turns the clown into the punch line. The words, on the other hand, are empirical. The message is what it is. Whether it's loathable or laudable, the message is always fair game, in my humble o.

Yes, now, as an adult who confronts discrimination, I sometimes jokingly use wordplay when I refer to the LGBT community's generalized political opponents as 'mo foes.

'mo foe |mō fō|
noun
One who denies homosexuals their piece of the humanity pie.
Johnny used to enjoy Ellen DeGeneres, but then he decided to become a 'mo foe.

And yes, I sometimes take the piss out of the seemingly single-minded obsessions of the professionally anti-gay players. But that's just silliness, meant to desensitize the debate with a humor injection, not to go after anyone on a personal level. My focus is the policy, not the people, and my underlying hope in all of this "culture war" nonsense is to lessen the aggression. For one thing, it's crucial that I do so in order to preserve my own sanity. But also, I hope that by highlighting not only the gravity of the situation but also the absurdity of it all, I can force at least some of the people who've been duped into embracing the discriminatory messages to see how senseless this fight truly is.

In a utopian society, we'd all be free to rib any and every group in equal measure, with no kind of targeted joke holding a higher weight. Regrettably, we do not exist in such a world. We live in a world of injustice, where needless affronts are waged against others. That being the case, it's not hypocritical to note that the keys of comedy are granted in unequal measure. It's simply the truth. While LGBT people can and should be the subject of comedy, our rights and worth and cores of beings are not as ripe for fodder as is an anti-gay's quest for discrimination. When some of us make jokes about the so-called "culture war" that is used to deny us of any of the aforementioned qualities, we are laughing so as not to cry. But what possible reason would someone who is working on the homo-hostile side of the "culture war" have to laugh at the battles that they willingly wage? So they won't look as mean when their organizations strip away a crucial right or protection? Sorry, but I don't think so! Activist comedy works when it's operating as a corrective and fails when it's helping to cause the nausea.

If the LGBT community's political opponents can deal with inflicting a degree of pain that's truly soul-crushing to LGBT people, then a 'mo foe here and a "ha ha" there (here a 'mo, there a 'mo, everywhere a 'mo foe) should in no way feel like a hit. Instead, it should strike him or her as surprising high road from a community who has every right and reason to take the low one! I mean, think about it. When we talk about anti-gay politicos, we're talking about people who are robbing others' civil rights, often marrying that political affront with the kind of faith-based condemnation that sends LGBT people straight to hell. That's *such* weighty stuff. If we pro-equality voices can find those little opportunities to inject a little bit of punch, a little bit of flare, a little bit of humor that shines a light on the absurdity of this figurative "war," well then, I think that's a good thing. We can show the other side that direct attacks on our lives and loves will not get us down. We can let them know that while they have the ability to inflict pain on us—a reality for which they can, must, and will take responsibility—they do not have the ability to rob us of our joy. We can show them that their rhetoric and actions are making them look like 'mo foes, but that it need only be a temporary state. Maybe, just maybe, we can teach them that there's a way out of that dangerous anti-gay lifestyle if they want it.

From the high road, we can avoid the sluggish effects of the base-level mire. However, the greater advantage is that we can launch far more strategic counterpunches than we could have from the ground level. There are teachable moments to be had; they all lie on the side that is pushing to keep kids safe from bullying, adults safe from civil unfairness, and government safe from religious oversteps. If we stoop down, then we lessen our ability to instruct. If we stand tall with principled steel in our spines and undaunted wit in our smirks, then we win.

Look, I don't expect jokes made at the LGBT community's expense to stop—and don't even want them to, specifically. I do, however, expect these quips to be made in the same spirit as ones that take the piss out of any other community. Just like with so many LGBT matters, right now our gay-targeted humor exists on an unlevel playing field where a premium is placed on aggression. That's not good comedy; it's hacky both in style and intent. I will challenge everyone to ask whether his or her words are witty or personally wounding. If it's the former, then we'll all share a laugh at the sheer ridiculousness that is humanity. But if the answer is the latter, then I'll encourage the could-be comic to at least have the fortitude to admit that he or she is bombing before even taking the stage. Because "just kidding" isn't enough to invalidate certain forms of aggression, and laughter is not the best medicine for curing all systemic problems.

I may have been clever enough, but I certainly wasn't confident enough to turn the tables on my junior high friends' jokes. I knew I would be someday, after just a little more figuring-it-out time.

6) CLEARLY IT'S AN ISSUE

It was my sixteenth birthday and the day I was to finally get my driver's license. Even so, it was my mother who'd manage to drive home the bigger life milestone on this date. Namely, the lack of license she'd give to a son whose own road diverged off the hetero highway.

First, some back-story. I adored *Entertainment Weekly* magazine to an almost unhealthy degree. This was pre-Internet and before celebrity culture pervaded every aspect of our daily lives, so for an entertainment junkie like me, this magazine provided a most-welcome, much-desired weekly insight into what the seemingly interesting folks on the coasts were doing. I would read each issue cover to cover, obsessively absorbing every detail, as I imagined the glamorous entertainment career I envisioned for my adult future. *EW* was the glossy coastal Bible; I, its flyover state disciple.

Having the magazine hit the mailbox was a major highlight of my week for most of the teen years, and everyone knew it. It was basically the only piece of mail that came in my name, and the family knew better than to interfere with my addiction. If someone else got the mail before me, *EW* was always laid out, untouched, ready for me to absorb when I got home from school. To read it before me was to taint it, and I could certainly detect a preemptive fingerprint on Julia Roberts' or Beavis' glossy face. I needed a crisp copy, spine unbroken and nary a staple even halfway loosened. Trust me, I could tell.

However, on this sixteenth b-day and all the excitement that comes with such a watershed, the magazine routine had completely slipped my mind. After all, this was the day—THE day—I was to finally get that Holy Grail of youthful privileges, and the thought of that shitty picture–adorned card in my wallet had clouded my mind to all other aspects of life. There was just so much to do. I had to find one of those ironic green tree air fresheners. I needed to figure out how to connect my Discman with that little cassette and cigarette lighter doohickey that all middle-class kids born on that bubble between tape decks and standard in-car CD players used as a musical stopgap. Then there'd be places to go and people to see, all in the few post-school hours that are even available to a boy-child on an autumn weeknight.

And, oh God, first I had to pass the thing! No time for frivolity. Little else mattered, not even my precious *EW.* Get ye to the DMV!

First came the driver's test, which was as smooth as yogurt. And I'm not talking about the fruit on the bottom kind—I'm talking the smooth, makes-you-regular kind that Jamie Leigh Curtis is always hawking at unorthodox locations like pools or gyms or houses where she switches bodies with Lindsay Lohan. Wait, I think I'm confusing my pop references. Where was I? Oh yeah, the test. I'd been warned I'd have to parallel park, get on a highway, and massage the steering wheel *just so*, without missing a beat in order to sing for my sweet supper. In actuality, all I had to do was drive around a quiet block, one where the low speed limit allowed a kid on a scooter to go whizzing right by, and where the complete and utter lack of cars limited crash potential to only the unexpected merging of expectation with uneventful reality. Needless to say, I passed that part.

For a somewhat-prone-to-procrastination peep like myself, [*note to editor: I'll finish this line at some point. What? No—I have to do it now? Grr, okay…*] the written portion of the test was much more daunting. I'd kind of studied for it, if by "studied" you mean kept the preparation book in my JanSport, mostly only bringing it out for toilet or nap breaks. I was convinced that the practical driving hours to which I truly had committed would see me through.

Well, I'm happy to report that experience did trump reading (but stay in school anyway, kids), as I did pass the written test with flying colors. I actually only missed one question; don't remember which one.

However, I'm less happy to report the one question onto which that day's later events would force my mind to focus for months and years and even decades to come. That question I do remember: "**Holy mother of mindfreak, does my mom think/fear I'm gay?**"

Allow me to explain.

On the ride away from my new favorite greater Nashville govern-ment office building, the familiarity of my parents' backseat and the com-fort of knowing I now had another vehicular option helped me to come down from the high of newly licensed euphoria. It was during this falling wave when I finally remembered that today was, in fact, *EW* delivery day. Excited about the thought, thinking it was just another win in this day of nothing but triumph, I instinctively asked, toward the general direction of my parents, if the precious mag had hit our street corner inbox the way it was wont to do on any other given week. To me, this question couldn't have been more benign, more rote. The response I received, however, was just—well, *weird.*

Not an emphatic "no" or "yes, it came," but rather a more mealy-mouthed "Uhm, well, ya, uhm . . . *maybe* . . . uh . . . what do you want for dinner, sweetie?" was the confusing reply my mother sent back. I can't remember if I immediately took pause at the bizarre, non-committal response, or if I just unconsciously answered, "O'Charley's, their salad sounds good," and went about my teenage business. With the knowledge of what came next and the time that has passed, I want to say I auto-matically knew something was up on the basis of mom's odd feedback. However, that probably wasn't the case, as I couldn't have realized at the time *why* my question was in any way controversial.

What I *do* know is that that evening, post–spinach dip and virgin daiquiris, when I discovered the magazine, apart from the other mail, carefully tucked away in another room's pile of papers and whatnots, I did manage to put all of the elements together—because it was pretty damn obvious. She'd never hide this magazine from me—no one in the family would. Moreover, she'd never play dumb about an action that was so clearly deliberate, about a magazine that was so important to me, on a day that was so *thoroughly mine* unless there was a bigger agenda.

But wait—how is this *Entertainment Weekly*–hiding nonsense leading to queer suspicions, you ask? Well, now comes the big reveal.

The particular *EW* issue for that week just so happened to feature a cover story titled "The Gay '90s." An exploration into all that was queer, the very cover itself featured more LGBT imagery than I had seen in my previous sixteen years of life. Elton John, Melissa Etheridge, Joel Schumacher's famously nippled versions of Batman & Robin—if there were to have been a Pride parade of 1995's magazines, this *EW* issue would've undoubtedly been the grand marshal.

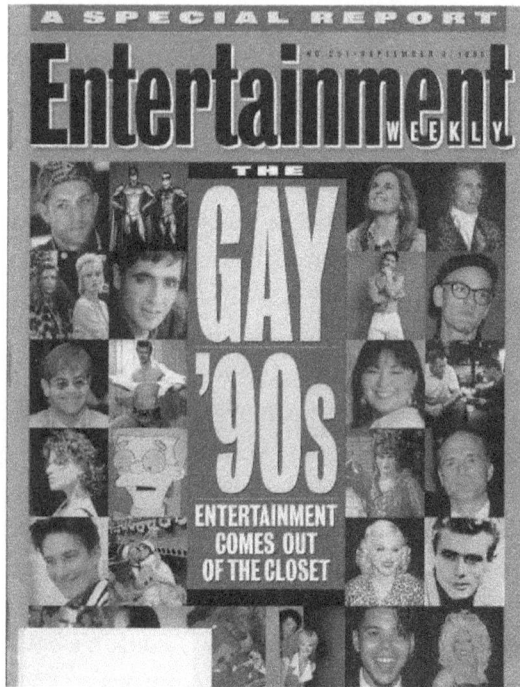

Gay, gay, gay, it was. Hidden, hidden, hidden, it had been. It was stuck in between a stack of household books and newspapers and junk we'd never gotten around to tossing, in a manner that a logical eye could only see as deliberate. Haste would've put it in the waste bin or halfway under the couch. Malice would have shredded the pages and left them in my bed. But placed where it was, on the kitchen table, apart from all of the other mail of that day, in between a Yellow Pages (kids, ask your parents) and an already-read Dean Koontz novel? How could that action have been anything other than methodical? Knowing what I knew about the operations of my house, I knew it couldn't have been an absent-minded act.

Placing on pause for just a second the fact that it had been hidden, my very first reaction, upon seeing it, was to simply fear the magazine itself.

---

[1] Jess Cagle, "Special Report: The Gay 90s," *Entertainment Weekly*, 8 September 1995, cover story.

By that time I had certainly had more than a few crushes, sexual thoughts, and masturbatory fantasies about guys to know that I had more than a passing interest in the male of the species. Exclusively about guys, if I was being honest. Yet despite my clear and ever-crystallizing feelings, I still didn't think of myself as gay yet. *How could I have?* In my household, gay was so bizarre, so foreign, and SO NOT ME. In fact, age fifteen had been the climax of my closet-dwelling and queer thoughts intersection—a trying collusion in which the former continued to stifle the latter. As one might expect, that age was also the nadir of my self-esteem.

All of this on the inside, at least—confined to only my own mind, shared only with Dr. Conscience. Outwardly I put up the all-American teen front that was expected of me, but internally I painted a truer (if equally American) portrait. Overburdened with what I now look back upon as my breaking point, my heart rate would increase and I'd become uncomfortable in my own skin whenever I saw anyone or anything that so much as looked or sounded gay, scared that my inner truth would show its colors. This so, I didn't even focus so much on where and how I'd found my favorite magazine, since I was instinctively more frightened of (yet intrigued by) its content.

However, once I started thinking about how weird it was for the magazine to have been hidden the way it had been, that's when I started asking myself some questions. As I've indicated, I knew that homo-centric feelings were now in the back of my mind most of the time and how, in turn, I felt like I should publicly avoid any and all exposure to gay things. I didn't, however, realize that anyone outside of my own head had an iota of insight into what was going on—most of all mom! She was the one person from whom I definitely wanted to shield the contents of my cranium!

As a scared, closeted teen, I desperately wanted to believe that somehow my mother had just placed the mag in a pile of assorted junk to keep anyone else reading my invaluable prize before I did. Over the course of the night, I kept going back to that possibility. But as a rational human being, this seemed unlikely. In fact, one would think that since it was my birthday and all, extra attention would be paid to me and my periodical needs. This was clearly less.

With uncomfortable acceptance of that one point out of the way, my thoughts quickly turned to how I should proceed with damage control. Should I just grab the now-rescued copy and go about my week of Time,

Inc., goodness as if nothing was out of the ordinary? After all, on normal weeks I'd read the magazine proudly and openly, filling anyone in earshot in on whatever totally pressing issues various Hollywood publicists wanted me to know in that given span. If I changed my own habits, might I make the situation more awkward for everyone? More telling?

Then again, what if I do decide to read it and it looks like I'm staring at it too closely? Its pages felt like a friggin' eclipse! I of course wanted to see it—hell, I'd waited ages to see something as queer-inclusive as this. But would looking for too long leave me with lasting scars? Sure, with verbal references, I could try to make clear that I was focusing on the mag's other articles rather than that pesky gay cover story. At ruse's rueful end, would it be my own story that seemed too much like a cover?

Coming right out and acknowledging the magazine's content felt *way* too risky. By then I was already shutting out, or at least reeling back, many of those wonderfully sensitive traits that I'd so easily cherished since I was a kid, making extra sure that my voice was appropriately masculine every time I opened my mouth and that any lunch room table where I parked my booty had at least one other male friend around for "dude" points. When it came to LGBT stuff, I purposely avoided any land mines that might make me address whatever mid-'90s 'moness was happening around me. If a gay discussion were to pop up on TV, it made me feel exposed and therefore went unaddressed, not only by myself but my entire family. Addressing this gay content now would've been wholly out of character for all involved. Plus no matter what actually came out of my mouth, it would sound in my head like I was saying, "I heart penis, I heart penis, I heart penis, I heart pecs, too." What closeted 'mo needed that? I was already uncomfortable enough as it was.

Even amid the fear and discomfort, denouncing the magazine wasn't something I ever would've done either. I may have still been struggling myself and may have been years away from anything that could be classified as LGBT activism. At the same time, I fully knew who I was in other areas, and I wasn't someone who was ever anti–any person or minority group. I still refused to be an anti-gay, even during these "butch it up" years. It might have sometimes led to clashes about how "cool" or "alternative" they thought I was trying to be, but basically my more conservative family knew and was okay with my burgeoning progressive heart. I was out of the closet in that area, so pointing to the magazine and embracing overcompensating bigotry would've been almost as foreign to my living room's jury as would a much-needed conversation about gay rights.

The nuclear option of tossing the *EW* altogether was totally out of the question. For one, it'd be the most revealing of all the possible actions, should someone notice my doing it. But also, if not for my weekly pop-culture pill, how would I ever know where Jennifer Aniston planned to take her hairstyle, where in the Nielsen's *Roseanne* placed that week, or whether this planned movie about the Titanic was going to be an epic failure? This was weighty stuff! LGBT content or not, I needed my weekly pop-culture lesson. Without a fix, I'd surely start to get the shakes by mid-week.

What to do, what to do? My drama was far worse than that of the straight boy whose mom finds a *Hustler* under his bed. Horniness might strike a parent as surprising, but it's usually not unexpected. However, acknowledging my truth would've revealed more than just my personal discovery of the orgasm: it would've made for a complete paradigm shift. I wasn't ready for that. The potential consequences still struck me like a mental paper cut, as jarring as it was painful.

This territory was just so uncharted. If my poor handling of the magazine dilemma somehow bore out the contents that had long been within my head, there was no guarantee that I wouldn't be hauled into the queer body shop to have a faith-based mechanic tell me I was in need of repair. I'd read enough substantive magazines to know about a little something called "ex-gay" therapy and was enough in touch with all other realities to know it was no place I ever wanted to be. Especially not before I'd even had a chance to test out either my dipstick or tailpipe!

There was also a fate that seemed even more unsettling to my self-involved teen priorities: that my "conversion" plan might include telling my friends as a way to embarrass me into heterosexuality. This seemed less likely, since my mother had always been private by nature. But again, this was all so unmapped. How was I to know whether or not the "de-gayification" of me would involve my public exposure? I certainly didn't believe that being the one openly gay kid in a rural high school would trend me more towards popularity rather than pariah-dom. There were always rumors about some past graduate, usually male, who had "turned gay" in college. Let's just say that "Wow, good for him—let's go to Nashville Pride and support him" was not the common response.

Then there was the matter of ease (or lack thereof). I was going through enough in my own head, figuring out who I was, what it all meant, and how it all fit into the world around me. I was in A.P. classes in high school and had similarly advanced college plans starting to shape up. Plus *The Real World* was particularly good that season. The last thing I needed in my life was an extra diversion—particularly a diversion that might in any way derail the grand plans I had for myself. No, no—I just wanted the interrogation to go away. For just a little longer, at least.

What to do? Where to turn? How to play this? But most importantly: who's that guy on the cover who's removing his shirt, and when can I learn more?!

I had only questions, no answers. This on a night when I thought the biggest question would involve nothing thornier than my preference for a cake slice with limited frosted roses.

This was truly the first moment I realized my mother thought I could be gay, and it scared the hell out of me. It scared the hell out of me because it so obviously scared the hell out of her! She had clearly wanted to keep the magazine from me for a reason—there was absolutely no doubt about that. Just knowing that she was suspicious, coupled with other contextual clues, told me everything I needed to know about the level of respect I'd receive from her if I were to acknowledge my truth. There may have eventually been cake on this, the night of my sixteenth; there most certainly wouldn't be anything sweet at whatever coming out party I might have been subconsciously planning for myself.

This is when fear of being "found out" really crept in, beginning a half-a-decade or so run within my being. *Happy birthday, paranoia!*

7) I COULD ALWAYS GROW A BEARD

At first they were experiments. Even if I'd never had an ounce of genuine interest in the physical female form, there was always the chance that I was some sort of late bloomer, right? After all, sexual awakening is uncharted territory for all of us. Who knows what one's supposed to feel and when?

But after one or two post-pubescent girlfriends, it was pretty damn clear that my lady lab should be closed down for good. Everything about opposite-sex love as it pertained to me was simply perverted—an abomination even. The kisses felt all wrong, way too soft and much too passive. The handholding made me feel as if I'd placed the wrong glove on the wrong meat hook. Sweet nothings were heavy on the latter and light on the former. There were no mixed signals. There never really had been. I knew that the extra X chromosome would never answer my Y.

In a perfect world, this long-overdue self-admission, coming not all that long after the *Entertainment Weekly* incident, would've immediately led me to open the door of truth. However, in my semi-rural Tennessee town during the 1990s, that door was still to remain padlocked shut. I've already established that there were no gay role models around me. Unless invisibility was a fashion trend for young Southeastern gays that escaped me during my high school years, there was not one out, much less *proud*, queer person in my midst. There was an abundant amount of fear and shame surrounding the subject, both in my home and in my town.

So even though late nights of soul-searching had freed me to admit to myself what I'd known to be true since I laid eyes on that cute guy at my kindergarten graduation, I also knew that my own mating was going to have to keep waiting until sometime after my high school commencement. There was bona fide risk in those halls, and it just wasn't worth it—especially not with my mother and perhaps others already on my trail. The one, focused fight was to retain sanity until I could get to college's greener, gayer pastures.

The major problem with this plan? I was a handsome kid with friends, a social life, and all of the common trappings of a typical teenage existence. Relative popularity is an odd thing to look back on as a problem, for sure. The cliché is for adult writers to bemoan their angsty days of tormented yore, right? Yeah, well in my nostalgic trips, the opposite is true. I don't say this as a way to gloat about past glory, mind you. I truly believe it would've been easier to go through high school as a loner with little to no extracurricular contact. If that were the case, I might not have been *expected* to date anyone. Sole satisfaction might've been understandable. But no, a shunned adolescence was not in my cards. Poor me [*sad trombone*].

Furthermore, my woes didn't stop at being fairly well adjusted in general. No, no—I was also cursed as being somewhat of a ladies' man. The girls simply loved me! It's probably because even through my faux macho trips, my ever-present sensitivity and strong emotions would find a way to seep out, sending subliminal messages that my female classmates found refreshing and intriguing. I also had the delicate features of a teen magazine regular, which surely exacerbated the situation. And who knows, maybe my scientific, girl-crazy brother had bottled some of his hetero pheromones in the cologne that I'd regularly borrow. Whatever the reason, teen me could not escape the eyes of the crushing lil' lasses.

"Not really interested," I'd say to this one or that one.

"I'm actually dating someone from church," I'd offer another.

Though after a while, I started to sense some raised eyebrows in my community, causing suspicion to grow within me. Most of it was probably in my overfilled head, like when I'd hear a teen boy do that oh-so-charming thing where he'd use the word "gay" as a generic insult and would have to remind myself that this was a school wide trend, not a targeted slam. Although I definitely *did* genuinely hear a family member suggest that I wasn't interested in girls, so it wasn't all paranoia. There was some curiosity swirling.

Petrified about being found out, it wasn't long before I determined that I'd have to take a lady-date or two if I wanted to keep up the charade. Plus, if I had a girlfriend, I reasoned that my mind would be less burdened with gay witch-hunt paranoia and therefore freer to focus on a less fallacious future. Internally, my cerebellum could host an all-out pride parade. My external being would do anything but.

So I dated. Females. It was as much of a game as my baseball matches, yet with much less arousal on my part (and far fewer bootie pats for my mates).

You know that cliché where the horny young guy in a movie theater fakes a yawn in order to put his arm around his date? Yeah, well, I was the hormonal teen who began with the arm in an embrace in order to get the uncomfortable act over with, only to then move into a yawn in order to justify my post-flick plan to go home and get some shuteye rather than make a romantic night out of it!

In fact, movies in general were pretty safe. There was popcorn breath to point toward as a reason not to smooch. The darkness allowed me to pretend to not see a come-hither look, and the THX-demanded silence meant less opportunity for gushy talk. Plus I didn't feel so guilty about my own play-acting if there were people on the big screen making a boatload of cash for the same kind of behavior.

Music was another safe haven. As a teen of the mid-'90s, I was fortunate enough to land within that small window where the longhaired, latte-sipping, "alternative" kids somehow became the popular ones. Forget football games and cheerleaders—to show off your best mall-bought flannel, it was all about all-ages rock shows housed in dark, dank, makeshift performance halls, where only *slightly* sticking to the floor meant you'd found a good spot. In terms of sexy, these venues were the anti-aphrodisiac. For my unnatural dating experiments, they were, in a word: *perfect*!

Yet teen social life can't be built on mosh pits and Brad Pitts alone, and there was certainly much more courting time that took place outside of these darkened spaces.

I actually enjoyed playing the stereotypical guy role at dinner. Taking charge of the seating, holding the doors, paying the bill—it all felt somewhat liberating. Plus it certainly felt good to be dating *anyone*. The gender might have been wrong, but schmoozing was fun. My instinctual chivalry was genuine.

The main problem at dinner was the very real chance of a gay male waiter. In the environs in and around Nashville, it seemed as if every Clinton-era queer dude had taken a job at a local chain restaurant.

"Our special tonight is manicotti with salad," said the aproned Adonis. Of course, he usually said this to the top of my head, as I was sure that looking up and making eye contact would cause some sort of revelatory rainbow to shoot forth from my peepers to his.

"Thanks, can you give us a minute?" I mumbled into my menu, looking it over so as not to do the same to him. Alas, the dessert I truly wanted was never on there.

Although even with gay waiter land mines, the dinner dates were still relatively easy. Chewing and chatting I could handle, as neither conversation nor consumption ever made the list of problems involving my lips. This was a dinner out with a friend, without any parental censorship or influence. Adult eyes would probably take that for granted, but for a teen, these moments of hands-off independence tend to be few and far between. So yeah, just in terms of the dining out aspect, the night was both enjoyable and effortless.

The hard part came at the end of the night. Or actually, no, that was precisely the problem—*the "hard part" never came*! There were no slabs of wood separating us after we left the dinner table, only two warm bodies, both built to send signals. At least *her body* sent direct signals. Mine? Let's just say that I knew that hips don't lie well before Shakira did!

I think my scrappy ass could have handled bullies—but these hits were below the belt! The faked kisses didn't hurt in the physical sense, but they certainly wounded the mind. They reminded me that while I'd come so far and achieved so much, I was still a fucking baby when it came to interpersonal relations that were in anyway personally stimulating.

If dad had given me enough money to spring for that brownie sundae I'd eyed earlier, there was always the chance to work the overstuffed and overplayed "if you hug me I'm gonna pop" line. Or even in the absence of a sweetened tooth, stomachaches were always possibilities. Although these kinds of food-borne denials were similar to lifelines on *Who Wants to Be a Millionaire*: they were limited and only paid off about half of the time. More often than not, I'd feel forced to sacrifice my gold-star gayness in order to maintain my hetero image. The fakery was really tough.

For starters, bras are insanely confusing! Of all of the research I did in order to pass off my supposed straightness, I was never prepared for the unexpectedly arduous task of removing a bra. Those things are frickin' labyrinthine! In fact, I'm sure there are women from my graduating class scattered around this nation to whom I owe a few bucks for the purpose of lingerie repair. If this is you, please get in touch with me on Facebook.

Not that the anatomy underneath or around the garment was any more familiar. I couldn't have had less of an internal roadmap when it came to the female form, and even repeated exposure didn't make any of it feel more relatable. The attempts started out somewhat interesting, in the way that seeing a celebrity in person is interesting. Once the initial novelty wore off, so too would the interest. I just never knew what to do with any of it!

According to sexy time edict, I probably should've been looking into my date's eyes. Instead, I was looking at the clock, longing for curfew to arrive in a way that no healthy teen should.

11:19: What's she doing with her leg?

11:21: Wait, is that a moan? Should I moan too?

11:21(and 30 secs): Oh God, why'd I just moan? Now I feel both opposite-horny and awkward.

11:23: Shouldn't we really have parental supervision? I did see a mother in that kitchen, right? Does anyone else want a cookie? I do.

11:24: Oh no, she's pushing my head south. DANGER. DANGER. Must abort mission!

"Oh crap, it's 11:25!" I'd say mid-leap. "Gotta jet."

Who knows if my dates saw right through me, filling their bathroom girl talk with swapped stories about the 'mo who thinks he's fooling them all. Regardless, I do know that *I* never felt good about any of it. On the drive home, I felt dirty. I felt guilty that I had just conducted a fairly elaborate lie. I was annoyed that I lived in a world that demanded the stifling of my truth. Ashamed that I didn't have the fortitude to be the one gay person in my tiny town willing to risk it all in order to save my sanity. All the while fixated on the idea of going back to the restaurant and waiting for that hot waiter to get off, both literally and figuratively.

Home was no saving grace. My tales of supposed teen love were a major, if not the *most* major, scene in this farce.

"It was great, mom," my teeth aching from the lie. "I really like her!"

Reciting outright bullshit only heightened the pain.

"We went to Olive Garden. The eggplant parmesan was awesome."

Having to pad the thoroughly underwhelming story with minutiae was almost more painful.

As I slugged up the stairs, I'd want nothing more than to turn on heel and shout at the top of my lungs: "I LIKE GUYS! THIS IS ALL A SHAM! IF YOU WOULD JUST GIVE ME SOME SIGN THAT MY TRUTH IS OKAY, THEN YOU COULD MAKE THIS SHITTY SENSE OF DREAD GO AWAY!"

But of course I said nothing. I instead brushed my teeth, the bristled stick sanitizing my failings. I was scrubbing away the meal; scrubbing away the kisses; scrubbing away the waiter. I wasn't scrubbing away my feelings, however. I didn't want to "change"—I wanted the world to.

Bedtime meant reflection. With head at rest on pillow yet mind still very much at play, I had to wonder where all of this was headed. The honesty within me was so rich and full, but if I didn't feel comfortable to express it now, where was the guarantee that I ever would? There certainly was no guarantee that any of my family or friends would ever be on board with my reality. Would I be able to handle that potential alienation, or would my existence carry on as an experiment rather than as a life? Would I ever drop this scraggly beard, no matter how itchy it may get?

In these questions I found pain—but at the end of the day, they only confirmed the predetermined answer.

DESPITE WHAT YOU MIGHT'VE HEARD . . . #2

➢ If a teen wants to pierce something, it doesn't mean he or she is gay. Unless that something is "a hole in the heterosexist paradigm," in which case they are (a) totally 'mo, so stop wondering; and (b) totally smart, so stop worrying.

➢ If you find heterosexual porn under your son's mattress, don't assume it's a sign of heteroness. He could be bi, he could desire a career in adult publishing, or he might be using the mag to stop the bed from squeaking whenever he spanks it to the gay smut in his closet.

➢ MTV will not teach your teen to be gay. Teaching your teen to be self-absorbed is another story.

➢ Masturbation is not a gay teen trait. It's a *breathing* teen trait.

➢ "Wait until marriage" is a pretty bad safe-sex strategy. "Wait until you're civil-unioned, since that's all your state will allow" is an even worse one.

➢ Lesbian teens actually *will* drive cars that are stick shift.

➢ Male gay teens actually *will* drive cars that have no rear entry.

➤ Starring in the school play will not turn your son gay. The hot guy playing Kenickie will.

Just kidding. Or am I? They didn't call me "greased lightning" for nothing.

➤ Books with LGBT characters are acceptable, and even responsible, reading for teens. If you oppose these kinds of books yet support *Romeo and Juliet*, a plot that revolves around teen suicide in the name of forbidden love, take one second and half as many brain cells to consider the message you might be sending to the adolescent set.

➤ Individuality deserves the premium we've long misapplied to conformity. **I demand that you all comply with that way of thinking and believe exactly as I do—en masse and right away!**

➤ There is no foreign language class that's any gayer than any other. Unless your child is hoping to start up an "Equal Marriage Vows in All Fifty States" class, there's probably nothing queer about his or her choice of non-native tongues.

➤ "Hope you won't be awkward to me and my same-sex date at the ten-year reunion" is a perfectly reasonable request to include in a yearbook signature. But it won't necessarily be heeded. I mean, did all of those kids "stay cool over the summer" like you commanded?

➤ Statistically, LGBT teens are targeted more often for bullying and harassment. If your child is on the "Smear the Queer" team or cheerleads for the same, then it's your responsibility to cancel the season.

➤ Sports moms and dads, I should remind you that spending days and nights around dudes, changing with them in the locker room, and patting them on the asses when they do a good job cannot successfully turn a boy straight. Shocking, I know.

➤ Teens can't help whom they like. They can, however, help saying "like" in every other breath. Seriously, young America: It's a word, not oxygen!

➢ Yes, you'll still want to take prom pictures, even if you know your kid is gay and that his or her hetero date is a total, utterly awkward ruse. And do it out of compassion for their coming-out process, not because you think that if they become famous, the Friar's Club might hit you up for roast material.

➢ Pro-gay teachers can't indoctrinate your kids. Your kids are likely not listening to him or her in the first place.

➢ No, non-accepting moms, the high school graduation gown will not de-dyke your lesbian teen. Though it might just turn your son into a drag queen.
   Just kidding. Or am I? They don't call me Lady Dee Ploma for nothing.

"Smile, kids! Say, '*By the ten-year reunion, we'll all have husbands!*'"

8) THE MIGRATORY PATTERN OF THE FLEDGLING HOMOSEXUAL

After having done it with two other kids, my parents and I both knew the whole see-the-campus, shake-hands-with-the-roommate, buy-the-books procedure to be standard college newbie protocol. It was never a question whether they were going up with me for my big move from Nashville to Knoxville. Whether it was out of requirement or actual desire, I was certainly glad they were, too. While I may have thought I was tough, this move felt so much bigger than anything I'd ever undertaken. To be honest, I was a little freaked out by the change.

Standing outside in the driveway, crisp yet warm air of an August morning teasing me with both a chill and a sweat, I didn't question whether or not I was packed. I'd had those bags ready for weeks. The real question: was *I* ready?

"Just 160 miles to go," dad said through his charmingly goofy smile. Of all of the family, dad was the only one who really ever smiled those super-wide smirks that would make for a proper cartoon. The rest of us were snitters and snorters whose good humor tended more towards a grin than an open-mouth chortle. Dad, on the other hand, was a laugher, getting tickled with the outside world or sometimes even his own jokes. I was going to miss that, even if I was way too Joe Cool to tell him so at the time.

We got into our respective cars, mom and dad in their sedan, me in my '96 Mustang. "Just follow me," said the pops.

I popped in a CD, probably Rusted Root, since I was just cheesy enough to soundtrack this experience with "Send Me on My Way." Whatever I chose as the backing track, it was to be the guiding voice of a surprisingly sentimental tour through my life thus far. And it was to be a lasting impression, too, since this would be one of the last times I'd drive down these familiar roads.

The first Jeremy landmark was the neighborhood shopping center sign that my mother had always told me was designed by my late grandfather. Since only one of my four grandparents made it to my birth (and she only stuck around until I was four), I was never able to actually verify this commercial art world claim. Mom had no reason to make it up. "My grandpa designed this sign," I'd tell one and all. He was an artist—a man of design. I know I would've loved him dearly, and he me.

We then came upon that one, peculiar building that was forever changing. In the past decade, the drab brick heap had been a seafood buffet, an Italian restaurant, a real estate office, a church, some sort of doctor's compound, and a severely lacking electronics store. Throughout every iteration, it remained a seemingly cursed conversation piece. Considering how much better it served the locals jokes than it did return visits, the owners probably should have seen if cashing in on the '80s comedy club boom was the building's predestined plan.

Ah, and there's the mega church that had become more like a *behemoth* church since its last remodel. So many of my friends belonged there. I never joined or took them up on the invite to attend. Not because I was gay, mind you, as while I knew that gays were frowned upon by this particular denomination, I really didn't know all that much about the anti-gay "clobber passages" then. I mainly didn't go because I loved *Saturday Night Live* and therefore embraced Sunday Morning Slumber. Plus, my family had always gone to a Methodist church, whenever we'd gone, and this was Baptist. The difference, explained to me at various points in my life, was that the Methodist congregations weren't as likely to talk about you if you didn't show up. That always made me laugh.

Moving a little further down the road, I knew what was outside my window without even looking. It was a big ass, well—*big ass*! Literally. This was a country ham sign, which was nothing more than a mockup of the cooked pig flesh, painted right on the broadside of a worn-down white barn. It had been there since well before I was. It's weird the kinds of things one just accepts as having always been around, yet that would surely be an instant conversation starter for any out-of-towner. This picture of cured pig butt was surely one of those things. Though what it lacked in artistic merit or compassionate eating, it more than made up for in down-home charm. Today, I was in the market for folksy.

I smirked at the sight of the nearby farm supply store. Correction: the *huge* farm supply store. Personally I had only been in it once or twice in my entire seventeen years living there, but it was always a booming place. I was sure there would be feed stores in Knoxville, since it wasn't like I was moving to some foreign urban jungle where lattes replaced fertilizer. But this was *my* feed store. It was the marker I'd known I had to hit by 8:07 a.m. if I wanted to make the 8:15 high school bell, as well as the place that some of the more agriculturally inclined members of my class had turned into a de facto Friday night hotspot. It too was feeding my heart and memory chain, if not my sow.

Interwoven through these touchstones of my childhood, our caravan also drove by this friend's and that friend's house. These were places where I'd played; they were faces that had just always kind of been there. I had to wonder who would stay and who would go? If I returned as an openly gay man, which of them would have built up a fence in my absence? Do I really want to leave all that I've known, or do I just know that I really have to if I really want to live?

In the distance, I could just see the Little League Park. I hadn't been there in a couple of years by that point, but it would always hold a special place in my heart. That park was and still is like mental shorthand for me. If ever I want an instant transport to a time of ease, when a stick and a crunched up drinking cup could turn into a game that occupied hours, where running the score board for a game felt like presidential power, or where a pack of Now & Laters were the only tools needed to broker any kind of peace deal, I can get back there with little effort. Can almost smell it, even now. That mud is in my blood, man.

Daydreaming about the ballpark, I almost miss the roller skating rink, just there past the turn. (*sigh*) The roller skating rink—one of the first places where I really felt alive and fully reconciled. In fifth grade, after a field trip on which some of the other room mothers had convinced her it was okay, my mom started letting me make regular social outings at the rink's Friday night, all-ages skates. There, on those rented rollers, in that blaring pop, no one could get me. If I wanted to be alone, I could push away from the pack. If I wanted the world to shut the fuck up so I could feel the Paula Adbul, I could point to the speaker and feign an inability to hear this friend's or that pal's pressing chatter. I could even dance on the skates if I wanted to, since all skaters kind of look like they are anyway. Everyone's cool points hinged on just showing up, so I didn't actually have to socialize if I didn't want to. Round and round. I was me, but free. The femme me who liked the rhythm, the more virile me who appreciated the athleticism—*all* of me cherished the ability to reconcile all of my parts. It was pure agony when I aged into the bracket where the place was deemed to be as lame as it had once been cool.

With both mind and rear view letting go of the rink, we next approached the old high school. It was here where I had just finished up with honors, but where I'd been so dishonorably sheltered in so many ways. There it all was: The parking lot where I snuck an occasional cigarette, even though I never really understood the appeal; the halls where I had dated, but not really; the classrooms where the Mark Twain quote "I have never let my schooling interfere with my education" became something of a personal motto to my angsty arse. For someone who knew and mostly rationalized that he was gay before graduation, I certainly came out the other side in amazingly unscathed shape, with a fairly impressive degree of popularity, even. But I had no plans to look back on the past four years of my life as the "best years." That kind of best was simply not good enough.

It was when we stopped at the red light outside the nearby Sonic drive-thru, oddly enough, when the sensation really flooded over me. Fully. Not a sudden hankering for a breakfast-time cherry limeade, mind you, nor a hunger for the fast food chain's uniquely soggy but astoundingly delicious grilled cheeses. The feeling had nothing to do with thirst, appetite, or trays that one attaches to a half-rolled-down window. It was instead a wave of finality. A realization that while the actual high school pomp and circumstance had taken place a few months before, this was the moment I was actually graduating out of my old skin and into whatever was next.

The speed limit on this tour was an ungodly 35 mph. For the first time driving this downtempo road, I didn't care. We'd be hitting the interstate in just a few minutes, continuing along its 65+ mph pace for the entire rest of the trip. For now I could afford to go slow. In fact, I was content sitting there at the stoplight—alone with my thoughts, some mid-'90s tunes, and the great question mark of life.

At Sonic, the carhops gave customers peppermints as a way of rounding out the fast food pigouts. My mom was always warning me about choking on them. Ironic that here, now, the time when I was moving away from her wing, a lump in my throat should feel so big.

The desire for stifled and denied people, especially ones from small towns, to move away and seek seemingly more conducive ground is nothing new. It's the thing of cliché. Most youthful realities contain some degree of longing; that's just the nature of the beast.

Although when you are demonstrably deprived of a certain form of liberty or happiness and there is the awareness that other places can give you a fairer shake, the drive towards flight can feel like something more: less like a chosen takeoff and more like the fulfillment of a demanded destiny. That's how I felt. I would tell people that I had chosen the farthest-away in-state school because of this benefit or that benefit, and much of it was true. But a greater truth was that I felt I *had* to get away if I was going to grow.

It's a weird feeling. No one should ever be pushed from his or her roots. The choice to leave should be exactly that. A flight shouldn't be informed by non-acceptance, nor should soul solace rank above washer and dryer connections in whatever real estate one seeks. The migration certainly shouldn't be driven by pain. Not ideally.

There on my farewell tour, I overlooked any and all pain. But it was there, of course. It was *always* there. The same town that was stirring my emotions on that August day had been stirring my discontent for far longer. It was such an incredibly great place to grow up in so many ways. It was home and it was oh-so-homey, but I knew I had been denied in ways greater than I would've been in some other places or in some other realities, and that I had no choice but to move on and find my own place of personal peace. First I'd go to college, then I'd move to a city with a demonstrable support system. Then—*then?*—*then?* Maybe I'd find that special "it" I was seeking?

Knoxville for college was just my first migration, and it was only a stepping-stone on the map I'd so loosely planned for my life. I suspected I would come home many weekends, and I even planned to return to bunk there the following summer, the same way my siblings had. Though I would never again be an artist-in-residence at my birth home—of that I was sure. I was taking with me a mixed bag of experiences and a boatload of sweet memories. I vowed to do my best to let those memories, the sugary sentiments that buoyed me on this day, always remain at the top of my sustainable consciousness. And when things got tough and recollections turned sullen? I knew I could always think of scoreboards and roller skates.

After we'd secured my books and grabbed some cafeteria grub, my parents were pretty much ready to leave Knoxville. They'd done the college thing twice before, and I was in many ways more independent than my siblings.

- Newly minted bank card with a whopping one-hundred-dollar balance? *Check.*
- Requisite parental-granted copy of *Oh the Places You'll Go? Check.*
- A values system that knew the basics and was ready to learn the rest? *Check, check, check.*

"We love you," said mom. "Remember, we're always just a phone call away."

"I love you too," I shot back, while reminding them in my endearingly snarky way of this newfangled technology known as email. "Hope you have a quick trip."

And with that, out the drab dorm room door they went, returning to their car and eventually back down the path we'd just travelled together. But while the trip out had been so warm and cozy, I certainly didn't envy my parents having to do it in reverse. I had arrived. It was time to look nothing but forward.

9) FINDING MY SEA(FOOD) LEGS

Of course the day-to-day freedom of college was so nice. Are you kidding me? After years of being treated like the stereotypical baby of the family, not having a curfew or an authority figure telling me "no" was a refreshing change of pace. Even if it was only to go to Taco Bell, there was something deliciously rebellious about doing that at 2:15 a.m. and paying for it with nickels.

The change in structure also suited me well. I've never been one to want to do the same exact thing, day in and day out, or to even stay in one narrowly defined location for too long. The more undefined pace of a college school day was a much nicer match for my sensibilities than K–12 had been. Going to this building, that building, then to that other one all the way across campus was far more invigorating than walking the same halls or seeing the same teachers who already knew you from your older siblings and a county Board of Education–employed mom.

Meeting new people was another perk. While I stayed in Tennessee for school, I did choose a national university with a student body of over twenty-five thousand. With numbers that high, diversity is something of a given. It was refreshing to get to meet, or even just *see*, multi-cultural, multi-faith, multi-race, multi-accented people. Even though I went away with a handful of my best and most lifelong friends, I wasn't shy about wanting to expand my horizons or mind.

On the whole, the entire collegiate experience was refreshingly different from moment one. Literally, on the first night away from the home where I had spent my prior seventeen years, I felt the shift. I can clearly remember talking to my friend Sarah on that inaugural night and having her offer up the unsolicited opinion that this new sense of freedom we were all sharing must feel especially heightened for me personally, since I'd been kept on such a short leash all of the years prior. She was right—it did feel major. I was determined to make the most of that first year.

However, even as that determined frosh year sped along its experimental course, with far more exposure to more liberal thinking than I'd known in my high school days, my eighteen-year-old self still couldn't see that I'd ever be in a place where I could admit my gay identity to anyone other than myself. Which sucked, because I felt so on course everywhere else—in school, in physical appearance, in general life trajectory, in Mario Kart rallies. But when it came to schmoozing and smooching the whosits that I wanted to dosits with, I was pretty much on a path to nowhere. With so many new friends and acquaintances from so many different backgrounds, I still hadn't become close with that one gay person who might've taken me by the hand and led me towards honesty.

How could I have even done so? I wasn't going to gay bars, joining progressive student groups, or making any real attempt. I was too scared to even seek out potential gay friends on the Internet, which, while still a "you've got mail"–bellowing novelty at that point, was certainly a connective option I, an early adopter, knew to be available to me. Yet I didn't use it, out of fear my roommate might find gay stuff in my history folder. Hell, my whole life seemed to have a user-accessible cache, and I was still too fucking scared of its contents rendering me some sort of social pariah.

The odd thing is that being gay itself wasn't even all that scary to me at this point, at least not when it came to mental anguish or tangible fears. I knew and accepted it as being my sexual orientation, as best I could tell without the sex part. Even so, I continued to succumb to the social pressure to present myself as one thing while holding on to a completely different truth. I was still dating females here and there because dating is what young, social people did. I was still going to bars with my straight male friends for the ostensible purposes of meeting girls. I still wasn't looking at males as even potential drunken smooch partners, much less husbands. Anything involving socialization and me was pretty much a ruse, a comedy show, a drunken bout of silliness, or a combination of the three.

I finished year one without even an inkling of when I could or would find enough fortitude to put honesty before ease. My true wants and expressed needs were wholly incongruent, and I still couldn't imagine the two halves would ever reconcile, even if the back of my mind must've known that they someday would. I was so fully wearing a mask, one so common for LGBT people. When one so totally lives a lie and presents a fallacy to everyone with whom he or she interacts, it's hard to even imagine conducting affairs in any other way. The mask may be constraining and ugly, its only available expressions inauthentic. But it *is* familiar—both uncomfortable and oddly comfy at the same time.

The mask of anti-emotion was certainly quite familiar to me in the summer of 1998, but quite honestly, it was one of the last things on my mind. I had moved back in with my parents for the summer between freshman and sophomore years, an action that comes with a certain degree of unsexiness in and of itself. Compounding matters further was the fact that I'd consciously chosen to shut down my social functioning for the warm weather season. Since I felt my former hometown could offer me none of the fun I'd enjoyed during year one away at school, I decided I'd simply work my ass off and save enough money, so that, come fall, I'd be able to get my own place and control my own spending. There would be no wasteful squandering. There certainly wouldn't be any faux dates (the most wasteful of all expenditures). Even the skunk beer that had been my freshman year lifewater was too rich for my newly focused blood. It was going to be an all work and no play summer, guided fully by my brain and in no way by my heart.

But ya know, it's a funny thing, this life. Plans. Expectations. They up and change. On a wedding day, there just might be rain. A fly might be just going about his life, when all of a sudden a bowl of soup comes along and drowns him to death. From a pile of turds might spring a flower. Out of spectacular mess can come great art.

And sometimes, when a southern teen is going about his best-laid plans, an out and proud gay man might just step in and show him a new set of ground rules.

Bryce was effeminate, loud, and bold in his statements. If I lived in a closet, he lived on the roof. Naked. While singing show tunes. Much to my surprise, he was also the most popular employee at the Red Lobster where I had found summer employment.

I hadn't counted on even making friends with my fellow Lobster servers, snobbily thinking the crab legs that united us would be quite enough
of a bond, thank you very much. But after spending forty hours together
for a few weeks, friendships just naturally came to be. I found myself
in meaningful relationships that were quite different from the bonds I
had with my college friends, as most of my fellow servers were people to
whom I probably would've never had exposure, if not for our shared job.
These were people in their twenties, thirties, and forties, who had actually lived a life beyond the bubble that comes from school-aged existence.
Diverse in viewpoints and backgrounds, I was intrigued by each and every
one of them. My comfort zone was being challenged by this new and more
representative microcosm, and I liked it. A lot.

One was an octogenarian server, the feistiest eighty-something I've
ever seen on two legs. Her big thing was to monitor how much dressing
we all were putting on our salads, having recently bought into the company's profit sharing plan herself. I respected her enough to dip the ladle
only twice. Although I respected my tip enough to grab my table another
ramekin of ranch when they'd inevitably ask. Sorry, Evie.

Then there was the hippy dippy palm reader with whom I shared
some glorious post-shift conversation. She opened my eyes to life. She also
had really good pot. Coincidence? Maybe, maybe not.

There was also a guy who up and decided to shorten his name to
"Christoph," even though he'd always been known as Christopher. I found
that choice pretentious, but I still found him fun in that early twenties
apartment party sort of way. He was dependable at factoring a keg stand's
trajectory, which was all the high-mindedness I needed during that summer break's rare respites.

Speaking of the odd break time, the aspiring country singer guy was
a good one to have a beer with. In New York City, the actor/waiter hybrid
is the cliché. In and around Nashville, the aspiring Opry star meme is far
more prevalent. As best I can remember, this would-be Garth actually did
have a good voice—I wonder if he found fame? I should go Google him.

Oh, and I can't forget the early-forties redhead who seemed to make
it her life's mission to convince me that the joy and revelry of one's third
decade could never rival one's fifth. I didn't put up an argument, mind
you. The argument seemed to be within herself. I guess we all have our
struggles.

And then there was Bryce, the one who'd most fully shape my days. The fact that he was so open in his sexuality, yet still so accepted, was nothing short of mesmerizing to me. I was not the least bit attracted to him, so I knew my little brother affection wasn't that of a crush; it was something more, something far more powerful. Basically, I just wanted to witness Bryce walking through life. I wanted to see how his customers reacted to having him as their waiter. I wanted to know if he talked about his relationships. I needed to see that he was not constantly on the butt end of the gruffest cook's jokes. Bryce was like a gift from some closet-busting God, and I was shocked at how willing I was to open up the wrapping.

When one night during post-shift cleaning he sprung up on a bench to sing "Let's Hear it For The Boy," I was a receptive audience member. Before, I would have run away, lest anyone see me smile at another dude singing this '80s ode to "loving one-man shows" into a mop handle. With Bryce, I simply didn't care. It was funny. To laugh was both honest and human.

Then there was the time I overheard him talking about the new man who had asked him out. I'm not sure how many times the line cooks had to scream my name before my daydreams left the realm of dude sex and turned back towards whatever lemon-encrusted swimmer they were serving up this meal. I didn't care. There was a gay story being told in a state where I'd never heard one, or at least not one that had a happy rather than tragic ending. My table could wait on turning Ariel's friend into a meal.

But those more overt moments with genuine gay connotations were of less importance than the ones where nothing greater than normalcy was the takeaway. When Bryce would throw on a hair net and join the line because we were long on servers but tight on cooks, it was the chorus of welcoming cheers from the tough guy mouths that greeted my ears in new and exciting ways. Or when a family of four would specifically request his waiter service, I couldn't help but be surprised that a mother and father with young children would actually be seeking out a proudly flamboyant man. It wasn't like anything I had ever known. These moments were like some alternate reality that looked and sounded like the Tennessee of my past, but with an injection of tolerance that was heretofore unimagined. I watched and watched closely.

Little did I know that Bryce had also been analyzing me.

Over Long Island Teas late one night after a double shift, another serving friend, Jesse, just came right out and said it. As naturally as if she were saying she liked my shirt, Jesse blurts out: "Bryce said he thinks you're gay but just don't know it yet."

What the friggin' room-elephant?! Warn a sleeping brother before you turn on the lights!

I froze, the words just hanging there. My blood pressure soared and my thoughts turned combative. "What the hell?" I exclaimed by face if not quite voice, as I searched for what words I'd use to challenge the assertion. You know the proverbial deer in the headlights? Yeah, well I must have looked like that deer's gay cousin, if he were standing two inches from the sun!

"No, but it's okay," Jesse calmly shot back, likely sensing my inner self struggling with the claim. "He didn't say it in a negative way; he just sees a lot of his younger self in you. He cares about you deeply, you know."

I then definitely pushed back a bit, still struggling to find my bearings. As best as I can remember, my tactic was to feign disdain for the fact that this older man would have the audacity to invade my privacy. But as I pushed this and that way, Jesse held firm. My faux outrage was no match for her reason. What came out of my mouth was not going to trump what she too had seen and heard with her own sensible senses.

But while I started out so shocked, what's most shocking was that it didn't take all that much time before my nerves started to calm. That's because while the confrontation was certainly blunt, I did genuinely realize this conversation wasn't coming from a place of hostility. It wasn't coming from my family or friends to whom I'd been so long trying to prove my desire for females. It wasn't coming from a place of judgment. It was coming from sincerity, from someone who had no reason to make me feel wrong or bad or *anything,* really. And so while I still felt denial was the best route on that night, it was clear that something had changed within me. This was the first time someone had suggested I might be gay but done so in a loving, not disparaging, way. Coincidentally, it was the first time the shock didn't end up ruining my night.

I can't remember how I eventually changed the subject, but looking back now, I know it wouldn't have mattered anyway. This was a liberal "fag hag" to whom I was talking and an out and proud gay man whom she was quoting—no words could combat what their life experience with gay folks had told them to be true. None of my routines would ever outsmart their finely honed gaydars. They'd seen 'em all. No way was I the first or last closeted teen to sling crab legs with them. I was simply one of the ones—the latest one—they looked on as a friend.

In the days and weeks that followed, nothing changed in my dealings with either Bryce or Jesse. I didn't go through the usual need to "prove" myself and instead just continued to *be* myself. I had admitted nothing at that table, but everyone involved knew that I totally had. It was like a pre–coming out, of sorts, a way for me to stick a toe in the water without even rolling up my cocktail sauce-stained pants.

Jesse and Bryce remained my closest Lobster friends, sharing loads more conversation and even more cocktails for the rest of July and August. I met one or two of Bryce's dates, which proved to be another step in my process. It was my first time seeing an actual man-date, complete with pecks and pokes and squabbles about who would pick up the tab. They looked and sounded like the dates that I'd third-wheeled on with my sister or the ones I had shammed my way through on several occasions. It let me know that gay life, even here in Tennessee, would not have to be secretive or sex-based. Bryce's dates gave me an introductory model of relationships, whereas previously I'd only thought about lust.

Also for the first time, my friendship with Bryce forced me to comprehend that by continuing to vehemently challenge the "you're gay" claim the way I'd been doing for the past few years, I'd be disparaging this man whom I'd grown to know and enjoy. I recommitted right then and there to fully supporting gay folks and gay equality, even if I couldn't yet verbalize that in doing so, I was actually supporting myself. This was a huge turning point for me, as it was then that others' claims that *I* might be a 'mosexual lost most of their ability to hurt me in any way. I wasn't ashamed of my friend. I wasn't ashamed of myself.

After taking that first step, the world started looking a little different. Over the next months and year, I would walk through life with a new sort of confidence. I started befriending other gay people fully and unconditionally. I stuck by the liberal convictions I'd always held rather than backing down when someone would challenge me to a game of reason. I lost loads of fear and, in turn, gained a new sort of confidence. Since I was no longer scared of being gay, I could step outside of the fear bubble and actually, truthfully, *empirically* determine if men were the cup of tea that

I predicted they would be. I could explore who I truly was without listening to others' assertions about who or what I should be.

A year later, I took my first sip of man. I will spare you the salacious details, but I will tell you that all questions vanished with the sort of immediacy that only human neurons could ever generate. My suspicions were confirmed, and that confirmation didn't scare me even a little bit.

I had lived with fear for long enough; it was time for trepidation and me to call it quits and break up. It had been real, but it hadn't been anything close to fun. I was leaving, taking custody of the kid I'd always been, as well as the man that I was destined to become. If someone was going to love me for me, then that was certainly preferable. If they were going to hate me for the same reason, then the problem was theirs and not mine. I was now ready to explore the joys, the pain, and the whole roller coaster of a life lived with truth.

Soon enough, I'd also stop eating fish.

10) ♫ SANDPAPER FACE ♫

Country music provided the background noise for so many Tennessee life experiences. Why should my first time batting for my own team be any different?

Were there a soundtrack to my first same-sex sexual adventure, at age nineteen, I'd imagine it would have gone something like this:

(Set to the tune of the worst country song you can possibly imagine)

♪ Ladies and gays let me have your attention
There's a little sumpthin' that we've just gotta mention
It's a warning tale about your first time
What they forget to tell ya should really be a crime

They tell ya to be safe and they tell ya to be careful
And to shave down below so you won't be too hairful
But why doesn't anybody ever make the case
About that little issue known as sandpaper face?
[twangy interlude]

You find someone ya like and you're just so darn excited
This virgin bill's overdue, tonight it will be righted
Your friends and the 'net have given ya advice
You feel you're all prepared so you don't think twice
But there's one place where you're bound to find trouble
Because you didn't consider the daggers that are stubble

You and your boy are hitting it off right
This here's the one who's gonna stay the night
Your lips are ready to make your case
And that's when you learn about sandpaper face

CHORUS: Sandpaper face
It'll surely cut you
Sandpaper face
Why'd no one warn you?
Sandpaper face
Dude, is that a head or a chainsaw?
But as long as there are frisky birds
There's gonna be sandpaper face
[interlude]

"Holy mother of shit!?" what the hell just happened?
Your lips might have touched but it's your cheek that was zappened
You look at Mr. Hottie and you don't see a beard
So why are you in a state that's near-teared?

Must have been a fluke, you say to yourself
You're surely not gonna put your feelings on the shelf
But as soon as your distance goes from separate to joined
There's a new term that your mind has just coined.
[spoken] It's called . . .

CHORUS: Sandpaper face
That's what just cut you
Sandpaper face
Why'd no one warn you?
Sandpaper face
Dude, is that a noggin or a tazer?
But as long as there are frisky bees
There's gonna be sandpaper face
[short interlude]

BRIDGE: Well you always hoped you'd need
to bite your lower lip

But you'd always thought that'd be because
of something happenin' below the hip

Who knew a kiss could make you want to scream?
Why ain't that face as smooth as it seemed?
He doesn't have a beard, which is what makes it weird
It's gettin' in the way of your dream…
{Long, twangy guitar solo}

But there's no use trying to resist it
Had you known you still would've kissed it
Sure you might prefer he go use a Schick
But you'll still want to play with his . . .

CHORUS: Sandpaper face
You're gonna have to deal with it
Sandpaper face
Why'd no one f-in' warn you?
Sandpaper face
Dude, is that a cheek or a porcupine?
But as long as there are frisky dudes
There's gonna be sandpaper face
As long as there are horny toads
There's gonna be sandpaper face
As long as there are orgasms
There's gonna be head-scratchin', cheek-matchin', pain-catchin',
sore-hatchin', pore-latchin', bandage-patchin',
Sandpaper face
Sandpaper face
Sandpaper face ♪

{spoken} Get a condom . . . and peroxide.

11) WHOSE "LIFESTYLE" IS IT ANYWAY?

"Language is very powerful. Language does not just describe reality. Language creates reality it describes. So when they call you a 'non-European' or a 'non-this,' you might think it is not working on you, but in fact, it is corrosive of your self-image. You end up wondering whether you are actually as human as others."
                    —Bishop Desmond Tutu[2]

The organized anti-LGBT crowd loves to tell us who and what we are. And by "us," I don't mean just gay, lesbian, bisexual, and transgender individuals, but rather anyone who champions acceptance. Because it's not really the sex or gender itself that the organized opposition turns into a public issue: it's the acceptance of certain so-called "lifestyles." The anti-LGBT movement, writ large, is hell-bent on believing that there exists (or, more accurately, forcing others to believe that there exists) some dark script that's been penned by radicals for the purposes of washing the world's brains in rainbow colors. In order to sell the play-acting to the citizenry, they say that those of us who dare to stand up for the equitable treatment of LGBT assets are buying into this certain "agenda," and that it—this secretive queer battle plan—is what has convinced society to embrace such supposed unsavoriness.

---

[2] Archbishop Desmond Tutu, interview by Bill Moyers, 27 April 1999, *Bill Moyers Journal* (PBS).

Within the collective body of religious right activists and like-minded allies, no one is free to his or her own motivations. Perhaps that's understandable, since the heart of their socio-political movement, if we are to boil it down, goes back to their unquestioning trust in their own personal interpretations of certain biblical "clobber passages." If they aren't acting out of free will, then why should anyone else? If they have no need to cull reality from the known world around them, then who else should have that right? If their movement sees no need to know and listen to actual LGBT people about their true wants and needs and goals, then where does that movement get off conducting their own anthropological examinations of the 'mo kingdom? And if they, the members of the self-declared "pro-family" crowd, have been so successful at selling their claims to the public at large, then what reasons have they to fix what ain't broke? Or so the thinking goes.

The ironic (read: insanely frustrating) truth is that by furthering an environment that doesn't support basic fairness and equality, the LGBT community's opposition in many ways nurtures the sort of gay "lifestyle" they so vigorously decry. They who have built careers around the lambasting of gay rights create the kinds of situations and occurrences towards which they then turn around and point fingers, not admitting that their own stone-casting has often played a pivotal role. Let me explain.

Gay kids can suffer cruelly in their own heads. No matter what sort of physical or psychological torment they may face from peers, family members, or those in positions of power, it can pale in comparison to their own internal unease. When one knows who he or she is, but also knows that actualizing this knowledge may lead to a loss of friends, family, or respect, it can create the sort of weightiness that plagues one's every thought. Frankly, it can be as frightening as being locked in a cage with a mad cow that's sick as a dog with chicken pox, swine flu, and a raging case of crabs. To put it mildly.

So what do most teenaged LGBTs end up doing with these feelings? More often than not, they bottle the thoughts. Some, like this writer, go through the adolescent motions as a pretend heterosexual, feigning interest in the opposite sex, thinking it will make life easier. But if gayness is the honesty lurking inside, then that truth never shuts up. For me, that voice of reason sounded like, *"Dude—you know the way it felt when you just kissed Laura? Yeah, um, it's not supposed to feel that way. See, I'm sure you've probably noticed that there, below that belt there, you have a biological gauge that sort of shows you what is and is not to your liking. Yeah, well— it's not so hard to see it's not so hard, now is it?"*

If the gay teen can't or won't listen to this voice and instead feels pressure to stay in the closet—and while great advancements in teenage truth revelation have developed in recent years, this is certainly still the adolescent norm—then he or she has been robbed of the chance to experience true love and connection. High school is a dating culture, with coupling the A-plot of most any cheesy teen flick tasked with selling us popcorn in the past century. Though for the LGBT teen, the pairing-off process is less of a John Hughes film and more of a war flick (*The Hurt Locker 2*, perhaps?). Rites of passage like prom and homecoming are muted or even rendered irrelevant due to the constraints typically placed upon them, yet are also more vivid and arresting than they'd be in the typical teen experience due to the added emotional burden attached to those same constraints. The eventual diploma is an exciting prospect, but graduating from this school of stifled sexuality can be an even more sought-after goal.

By the time he or she gets to college or similar post-grad post, the gay teen's ideas regarding the possibility of love, marriage, finding his or her soul mate, and settling down in a picket-fenced casa are in a far different place than those of most hetero friends. Maybe he or she is now in a more welcoming environment and can finally live a truthful life. The problem is that now, at eighteen or nineteen, there tends to be a very low maturity level in terms of the whole dating arena. There's certainly a bit of a learning curve when it comes to romance. One has to get the hang of all the ins and outs, from learning how to compromise to remembering to pack a toothbrush for overnight stays. Early teen dating is like a trial run, one that most LGBT folks missed out on, at least in the way they truly wanted it to go down. For a now nearly twenty-something gay or lesbian, what should be old hat can instead feel like a baby bonnet.

Not to mention, the idea that he or she could find a perfect mate and get hitched once they both graduate is still a notion largely unsupported, as true marriage equality is still far from fully realized in this nation and in this world. Many heterosexual people will forego the freedom to marry, for any number of reasons. At least they'll still know they *have* the freedom and know the world around them has implanted a figurative staircase on which to progress to their commitments. By denying gay and lesbian couples marriage amid claims of "controversy" and "societal protection," society gives young people the message that same-sex dating is a dead end. Whether the gay person even wants to marry or not is beside the point. Just the fact that civil government and self-appointed morality police are putting up a discriminatory roadblock sends a harmful message that weakens psyches. It's just one more obstacle on the path to peace.

Once my actualized version of the aforementioned teen took the first steps out of the closet in my second year of college, this enforced differentiation meant I'd spend at least four nights a week in a bar or club. I didn't always *want* to be out at these places—hell, a boy only has so many sleeveless tees (the required uniform for a turn-of-the-millennium gay club kid). But I desperately wanted to meet fellow gay friends and reliable straight allies who could help me feel connected at a time when feeling alone would've been all too easy, here in a town where there were few options other than clubs to form these bonds. Despite affording me a far greater sense of peace than I had known in high school, my college town was still undeniably conservative. There was that charming mixed bag of politics, religions, and viewpoints that can be found in almost any city that's near a university quad, but looking lovingly in a same-sex date's eyes over a Valentine's dinner was still guaranteed to elicit a share of stares, at the very least, with harsh confrontation not out of the realm of possibility. Reliably supportive places, like maybe bookstores or coffee shops, were few and far between, meaning that once I was out as a man-dater, if I wanted to have a comfortable conversation with a potential friend or possibly a beau, it was only to be had in the dark, thumping environment of an establishment that peaked at 1:30 a.m.

Now this being said, I did find some enjoyment at these clubs and bars. My heterosexual friends certainly did the same at both "my" and "their" establishments. Gay clubs were, quite undeniably, the most fun ones in town. But to not acknowledge that certain situations and substances were more readily available in this environment would be disingenuous of me. The club scene is, by design, party-centric. I certainly partook in some of these nightlife indulgences, but fortunately I had the capacity to know myself and to know my limits. Not everyone does. Clubbing can and does sometimes turn into one's total life. If you're someone who only fully feels comfortable in this nightlife environment, as many young gays do, the lures of the "thumpa thumpa" are only increased. If you're someone who has craved a place—some place, any place—where you could finally feel free, then the freedom can turn into abandon.

Call me a prude if you must, but I've simply seen far too many friends chewed up and spit out by this underground environment to not have some desire to reform the all-too-familiar system. Again, I'd like to reinforce my cred by saying I'm no stranger to the indulgences, and to also admit I look back fondly on many of my post-midnight college memories. Some of the best and truest stuff happened then. But as for the friends who were more gaunt every time I returned to the nearby big city; the gorgeous overachiever whose crystal clear future was destroyed by a cloudy crystal pipe; the kid who thought he'd found an easy way to pay bills but instead paid a steep penalty—all these recollections still haunt me. Even though they were the exception and not the rule, they were still living, breathing human beings whom I came to know. Living, breathing beings who came to know their own lives as disposable, sadly.

Then there's also value, or lack thereof, in terms of sex. In college I made a good friend, let's call him Max, who was kicked out of his home before he was old enough to vote. When his family abandoned him, Max took shelter with friends who were a decade or more older than he was. Max moved fast. Max moved hard. Max moved, so that he wouldn't have to stop and think.

"We didn't have sex. Just oral," Max once said to me about a sketchy character he'd bedded then rejected by the light of day.

"Girl, I had to sneak out of a frat house last night," he confessed on another occasion, this time sitting in the lap of another someone new.

"I'm gonna find me someone tonight," was a regular pre-club refrain.

Not that there's anything wrong with being young and having fun. I certainly was and did. Max, however, was undeniably different in the way he dated. There was absolutely no mental connection between his active sexuality and his life as a bright, charming, adorable college student who had big plans in terms of career, future moves, and life as a whole. It's one thing to date around as a form of experiment—hell, modern TV writers seem unable write a show with a primarily female cast unless they use such a plot device. Max, though, was a bit of a sexual vampire, going from night to night, sucking on another neck in order to sustain some sort of need—a need that I knew, from tearful conversations

in which he said plenty on a verbal plane but even more on a subtex-
tual level, directly arose from the intense drama in his family and their
Catholic-motivated rejection. Max had been so devalued that he devalued
his own right to have concrete love. And boy, he wanted it, too. He so,
so, *so* wanted love, he just didn't feel it was owed to him. That's what was
so damn sad.

Why do I say gay rights opponents deserve responsibility for these
kinds of situational patterns? Well, because the attitude telling kids
from day one that gay equals lesser than and wrong leads way too many
young gay kids to accept these descriptions and actualize their realities as if they exist in a realm separate from that of mainstream society.
The results may materialize as club drug addictions, risky situations,
or wanton promiscuity that's emboldened in large measure by the way
anti-gay people shun gay commitments through both word and vote.
In any case, it's high time those whose actions and rhetoric help foster
non-acceptance realize that their oh-so-cherished talking points can
and do lead a great number of individuals to seek acceptance through
other means.

Frankly, it's quite shocking how much the LGBT community's organized opposition wants to think about gay sex, since I've met virtually no
one on the pro-LGBT side who devotes more than a passing thought to
any form of sex that he or she does not personally desire. Whatever the
reason, our opposition does think about gay sex often, and the messages
they send out are enough to make even the most adjusted person internal-
ize the "gay bedrooms = biohazards" meme. Not a great framework for
healthy sexual awakening.

Of course the anti-LGBT social conservatives' claims also go well
beyond sex, cutting right into the various aspects of gays lives they feel
they can exploit as being components of some sort of unsavory "lifestyle."
It wasn't long after I came out that I began hearing the claims about who
I supposedly was and what I supposedly wanted for the world. Or I sup-
pose I had always heard them, but once I was out I started connecting the
dots, and I finally understood why the organized opposition used the lines
they did and do. I realized these folks truly are students of LGBT people
and the LGBT political movement who have learned where the exploit-
able vulnerabilities lie—knowledge that tells them which lies will keep
LGBT people most vulnerable.

Let's now break down some of the more popular ones and pick them apart.

CLAIM: LGBTs ARE "IMMORAL"

I think that for many, "immoral" has become one of those socio-political terms whose actual connotation matters much less than its weight. Rather than carefully considering it along the genuine range of morality and against the true social ills that plague this world, many of the term's most stalwart users carelessly abuse it as a rhetorical talking point to pad their otherwise empty cases. So many people casually toss it around— accompanied alongside phrases like "gays will destroy marriage," "protect the children," and "ignore all that other stuff in the Bible about eating shellfish"—that it's become much more of a verbal tic than a referendum pertaining in any way to right versus wrong.

This sounds like I'm excusing it a bit, but I can promise you I'm not. In fact, this casual usage of this term "immoral" strikes me as *more* sinister than an actual, legitimate use of the word, as the lack of processing has placed it not only in the realm of offense but also in the arena of intellectual laziness. It's the same way I feel about "socialism," a term that has been misappropriated so many times by conservatives of the modern era that it's close to losing a connotation that is anywhere near its intended one. In both cases, the goal is unquestioned adoption, not deep thought. In both cases, genuine information takes a back seat to personal motivation, which is a recurring theme in most anti-LGBT claims.

Regardless of reasons for the word "immoral" being so used and abused, there is no doubt that the careless tone that monolithically puts gays in morality's penalty box is one of the anti-gay movement's most fundamentally negligent contributions to this so-called "culture war." If you're blessed enough to lack firsthand subjection to the label, just imagine for a second how out-of-whack your moral compass might become if you were brought up from day one hearing how you are out-of-touch with God's plan for humanity. It's certainly not an insurmountable obstacle for those who choose to get their own education on the subject, but it's definitely an obstacle—a particularly formidable one for those with certain faith backgrounds.

CLAIM: LGBTs ARE "SICK"

"Sick" is a uniquely favored label among those who've chosen to foe the
'mos. It's a particularly interesting word, to boot, mainly because of its
sheer adaptability. There's the literal usage, which took on a crazy new
light during the early AIDS days:

> *"All gays deserve to get sick and die"*

Though the branding actually dates back to way before that. There were
certainly nuggets from the days when homosexuality was still listed as a
mental disorder:

> *"Honey, those homosexual sodomites are sick and twisted! Kind of like someone
> of one race marrying another. Now get back in that kitchen, woman!"*

Although I imagine we could trace it back even further:

> *"Fire, good. 'Mos, sick."*

In modern days, there's the visceral reaction that gender-matched love
brings about in some:

> *"Two guys holding hands is so sick."*

It can also find itself on the tongue of a loved one who turns on his or her
own blood kin when he or she finds out his secret:

> *"Mom, he's a sickness to our family—always has been."*

And of course the organized anti-LGBT community uses it to describe the
push for equality in general:

> *"The militant gays have a sick agenda."*

On the flip side, it's also a term that can sometimes be used in the
good way:

> *"Girl, that was a sick drag show—she to' it up!"*

As well as a term that's sometimes used by gays to describe their own
treatment:

> *"The National Organization for Marriage has a sick new TV spot."*

Or used by distraught gay and lesbians, who utilize the word when they
consider how they'll protect the love that has been denied by the law:

> *"How will I care for her if she gets sick? It's making me sick with worry!"*

The word also makes up the line that the anti-gays deny us:

> *"In sickness and in health"*

Or drop or add a letter, and you might find a version of the word in print:

> *"Hatred iss {sic}"*

But my favorite summation of the whole "sick" game:

"It's just plain sick that LGBT people would have to feel this sick sense."

And if we're to remain dogs to whom our organized opposition won't even throw the bone that comes from basic tolerance (at the very least), then we have no choice but to

"Sick 'em!"

Not 'em personally, but certainly the sick machine that's spun the ill will.

CLAIM: GAYS CAN/NEED TO BE "CHANGED"

Listen up, I have an announcement. Through faith and strong will, I've decided I'm no longer right-handed and would now like to be identified as an "ex-rightie." Although I may fumble and find embracing my left-handedness a great effort, I'm simply no longer right-handed, and you must accept that fact. Who cares that I've always felt inclined towards right-handed relations; I'm simply tired of utilizing my eastern palm, so I'm giving my own dexterity and former community of like-minded hand-users the proverbial middle finger. Goodbye dextral life, for I am now a sinistral being.

But why don't I just now identify myself as a leftie, you may ask? Well, see that's the genius part. If I were to present myself as the new thing that I've seemingly become, you may forget that I ever identified the other way in the first place, and I wouldn't be able to use my struggle for political purposes. For you see, I've noticed more and more folks accepting right-handed relations as "normal" in days of recent, and I simply do not think they are. In fact, I, along with many of my similarly minded friends, find right-on-right handshakes to be downright disgusting, as well as a threat to society. For that simplistic reason, I will keep identifying myself as an "ex-rightie" to show you that if *I* can overcome my former below-the-wrist desires, then change is possible for *anyone*.

And don't even try to indicate that maybe I'm ambidextrous, thus capable and designed to use both of my hands for joy, pleasure, and companionship. I'm an "ex-rightie" because I say so, and there is nothing you can do about it. If you try to refute my existence as an "ex-rightie" and my new career decrying my former community, I will simply call you intolerant of the thousands of undocumented people who I will claim have also changed their hand usage. Oh, and you'll have to ignore the fact that you're unlikely to know even one and just trust me when I tell you we're everywhere. I'll say there are millions of us roaming this Earth because how the hell will you ever prove me wrong?

It's a flawless plan, I tell ya. I will join with any group whose political and spiritual interests are focused on demonizing righties, as my new campaign of morphing dexterities will give these folks an easier way to stigmatize and not feel guilty. I plan to hold "ex-rightie" conferences, where I will specifically target parents who don't understand their child's right-focused biology and are willing to do almost anything to see that their kid doesn't grow up in such a "lifestyle." Perhaps I'll host a radio show to be syndicated on the anti-right's network of airwaves, in which my left hand and I will dedicate every edition to our version of truth about my former community of righties. Ooh, and whenever there is some sort of convention in which tolerance for righties is encouraged, I'll demand equal representation as a member of the poor, discriminated against "ex-rightie" community.

It's all so genius. Bwa ha ha ha ha ha ha!

Okay, so you got me—I'm not talking about hands. I'm still an out and proud member of the prestigious right. I'm a naturally born rightie and will surely die a rightie (handily, not politically).

The bizarre metamorphosis I'd like to talk about is one in which normal folks are convinced that a part of their being is innately flawed and that through faith, therapy, prayer, or a combination of the three, they can change into a creature that's unknown to many, but one that is widely supported and encouraged by the professionally 'mo foey. My friends, I'm referring to the "ex-gay."

The "ex-gay" or "former homosexual" or "total and utter bullshit" movement has been gaining more and more attention in recent years. However, that movement's battle plan has remained pretty much the same. Despite what every international medical and mental health association says, despite the biological evidence that exists, despite the insistency of nine-tenths of the gay community that change is impossible, and despite common sense, they actively persuade impressionable folks into believing that they have the key to turning homosexuals into a construct known as an "ex-gay." They strongly focus on targeting parents (especially in the red states), as they know many of them are scared/confused/in denial about their child's sexuality. They trot out the same four or five speakers as PROOF that "ex-gays" (never identified as heterosexuals, mind you) do exist. All the while, they'll neglect to tell you about the COUNTLESS folks who have tried their programs and now see them as the dangers that they are; in some cases, they'll even continue to use these ex–"ex-gays" in their advertisements and literature. When protested by the gay community, they counter by simply quoting various passages from the Bible, so that they can position themselves as being on the side of good, while they work day and night to paint the gay activists as the bad. The religious right adherents fully support and propagate these efforts because they know if they can present the illusion that homosexuality is a fixable choice, they can justify their biases against homosexuality. After all, that way they can hate the SIN, not the SINNER, as the SINNER is "choosing" his SIN.

Got all that? Well, if you're heterosexual, you probably don't have the full grasp because it all sounds so far-fetched and fictional. For LGBTs, however, it's all too real. Real, even though the fact that there are grown adults out there encouraging such "change" is a uniquely pointed, multi-faceted, mindfuckity claim of which no human being should ever have to be aware.

CLAIM: GAYS' PARENTS SCREWED THEM UP

Overbearing mother and absent father—those are the parental archetypes that anti-gays like to cite as common threads connecting most, if not all, homosexual males. The causation claim is Freudian in its root, flawed in its simplicity. And while most credible mental health associations have rejected the claim for decades, many anti-gays still present this ridiculousness as "logic":

> I think we can still say that the most common home environment of a future male homosexual is a home where the mother is dominating, overprotective and possessive, while the father rejects and ridicules the child. The opposite situation occurs too, where the mother rejects her son because he is a male. Generally, the same kinds of role confusion in the home contribute to female homosexual tendencies. In some sense, the girl feels rejection because of her gender and comes to believe only a male identity carries worth.
>
> . . .

The best prevention of gender confusion remains a strong home life. Homosexuality is much less likely to occur in the context of a loving home where parents are reasonably well-adjusted sexually themselves. I don't think it is necessary to react with paranoia even in this aberrant culture. If parents provide a healthy, stable home life and do not interfere with the child's appropriate sex role, homosexuality is highly unlikely to occur.[3]

In certain situations (such as when they're trying to "convert" us), the organized anti-gays will try to convince gay men that this kind of family scenario is their past truth, even if it isn't apparent. They're often quite successful, unfortunately, since it's fairly easy to convince a grown child of this, especially if there is any sort of parental strife at play in his or her life. Just think about it. In terms of mothers, who among us who was raised by a maternal figure can't think of a few instances when she was a bit meddling or autocratic? Mamas have a way of being a little too involved sometimes. And in terms of fathers, who among us had a dad who was forced to work more than he might have liked? Such is not uncommon. When looked back upon through the filter of stigmatization, however, both sorts of common parental traits can be easily misconstrued as more than they actually were. That's what they want.

What practitioners of the simplistic causation claim also fail to present is the possibility that even if they *were* to find such types of parent-child relationships as having existed in adult male gays, that perhaps it was the person's nature that led to the familial dynamic, not the dynamic itself that nurtured the person to become gay. For example, if an adult gay male says he always preferred watching the Miss America pageant with his mom over fishing with his dad, the anti-LGBT crowd rarely or never considers that this was an instance where his true characteristics guided his behavior. Instead they would say that it was the pageantry and the extended mother time that brought out the inner 'mo (and not vice versa) because that's what the preconceived script tells them to say.

---

[3] Dr. James Dobson, *Building Confidence in Your Child* (Grand Rapids: Revell, 2010), 195-196. Previously published as *The New Hide or Seek* (Grand Rapids: Revell, 1999). Until I brought them to attention in 2010, quotes were prominently featured on FocusontheFamily.com, 'Parenting' section.

That's just one of many instances in which the anti-gays put the cart before the gay horse, so to speak, in claiming that it's the behavior that contributes to the gayness, not the gayness that contributes to the behavior. One that involves both gay men and lesbians is the way the anti-gays will cite gender variances in a child's personality as a factor for a later "preference" of homosexuality. They say that being the "sissy" kid (for a boy) or the "tomboy" (for a girl) in school is a contributor to that child's "choosing" of gayness at puberty. What I've never once heard them acknowledge is the possibility that these kids might be acting in their stereotypically "effeminate" or "tomboy" manners because—*wait for it, wait for it*—THEY'RE GAY! Because let's be honest here and say that, while many people defy their various stereotypes in different ways, there is some degree of truth behind all of them. If you go to a mass event of LGBTs, you are going to see scores of what are considered to be effeminate men and scores of what are considered to be butch lesbians. Is it that these folks had such an easy ride playing this role as a kid that they decided to stick with it for life? *Unlikely!* It's far more likely that the biological factors that play a role in homosexuality also have a little something to do with what we think of as being homo-associated stereotypes, but the agenda-motivated anti-gays don't want to consider this possibility.

Along those same lines, anti-gays often say that gay and lesbian adults tended to have been shy kids. It's not a far-fetched claim on the surface. It probably even holds some truth, based on the considerable obstacles that can come with being an LGBT young person. Unfortunately, the 'mo foes take that information and spin it as if it was this kid's shyness that later helped his or her homosexuality take root. Again, they don't present the most common conclusion one would seemingly draw from such data, which is that many gay kids feel different and sometimes have trouble relating to their peers, which is what caused them to come across as shy. Shyness is, after all, a natural response to feeling like an outsider. However, you will not hear an anti-gay give much credence to this far-more-likely root of the bashfulness, since (a) such reasoning is not conducive to their bashings, and (b) such reasoning shines a great light on the role their work has in making LGBT kids feel vulnerable.

Pulling homosexuality far away from the nature side of the nature/nurture debate is the number one key to virtually all of organized anti-LGBT movement's strategic doors. That's why in terms of gays, they pick apart every aspect of character and upbringing to pinpoint what they consider to be the faults therein. Whereas childhood personality manifestations and family dynamics for heterosexuals are seen as nothing more than traits and upbringings, for the gay person they are painted as impetuses for future Pride flag ownership. Because it doesn't seem to be enough for the 'mo foes to gun for gay's presents and marriage-desiring futures—*they also want to rob us of our pasts!*

CLAIM: GAYS RECRUIT

If gays and allies say we want bullying eliminated in public schools, the 'mo foes say we're "recruiting." When we try to help the next genera- tion of gays from suffering in the ways we did, they say we're coercing them into the "homosexual lifestyle™." If we step up and do the righteous thing, we're accused of being predatory. Yet if we sit back and let them control the hearts and minds of America's youth, we will be the ones who continue to be preyed upon. We simply can't win in the eyes of those who foster the "gay recruitment" claims, and that is precisely how they want it.

The idea of gay recruitment can be seen as far back as those campy 1950s instructional videos, with boxy-suit-wearing men warning of the dangers of the menacing 'mo. However, the idea was really brought to the forefront by infamous gay rights opponent Anita Bryant, who named her 1970s campaign against homosexuality "Save Our Children" and who infamously stated: "As a mother, I know that homosexuals cannot biologically reproduce children; therefore, they must recruit our children." Anita made this idea of recruit- ment and child endangerment the crux of her argument, and since her efforts were instrumental in having an anti-discrimination ordinance repealed in Dade County, FL, (which was reinstated in 1998) and gay adoption banned in the entire state (which finally ended in 2010, due to court action), 'mo foes nationwide caught on to how beneficial this message of gay recruitment could be to any campaign designed to wipe the same-sexers off the map of humanity. A *"Eureka!"* moment was born in the heads of America's anti- gays, and they've never strayed from the tired "recruitment" lines.

> [I]n at least one sense, pro-homosexual activists in our schools do indeed "recruit children." What they seek to do is "recruit chil- dren"—100 percent of our children, "gay" or straight—as soldiers in their war against truth, common sense, and traditional moral values.

That's one recruitment drive that has no place on the campuses of America's public schools.[4]

Or in modern days, the nothing-if-not-savvy religious right has adapted the word "recruitment," knowing it can come across as loaded. They have largely changed it to "indoctrination" instead. It goes something like this:

> You know, it's not a lifestyle that is good for this nation. Matter of fact, studies show that no society that has totally embraced homosexuality has lasted more than, you know, a few decades. So it's the death knell for this country. I honestly think it's the biggest threat… that our nation has, even more so than terrorism or Islam, which I think is a big threat. Okay? Because what's happening now, they're going after, in schools, two-year-olds. You know why they're trying to get early childhood education? They want to get our young children into the government schools so they can indoctrinate them. I taught school for close to twenty years and we're not teaching facts and knowledge anymore, folks, we're teaching indoctrination.[5]

Charming, huh?

Like almost all of the gay rights opponents' tactics, the recruitment/indoctrination concept works because it plays on the greatest fears. It's designed to paint gays as raptorial hunters, a characterization that feeds into a number of other anti-LGBT claims. After all, if you convincingly frame *any* debate as if your opposition is out to harm children, you're going to automatically have a team of scared parents who are willing to join your side. Casting LGBTs as the witches who want to cook Hansel and Gretel in our rainbow-colored ovens until they come out golden gay helps the "pro-family" movement to fill the roles in this fictive "We Don't Care for Fairies" tale.

Perhaps even more important to the ultimate cause is that the claim also propagates the illusion that homosexuality is a "choice." After all, if

---

[4] Peter Sprigg, *Homosexuality in Your Child's School* (Washington: Family Research Council, 2006), 22, http://downloads.frc.org/EF/EF06K26.pdf
[5] Oklahoma state representative Sally Kern, speech to a Republican club in Oklahoma City, OK, 10 January 2008.

we gays recruit, we must have a reason to do so, right? If you are to follow Ms. Bryant's *obscenely simplistic* groundwork, then the answer is that
we enlist America's kids into our homo realm as a way of reproducing our
kind. The anti-gays make it sound as if we queer folk are standing outside
playgrounds, waving around candy and Kathy Griffin DVDs, in order to
build up our base.

The most annoying aspect of the "gays recruit" claim, however, is that
as LGBT equality becomes a more widely accepted topic of discussion
with younger kids, that acceptance only fuels the flames of this particular
anti-gay tactic. Since any attempt to encourage gay acceptance to kids and
teens is, to the ones who make the recruitment/indoctrination claims, an
attack on America's youth, they only increase their nonsense whenever a
Gay-Straight Alliance club or queer-inclusive Diversity Day is established
in one of the nation's schools. If we pass bills that discourage bullying and
harassment, then they misappropriate our motives so that enlisting adolescent 'mos, not removing "Smear the Queer" from schools' varsity sport
list, appears to be the goal. The more we cheer progress, the more they
hear, "WE'RE COMING FOR YOUR BABIES!"

The only true way for gay rights advocates to quiet the recruitment
claims would be to stop the fight for acceptance in the area where it's
most needed. But guess what? We're not going to stop telling kids that
we're normal parts of humanity's spectrum! And *why?* Well, because we
do want to recruit America's kids! We want to draft them into the ranks of
decency, wherein non-acceptance and bias will not be tolerated. We want
to target all potential high school bullies while they are still relatively
innocent, before uninformed gay stigma turns them into rabid, or even
violent, anti-gay aggressors. Those who claim that gays recruit try to pass
off half-truths and outright lies to anyone and everyone who will swallow
their messages. If we are not to challenge those messages, then who will?

So yes, we *do* want your kids, America: we want them to not mali-
ciously use the word "fag."

CLAIM: LGBTs DESERVE TO BE UNEQUAL

More a tone than a term, the idea of being less than equal is one every
LGBT person feels at some point in his or her life. Of all the B.S. in the

anti-gay side's preconceived script, this is the component that most fully causes LGBT people to see disparity as their predetermined answer. Why would adults expect a kid to value a nation if they are using that nation's precious governing documents to devalue his or her life?

Since marriage is the big headline grabber, let's look at that particular matter of asymmetry. Here in America, we have a coalition of groups, churches, and everyday citizens who have taken on gays' ring fingers for sport. The '70s had pet rocks; the '80s saw leg warmers; Flannel and Doc Martens garbed the grungy '90s. For the first part of the twenty-first century, it just might be marriage inequality that goes down as the unfortunate trend we'll all be embarrassed to have foisted into pop culture. It is, after all, more restrictive than a leisure suit and more of a time-waster than anything Rubik ever invented.

If one had been cryogenically frozen for sixty years with first re-exposure to human life coming in the form of a '00s "protect traditional marriage" rally, one would likely think there was a group of homicidal madmen running through this country on a maniacal rampage, killing every married or marriage-bound hetero along the way. The anti-gays truly present the fight for marriage equality in terms extreme enough to convince an unsuspecting person that the threat is that frighteningly bone-chilling. It's all fear, fear, and more fear in order to incite an angry mob mentality within the impressionable ranks. As with virtually all of their claims, they use a fear-mongering approach on marriage so they can once again put gays in the position of aggressor. Just as they say we prey on children through our "recruitment" campaigns, that we gay men possess a heightened desire to molest, or that our own struggle for equality "hijacks" other civil rights movements, they say we're poaching marriage to make us look insidious. The opposition casts gays as the big bad wolves who are out to ruin Little Red Riding Bride's trip down the aisle, taking advantage of the fact that human brains like to view things in ways that are this storybook simple.

This is an actual photo that the North Carolina "protect marriage" movement ran in the winter of 2012 in order to drum up support for a proposed constitutional ban on same-sex marriage:

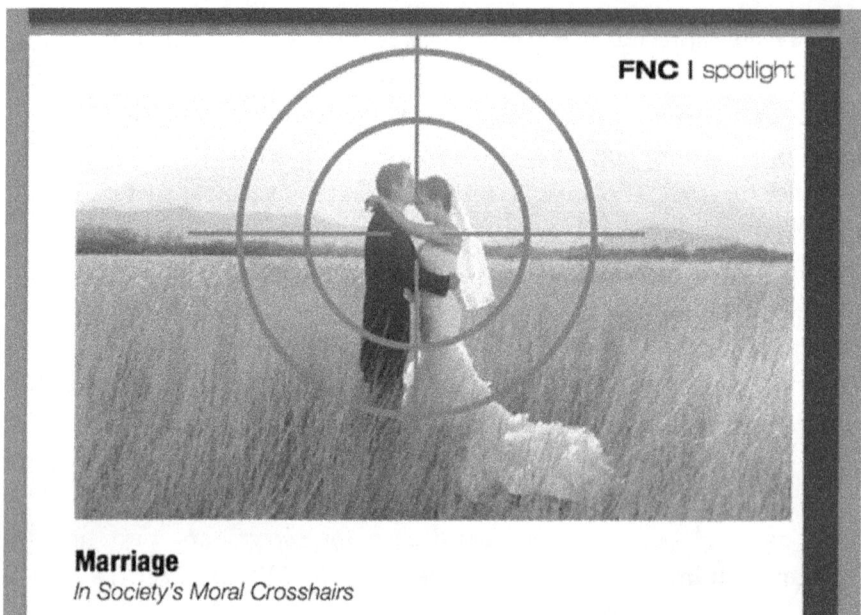

Marriage
In Society's Moral Crosshairs

Framing the marriage equality debate as if those of us on the gay side are the ones on the offensive is a claim from which the anti-gay team will *never* stray. They've been quite successful in creating and selling this illusion by doing what their team does best: STAYING FIRMLY ON MESSAGE. Sadly they've learned that heated and divisive messaging will turn out their vote in ways far stronger than will a reasoned consideration of what civil equality would and would not mean for gay people and the greater good, thus we get crosshairs placed on heterosexual newlyweds as they embrace in wheat fields.

In waging these condemnatory campaigns, gay rights opponents have cultivated the inequality message for an entire generation. Whereas invisibility defined the struggles of prior LGBT people, the acknowledgement and subsequent denial of modern gays has put the unlevel playing field on full display. This is good, in that it has heightened public sympathies. It's also dangerous, in that young LGBT kids are now more aware of their forced differentiation than in any prior time.

---

[6] Jacqueline Schaffer, J.D., "In Society's Moral Crosshairs," *Family North Carolina*, Winter 2010 ed., http://ncfpc.org/FNC/1201-MoralCrosshairs.pdf (accessed 30 Dec. 2011)

CLAIM: GAYS ARE SEX-OBSESSED

EXHIBIT A: The Bunny Ranch is a legal brothel in Nevada. Heterosexual only.
EXHIBIT B: AshleyMadison.com is a website designed exclusively for the purposes of infidelity for married heterosexuals. The company claims over 10 million members.[7]
EXHIBIT C: *Playboy* magazine is in its 57th year. There is overlap in readership, but heterosexual men are undeniably the target market.
EXHIBIT D: Reality shows built around heterosexual hooking up are all over the program guide.
EXHIBIT E: Tiger Woods circa 2010.
EXHIBIT F: Charlie Sheen circa 2011.
EXHIBIT G: Herman Cain circa the 2012 Republican primary.

Do gay people like sex? You bet your sweet orgasms. But if the organized anti-LGBT crowd wants to paint us as unduly sex-focused, then I'm going to take every single opportunity to remind them that the "sex sells" concept was pioneered around heterosexuality. Forget recession-proof business—heterosexual sex obsession would seem to be *nuclear war*–proof!

So rest assured, straights. Even if we do "destroy marriage," heterosexual coitus will likely endure. It did survive the Lorena Bobbitt incident, after all (look it up if you're under thirty).

CLAIM: GAYS ARE ANTI-RELIGION

The water carriers for the American religious right have long brandished the Bible as a bully club, telling all who will listen that their personal belief in their personal denomination of their personally chosen faith determines LGBT people to be an "abomination." Fair enough. This is a nation with true religious freedom. Thank God.

But religious freedom does not mean freedom for people of any certain faith to hijack all debate or to unjustly come down against others'

---

[7] Suzanne Choney, "Extramarital 'dating' site has 10 million members," Digital Life on Today, 9 Aug. 2011, http://digitallife.today.msnbc.msn.com/_news/2011/08/09/7320489-extramarital-dating-site-hits-10-million-members (accessed 29 Dec. 2011).

civil equality. And this, my friends, is what those within the anti-LGBT movement simply do not understand. Or in most cases they likely *do* understand it, but they also understand that exploiting religious-based fears comes with a built-in base—a sizeable, well-connected base that will fill the coffers, since the money comes via a decree from God. Right?

Through this process, the American anti-LGBT crowd has cultivated a meme suggesting that anyone who resists their overreaching is an irreligious hostile. In evangelical Christianity, the stated and unabashed goal is to win followers, and following means agreeing around 99.9 percent of the time (at least). A citizen's resistance to biblically-based measures such as a federal marriage amendment or limitations on reproductive freedom are not seen, to many (if not most) within the "pro-values" crowd, as pushback. They instead turn the political resistance into a referendum on them and their right to pray, when in fact, it's their right to *prey* on a nation's *true* sense of religious freedom that is the point of contention.

Which takes us to the LGBT crowd. No target is more in the religious social conservatives' crosshairs, so there is no flock with more of a reason to resist the threats. When those who oppose basic protections like employment non-discrimination, military fairness, or measures meant to reduce bias-motivated crimes launch an attack in the civil sector, pro-LGBT people naturally stand up against the aggression. What other choices have we?

But what inevitably happens? We LGBT people are immediately and absent-mindedly positioned as "anti-religion." Never mind that LGBT people are far from a monolith, and that sexual orientation and gender identity are in no way religion's logical opposites. All LGBTs, from those who are in the pews every Sunday to those who are into their third Bloody Mary by the time the sermon rolls around, are simply written off as militants to a God who loves them but not their "lifestyles." Religious gays are said to be heretical, buying into liberal biblical revisionism. Non-believing gays and their allies are just plain in need of saving.

Focus on the Family's Director for Family Formation Studies, Glenn Stanton, puts it like this:

> All sexual sin is wrong because it fails to mirror the Trinitarian image, but homosexuality does more than fail. It's a particularly evil lie of Satan because he knows that it overthrows the very image of the Trinitarian God in creation, revealed in the union of male and female.

This is why this issue has become such a flashpoint. It will become even more contentious because nothing else challenges this image of the Triune God so profoundly and thoroughly as homosexuality. It's not what we were made for.[8]

I mean, seriously—how do you even have a discussion with someone whose starting point has you as a "particularly evil lie of Satan"?

It's not just gays who are shunned, either. People from other, less "traditional" faiths are essentially ignored altogether, unless in an area where engagement might be of benefit (see: Mormons in California's Prop 8 fight). Affirming faiths are a complete non-starter. Keep in mind that all of this exclusion is done *in the name of* faith, which one would think is supposed to involve a deep understanding of God's natural realm and all of the people who were created to exist within it, not a myopic shunning of the same. But no, the general message of the organized anti-LGBT crowd is that most of the world is "fallen," with dissent being just another ill.

The most frustrating part? That it's actually LGBTs, atheists, progressive people of any faith, and the like who are more inclined to understand and support true religious freedom. LGBT people know what it's like to be told to sit down and shut up, and are often very sensitive to anyone's attempts to roll back the speech or expression rights of any group—including people of faith with whom they strongly disagree. For just one case in point, look to openly gay Representative Barney Frank, one of three members of Congress to vote against 2006's Respect for America's Fallen Heroes Act, a piece of legislation specifically designed to limit the notorious "God Hates Fags" family's novel form of religious expression at soldiers' funerals.[9] This vote despite the fact that the out, gay Frank had been personally targeted by this so-called church on a number of occasions. Frank put the freedom of expression above his freedom from religious criticism, as so many on our side do.

It also must be mentioned that atheists typically have no need or desire to convert anyone, only to ask questions and foster conversation. Likewise, liberal religions that practice acceptance are generally not in

---

[8] Glenn T. Stanton, *My Crazy Imperfect Christian Family* (Colorado Springs: NavPress, 2004), 86.

[9] US. House of Representatives, *Vote On Passage: H.R. 5037 {109th}: Respect for America's Fallen Heroes Act*, http://clerk.house.gov/evs/2006/roll129.xml (accessed 10 May 2011).

the market of closing down their more exclusive cousins. Live and let live is undeniably in larger supply on the pro-inclusion side of the fence, and it's a mindset that seems to most fully understand and respect the right to call up God in whatever way one sees fit, just as long as that call doesn't harm another's liberty.

Here again, the team that wants to turn its movement into the supposed victims of persecution doesn't want to hear any of this. Gays hate God. Period. End of story. Conversation stopped. I can't hear you [*fingers in ears*]—la la la la la la la la la.

It damages our discourse. It damages many LGBT people's souls. For the love of God, this aggressively self-involved myopia needs to stop.

CLAIM: "THEY'LL TREAT US LIKE BIGOTS"

This piece of witness-leading comes from the National Organization for Marriage's "Same-Sex Marriage Talking Points":

FREQUENTLY ASKED QUESTIONS
Are you a bigot? *"Why do you want to take away people's rights?" "Isn't it wrong to write discrimination into the Constitution?"*
A: "Do you really believe people like me who believe mothers and fathers both matter to kids are **like bigots** and racists? I think that's pretty offensive, don't you? Particularly to the 60 percent of African-Americans who oppose same-sex marriage. Marriage as the union of husband and wife isn't new; it's not taking away anyone's rights. It's common sense."[10]

And this quote comes from the National Organization for Marriage Founding Chair Maggie Gallagher, writing for National Review Online:

It's sad and disturbing, and a confirmation of what I began saying seven years ago: When they say you are a bigot, comparable to those who opposed interracial marriage, if you think marriage is the union of husband and wife, believe them. They say it because they think it's true.

[10] "Same Sex Marriage: Answering The Toughest Questions," National Organization for Marriage website, http://www.nationformarriage.org (accessed 2 Jan. 2012).

The movement goal is to use the power of law to help reshape the culture, as was done for race. Those who didn't realize this in 2003 will start acting that way in 2010, because framing ideas have consequences.[11]

I chose this quote, but there are a million others just like it. The basic assertion is that marriage equality for same-sex couples will eventually make Maggie, NOM, and the rest of the "protect marriage" crowd seem like bigots, much in the same way that the elimination of anti-miscegenation laws has helped foist those who oppose interracial marriage into a negative light.

In the post–Prop 8 world, this has become the talking point de rigueur for this team of activists, all part of their strategy of flipping the script so that the ones *banning* same-sex marriage seem like the true victims. Admittedly they state it ably and clearly enough—an ability to convey a message is not a skill I would ever deny to Maggie or NOM. However, in using this meme, people like Maggie always overlook the most key element at play here. That element is the nature of right versus wrong—the truth that views and laws regarding racist behavior have *rightly* changed over the years because society has evolved and corrected its past biased thinking. In fact, I would argue that these comparisons actually hurt the anti–marriage equality cause, as they remind folks of all of the other mistakes that we as a nation—whether through courts, votes, or legislative action—have stepped up and remedied.

Many of us would love to think the pro-equality community has the power and influence that Maggie Gallagher ascribes to it. The reality, however, is that our movement pales in comparison to the anti-gay forces in most every area. The opposition is bigger, more connected, better financed (Focus on the Family/CitizenLink alone has a larger annual budget than thirty-nine national LGBT groups combined[12]), have a much easier ability to rally through their churches and parachurch networks, and have always held public opinion regarding marriage on their side. It's illogical to assume that our gains are due to our ability to outpace their

---

[11] Maggie Gallagher, "Is David Blankehorn a Bigot?" *National Review* Online, 9 July 2010, http://www.nationalreview.com/corner/232910/david-blankenhorn-bigot-maggie-gallagher (accessed 4 Nov. 2011).

[12] Matt Foreman, "Celebrating The Gains of Underdog LGBT Groups," *Huffington Post*, 30 June 2011, http://www.huffingtonpost.com/matt-foreman/celebrating-underdog-lgbt-organizations_b_888179.html (accessed 12 Sept. 2011).

considerable public front. In truth, the equality movement has made all of our gains *despite* the opposing muscle. We haven't out-PRed or even outsmarted them, necessarily; we certainly haven't outspent them. We've simply outed the reality of this conversation, where both the facts and feelings undeniably fall in our favor.

That takes us back to the righteousness of the fight, the key variable I feel this crew is failing to acknowledge. It's very easy for the "pro-marriage" rock stars like Maggie Gallagher to make it sound as if we've whipped society into P.C. submission, but it's simply untrue. In truth, we've stated our case in the face of a considerable adversary and have managed to slowly connect with the public. We've come out and shown who we are, using our visibility to open hearts, minds, and others' previously sealed closet doors. We have stood up for that which we feel we deserve yet are still largely denied. Over time, we've come to where we are today, when public opinion polls are mixed-to-slightly-negative bags, but where the tide seems to be carrying us to a brighter shore. More and more, those polls are starting to tip in our favor.

It is that tide and all of its variables that Maggie Gallagher and her pals must both acknowledge and examine in full. Not just acknowledge in terms of the marriage fight, because that fight cannot be accurately disassociated from LGBT lives and loves as a whole. Instead, they need to examine the variable of their own team's anti-gay activism, as well as any and all public rejection of the same. They have yet to take a hard, objective look at the basis for their marriage views, and they must. No matter how fully they believe in these views, they must. They must look at why we in the queer community have been able to progress against all odds; they must ask why bigotry and bias is more readily associated with their side; they must stop looking only at what marriage equality will supposedly mean for anti-equality people's operations in American society; they must ask WHY they think that this will be the one time in American history that a valid, recognized minority group's ability to achieve their desired gains, both in public opinion and civil law, would produce a negative outcome. Why is that, Maggie?

Regarding the idea that same-sex marriage victories will bring on a slew of problems that will plague and ultimately disfavor certain people of faith, I would argue that nearly all of the people who work these lines are doing so out of tactic rather than belief. But even taking them on their word, one can't just look to what may or may not flower—one has to most fully examine the root. I would argue that if you were to look at the roots of marriage equality, you'd see that they, like the roots of so many other virtuous fights, were always strong and conducive to growth—it has just taken society a very long time to dig through the mounds of withering talking points, rhetoric, code words, and false compassion under which they had been buried!

· · ·

These are just some of the claims that the professional foes of the 'mos use to suggest that gay people, by virtue of nothing more than birth, have secured a less-than-stellar, less-than-normal, less-than-easy placement in society as their fait accompli. The anti-LGBTs attach a heightened form of "original sin" onto good and decent people's existences, with their suggested purification methods ranging from offensive to anti-scientific to unconstitutional to downright frightening. Nobody should be surprised that this degrading worldview causes problems for many, many, *many* LGBT people. Perhaps the greater shock is that *any* LGBT person manages to reach adulthood with his or her faculties intact!

But the beautiful part? The opposition movement has overplayed its overreaching hands. While they have cultivated such harm through these and oh-so-many more claims, in doing so, our political opponents have also awakened an activist spirit that would've been far more dormant in their absence. Groups from the National Organization for Marriage to the Family Research Council to the Holier Than Thou Consortium of Conservative Family Values Voters Who Have A Big-Ass American Flag In Their Logo and An Even Bigger-Assed Anti-Gay Chip On Their Shoulders have given history a face of bias. New and greater technologies have brought them more exposure. Yes, some Americans have bought into the deception, and that really eats it in the short term. The truth we can hang our hat on is that those who chose temporal hurt will not write history—instead, the principled resistance will pen our story. The final mark will come from the stamp of a fair-minded foot. *Harumph!*

It's too late to repair countless expired souls that were ripped apart by the unequal messaging, but it's up to us to repair the present and win the future. Until we remove the campaigns of marginalization associated with every malicious uttering of "faggot," many gay, lesbian, bisexual, transgender, and questioning human beings will continue to live their lives in the margins.

The organized anti-gays are quick to point the finger when the supposed negatives of the supposed "lifestyle" come to light. So many want so much to paint LGBT lives and loves as, at the very least, dangerous, and often downright evil. It's time we shine the brightest light on the considerable negatives they foster because of *their* lifestyle choice to be hostile to certain people. Holy water cannot and should not wash this organized movement's hands of the unnecessary strife they have caused!

12) HOMO-PHONE

WHAT I SAID: "Hi Mom."
WHAT I MEANT: *Hi Mom.*

WHAT I SAID: "Sorry I'm calling so late. Just got in not too long ago."
WHAT I MEANT: *Sorry I'm calling so straight. Just got out not too long ago.*

WHAT I SAID: "Yeah, Kelly and I had a really nice time tonight."
WHAT I MEANT: *But his name was actually Jeff.*

SAID: "We went to dinner. Hooters, for the wings."
MEANT: *Hooters, for the irony.*

SAID: "Then we went to see Janet Jackson."
MEANT: *Or the drag approximation thereof.*

SAID: "What's she look like? Kelly? Hmm, let's see. She's kind of short . . ."
MEANT: *But built like a brick shithouse.*

SAID: "Has brown hair . . ."
MEANT: *On both head and chest.*

SAID: "I think her eyes are blue . . ."
MEANT: *I know his eyes are brown.*

SAID: "She's cute. She likes to laugh, too."
MEANT: *Trust me, you should hear him cackling at me in the next room while I keep up this charade.*

SAID: "Is she in school? Yep, she's studying film."
MEANT: *He is in fact studying film. And you'd actually like him, if only his personal movie was cast with a female rather than a male lead.*

SAID: "No, I haven't met her parents."
MEANT: *Because to his parents, I'm also a "she."*

SAID: "I mean, I'm not looking to get tied down or anything."
MEANT: *Especially since my state and federal government legally prevents the kind of tying you're talking about.*

SAID: "But we are having fun together."
MEANT: *Even if we only feel comfortable in certain places.*

SAID: "So we'll see how it goes."
MEANT: *Will you see it too? Someday? Possibly?*

SAID: "Maybe I'll bring her to visit sometime. Like next weekend or something."
MEANT: *Or when it's feasible for us to go ice skating in hell. I hear the 12th of Never's a good time for that. Does that work for you, dad, and the pigs that will fly on that day?*

SAID: "Oh. Uh. Yeah. Or you could come here too. Sure."
MEANT: *Oh god, I wonder if that fake Janet Jackson does daytime performances as stand-in girlfriends?*

SAID: "Except my house is filled with junk . . ."
MEANT: *Especially the closet.*

SAID: ". . . so I should probably just come to you. I'll see if maybe Kelly can join."
MEANT: *Her name was Kelly, right?*

SAID: "Alright, let me run. I need to study."
MEANT: *Drink.*

SAID: "I love you too."
MEANT: *I love you too.*

SAID: "I will. I'll definitely tell *her* you said hi."
MEANT: *And then I'll tell* him *how much it hurts to lie.*

SAID: "Bye."
MEANT: *Gay.*

How long could I keep on with these kinds of hang-ups?

13) MY "BOTHER," MY "SHEPARD"

The first couple of years of the twenty-first century are among the gayest ones this country has ever known. Or at least it was the first wave of a new visibility. I can remember walking down the magazine aisle of one of those mega books/movies/music chains circa 2000 and seeing no less than five mainstream publications with some sort of gay content on the cover. In film, the gay best friend had by that point become a cinematic stock character, used with varying artistic merit and success. There was also the world of advertising, where gay and gay-vague had seemed to have replaced passé hetero-sex as the new way to sell. Then there was Britney and Christina and the Backstreet Boys and that whole youth culture pop explosion that took over music around that time, which, even if not officially queer, had a tinge of 'mo-ocity. The fact that this time period coincided with my own transition into a happy homosexual only furthers my long-held belief that the world revolves around me.

I, of course, say that last sentence in jest. My summer of 2001 self, however, may have said it and fully meant it. After a year or two of slow advancement, I was finally fully in touch with my sexual orientation, and I no longer cared who among my friends and fellow Knoxville travelers knew. Quite simply, I loved being free from the shackles of self-checking or being found out. It was like stepping into my true skin for the first time and finding the flesh was as form fitting as the tight, slit-sided message tanks I now wore out to the clubs. Of newly legal age to do everything but rent a car (why is that twenty-five, seriously?), I immersed myself in the culture, the bars—*the absolutely everything*. No matter what was going on in my life, *Queer As Folk* and *Will & Grace* were on the television, which meant people who were in the know were supporting a gay-friendly environment. I was now part of a wonderful, vibrant community, and I was ecstatic. I was convinced the country, despite its recently inaugurated conservative figurehead, was also on the same page.

Still living in Tennessee, I knew in the back of my mind that there were many in my immediate and extended community who didn't support me and even might, in extreme circumstances, wish me harm. However, living in the bubble that comes with being a student at a large university, I was surrounded by enough people who *did* support me to fully drown out those who I considered to be my poor, misguided opposition. By this point I had more than found the gays I'd been missing during my first couple of years at school, and had more friends in my cell than I knew what to do with. It felt weird that I had ever considered alienation to be an argument for staying in the closet, considering how easily and rapidly my post-out social card exploded.

Yes, I heard the claims that the Falwells and the James Dobsons made about my peeps and me. Sure I saw the "God Hates Fags" protesters at some events. But these were figureheads, not factors. They were pundits, not people. My bubble kept me from connecting the organized opposition from my day-to-day life, and it kept me from processing all of those claims from the last chapter.

As far as actual personal dangers go? Well first and foremost, I knew that safe sex was not just the best bet but rather the ONLY option. I never slipped on this point, no matter how hot the situation or drunken the participants. Condoms and food were neck-in-neck in terms of where I'd allot my meager financial means.

Also, I was told early on that I was "too pretty" to leave the local gay bar by myself and that I should always venture back to my car amongst a pack of friends. My naïve self saw this more as a precaution than as any real danger. The worst I could perceive in terms of harassment involved a pack of straight boys mocking and teasing me, not causing literal harm. Nevertheless, I did basically heed this warning as well, making sure to adopt a buddy system when leaving the bar. Typically this was my drag queen pal Gabby, whose stiletto was as intimidating as it was stylish. I felt safe.

Showing public affection with a date was something else I knew to be a bit risky. Same-sex smooches or even handholds were not to be put on display. Here again, my concerns revolved less around bodily harm and more around stares and shitty comments. But since those could be enough to at least press against my bubble and put me in a bad mood, it was rare for my date and me to look like anything more than colleagues. Unless we were in the most reliably progressive establishments in town, we'd keep the "they could just be brothers" distance: close enough to get a second look, yet distant enough to let the angry or intimidated free their minds from visions of the dirty dude sex.

So yeah, some stuff was on the mind. For the most part, though, I genuinely felt that my days of fearing for my safety were pretty much behind me. Want to see how wacky my priorities were towards the end of '01? Well check out this page from my journal:

10/29/01 approx. 7 AM.

Hello. I have not posted an entry in months . . . I've neglected this beautiful book for my online journal . . . .Well . . . in 10 points, the major events of the past months:

1) [Juan] and I broke up
2) I got a bartending job at Rainbow
3) My dad had open heart surgery
4) I'm ready for school to be over
5) [Will] and I began a long distance flirtatious relationship
6) I met [Roman], my current boy toy
7) The World Trade Center was destroyed
8) Aaliyah died
9) My family pretty much knows I'm gay
10) I love and accept myself more than ever
Things I need/want: Gym membership, Margaret Cho tickets, DVDs, winter clothes, to sleep with [Will]

• • •

Dad gets number 4 priority? Three boys get shout outs before even one 9/11 mention? I *needed* DVDs, when I had to use a credit card just to buy generic groceries? As I said, a bubble.

As college progressed, there were some punctures. As stated in the journal entry, my family was by then almost unanimously aware of or at least suspicious about my sexuality. My pronouns had slipped more and more, and my club shirts were creeping ever more into my everyday wear. There was speculation and even some mild forms of interrogation. Because of that speculation as well as my own negative reaction to it, my relationship with them was becoming somewhat strained, even turning outright hostile on occasion. But since they weren't in the same city as I was (remember, my parents lived in Nashville; I was 160 miles away in Knoxville), I viewed any issue with them as separate from my daily life. I hoped they would always be part of my future, but their antipathy or even antagonism at the present seemed like part of my past. I thought they'd come around, eventually, so I didn't let what I perceived as their hang-ups fully permeate my protective layer. It was as if they were still focused on the old me, which was the skin I would step into whenever forced into a family fight. The new me was someone else, someone who I understood and, quite frankly, really liked. I wanted them to come to know and enjoy the new, real me too; in the meantime, my bubble protected me from harshness.

The bubble wasn't visible to anyone's eyes but my own, but I could feel it around me. It was a shield I'd been building up for two decades, with every "what doesn't kill me makes me stronger" moment used to patch together its surface. It gave me more than just the usual early twenties cockiness. My bubble afforded me the confidence to obtain a fast-tracked education that had nothing to do with my schoolwork. It gave me the ability to laugh with a delicious, even childlike, ease. It gave me clarity, letting me see both the world and myself through refreshed eyes. It gave me the kind of nerve to rip off my shirt and shake my little booty on the dance floor.

My slightly narcissistic bubble offered me a respite. Peace.

My bubble effectively popped in the spring of 2002.

Less than four months from when I was scheduled to flee college life for unknown Manhattan adventures, I was spending yet another night in one of the local gay watering holes, drinking a beer on the outside deck of the bar with a collection of locals whom I'd come to know and love over the past couple of nightlife years. Varied in both ages and outlooks, our motley crew was enjoying the spring weather and uneventful conversation, likely bitching about how boring our town was. "Nothing ever happens here" was a refrain often echoed at such tables, generally in a tone implying that something, *anything* happening would break up the monotony that came from the same old Michelob Lights, thumping music, and drag performances we'd all seen a hundred times. Little did we know that the *something* that had happened the night before would have us wishing for monotony's return.

We're going to call him Jon. He was a bartender at the biggest, most popular of the local gay clubs. While he carried himself with a presence that was unassuming and just a little bit shy, I had come to know Jon as a super-friendly, stand-up guy who was certainly confident enough to give me free shots around last call time. I always suspected that he had a little crush on me. He may have just been a genuinely nice man who considered me to be the same. Either way, I enjoyed him greatly and found that his presence behind the bar provided a comforting, reassuring, reliable place of calm.

Jon was murdered on his thirty-sixth birthday. Tricked by a potential trick into a homicidal situation.

Jon was murdered on his thirty-sixth birthday. Robbed of life for no greater reason than that he was a gay man.

Jon was murdered on his thirty-sixth birthday. Strangled so hard his windpipe was crushed.

Jon was murdered on his thirty-sixth birthday. It was a hate crime, undoubtedly, even if local authorities were later reluctant to admit it.

I said it four times, but I'd have to say it a million more and a trillion times louder to tell you how it reverberated in my head when I first heard it. The news rocked me. So hard.

What jarred me at least as much, if not more, in the immediate moments following the tragic news was the fact that so many others were still capable of playing pool and talking about whatever silliness they'd encountered during their week. The shock was definitely there, don't get me wrong—but whereas my level of disbelief was at 99.9 percent, most of the elders with whom I was I having a cocktail seemed to only be at about a 63 percent or so. I didn't understand how we could even talk about the minutiae of our existence—one of us had been murdered, seemingly because he was gay.

I couldn't speak, so I listened.

"Girl, did you see Kylie Minogue on *SNL*? She was fab!"

Wait, what? Seriously? What was I missing?

"Oh, I know she was. Did you hear her next single? It's okay, not as good as the first. I have a burned CD in my car; I'll play it for you later."

Where was the compassion?

"Darling, will you get me another Jack and Coke? Tell 'em to make it strong this time. I'm tired of that new bartender shittin' me out of drinks!"

Oh my God, a drink? Where were the priorities?

I heard the eight ball clacking against the cue. I heard laughter. I heard the touch screen video game doing its picture matching thing, as well as the over-the-shoulder player doing his best to coach the seated one to another, if not pyrrhic, then at least quarter-wasting, victory. The collection of sounds weren't any louder than on any other night. That the collection wasn't any softer was what I found so disturbing.

Feeling a strong need to talk but not wanting to poop on the party that, while surely somewhat lessened, was not going to stop, I decided to make my way over to Mother Mather's house. Mother Mather was a legend in the Knoxville gay scene, partly because of his past performances as a female impersonator, partly because of his always-friendly disposition, but mainly because he'd been so omnipresent in the scene for so many decades. As the grande dame of the midnight to 3 a.m. set, he'd seen many come and go—but he was still here. A reasoned voice who still drained his clock in a club scene where reason can sometimes take a back seat, Mother Mather had become a unique presence in my life. He was always there for a bitch session, a hug, or a hard truth. We'd developed a parent/child-like bond, and in many ways, he'd become a grounding influence. Tonight I needed a Mother's concern.

"Can you believe what happened," I asked Mother Mather before I was even fully through his front door. I was fairly certain that since he wasn't at the bar from which I'd just ventured, his heart-heavy self must've been at home contemplating the tragedy. After all, he sat at Jon's bar perhaps more than anyone, engaging in light conversation whenever he'd refill his plastic beer cup. The sad outrage I'd been looking for was surely going to pepper *his* response.

"What happened?" he asked. His voice suggested the tragedy was still unbeknownst to him, but how could that be possible? While I had no clue, I was surely going to clue Mother in on what he'd apparently missed.

"Jon!" I replied. "Jon was murdered!" I said, voice now approaching shout.

"Oh, yeah, I heard—it's just awful" was the casual, almost flippant way in which he responded. I wasn't prepared for that. His seemingly dismissive words bothered me on a deeper level than the ones I had heard earlier that night. He was the one who was supposed to "get it." Mother was my rock, my voice of reason. I wasn't going to just let this one go by unchallenged.

"Awful? That's it? Just . . . awful?" I asked, now in undeniable shout mode.

His feedback was still stuck at only a stare. Did he not hear me?

I pressed him to go further. I needed him to show that he was as on the verge of tears as I was. I was truly playing the role of child, pestering and prodding my adopted nighttime guardian to go on this sad journey. Petulance wasn't the act: I wanted him to feel so heartsick that he, like me, could hardly look at a heterosexual neighbor without pointing a finger of accusation. I wanted him to help me gather a band of troops to march down to the police station and demand action. I wanted—something.

"Child," he drawled in a Tennessee-by-way-of-Vanessa-Williams tone, "come in the living room and sit down."

Here it comes, I thought. That's it. He just needs to sit to find his bearings.

But as it turned out, all Mother seemed interested in discussing was the then-simmering Catholic priest scandal. In fact, while sitting there in his ornately decorated chambers sipping the Bud Light that was placed into my hands (Mother must have been out of milk), it was as if I was *deliberately* being led from the buzz-killing subject my tongue had brought into this house. The TV was on and marijuana was offered (Mother must have been out of cookies). Distractions abounded.

"They've been doing this for years," Mother offered. "I was an altar boy—trust me, I know. It's just now catching up with them!"

"Oh...um...so...but—" I tried to get a word in edgewise, the beer doing little to garble my discontent.

"And this is just the beginning. You watch! I bet it goes all the way up to the top."

"Yeah, um—can we please talk about Jon?!," I finally demanded, raised voice and all. "This is so messed up and it's like nobody cares! You should have heard the people at the bar!"

"Jeremy . . ." [long exhale]

It was then, as I persisted in directly combating the non-concern I perceived in his words, that I learned some truths that haunt me until this day.

"Let me tell you something, child . . ."

And he did. Many somethings.

His tales of brutal beatings spanned the decades. There were Kennedy-era smacks and pushes; disco-era brawls; group assaults that were even more unbalanced than the Mondale versus Reagan matchup. Making his way through the '90s and right up into present day, Mother railed off a string of pain that had greeted him and his considerable cast of friends, past and present.

Or what about the bars that had been burned to the ground? Mother fired off a list of Southeastern U.S. haunts that had been put to fire. His ease in rattling off the names told me he'd shared this list many times in his life.

There were epithets that had been scrawled upon various buildings and property. These too spanned space and time—though despite the nearly half-century these slurs traversed, the verbiage and the intent remained mostly unchanged.

Of course there was the tragedy that the early days of the AIDS epidemic had presented to his unsuspecting friends and loved ones. Mother had been around before, during, and after it hit. He didn't share these kinds of tales with me on this night, but I had chatted with him about them before. I knew that his mind and body would never forget the battle wounds he acquired, brought on by both the disease's asteroid of impact and the religious right's callous reaction to the same.

But perhaps most shocking of all was Mother Mather's own detailed story of being chased down a local road by a knife-wielding masked man, putting within him the fear that his own life was about to come to an early end. He told me how he ran without looking back. He told me how he never thought he'd live to see another day. He told me of the sweet relief that fell over him as he rounded the bend and found a place of business (a market, I believe) that was still open at that late hour. He was either telling me the truth or he'd been ghostwriting for Stephen King all of these years. The stories were so vivid, so harrowing.

For you see, Jon was far from the first such tragedy Mother Mather had witnessed in his almost thirty years in the local gay community. Jon was just one on a long list of victims and almost-victims Mother Mather had known, self included. Mother rattled off all of the offenses with such precision and clarity, it told me they were thoughts that were always on his mind in some capacity.

That's when I finally got it. I realized that for Mother Mather and many others, their sadness over the news of Jon's death was in no way lessened because of the past incidents, but the self-protective way in which they dealt with this latest murder was a tactic that had surely been learned over time. My older friends at the bar were, indeed, as sad and outraged as me, many of them more so. It was the shock that some of my younger friends and I were experiencing to which they could no longer fully relate. Many of them grew up in times and communities much more stifling than the one we were all now experiencing. With such difficult memories in their collective subconscious, offenses against the gay community, even on such a grand scale, were no longer all that astonishing.

Bubbles are not uniform. Bubbles come in different varieties. Some patch together the pain of the closet into a barrier that allows for wide-eyed, somewhat oblivious protection to harm. Others string together real-life experiences, an almost unimaginable laundry list of painful scenarios, creating a shield that prevents too much emotion from escaping. Perhaps the latter group once lived in a starry-eyed bubble as well. Perhaps not, since the advancement of time has certainly supplied modern young gays with a more protective solution than was offered to earlier generations. Whatever the case, we all, as humans, build up layers that allow us to stave off the proverbial *and* literal jabs and stabs of life. We protect our bubbles. No group has had to do this more so than the population that's faced such a lion's share of pricks.

By the next night, people had had a chance to go through the processes. Reality had set in, and shocked shells had largely given way to remembrance and resilience. Memorial benefits were being planned and informative campaigns about the need to protect each other were gearing up in earnest. People did care. Deeply. The setting-in process had begun; emotions were on display.

Some were dancing; others were in deep conversation about the latest news report. It was not for me to judge anyone else's grieving process. One person's tears were another person's laughter, and vice versa. In fact, maybe it'd be good for me to let it go and have a beer, to relax. After all, relaxed was the only kind of Jon I had ever known. Maybe tonight it would be okay to crack a smile, in memory not neglect?

Meanwhile, at the dark end of the bar sat a lone, melancholy patron. He was staring into the mirror behind the bottles but focusing on nothing in particular, not even the empty cup in front of him.

"Another one?" asked a bartender who was decidedly not Jon as he grabbed the bubbling beer tap.

"No, child," a Mother replies while grabbing a tattered jacket. "I've more than had my fill."

DESPITE WHAT YOU MIGHT'VE HEARD . . . #3

➤ Just because your kid gives homosexuality "that old college try," it doesn't necessarily mean said kid is gay. When he or she gives it "that old graduate school dissertation," then you might be on to something.

➤ College is not right for everyone. In fact, most of them are quite left-leaning.

➤ Queer Theory classes are a nice addition to any school. Especially if the school itself has a theory that queers are not.

➤ Sending your gay kid to a religious school in order to force him or her into heterosexuality makes no more sense than sending your straight kid to that same school in order to force him or her into a marriage with that one kid who seems to not care in the slightest about physical intimacy with the opposite sex.

➤ Free condom distribution is an awesome college perk. On one hand, you may not need them. When you move past that one hand, you'll be glad you grabbed several.

➤ The Gay-Straight Alliance is not the gayest thing on campus. Not as long as fraternity hazing rituals still happen.

➤ "We're just testing whether his underwear matches the carpet" is not a convincing explanation for why you're in bed with your same-sex friend. No, not even if you're an art student.

➤ The early twenties can and should be a time to find oneself. It can but shouldn't be a time to lose oneself. Don't make freedom the enemy of standards.

➤ Let's keep those over-macho acts in check, fraternity bros. Because let's be honest: "*Toga! Toga! Toga!*" is essentially the chant of an underprepared drag show.

➤ A college student must remember to eat. The "freshman fifteen" can look unbecoming on certain frames, but nowhere more so than on the emaciated twink for whom that weight gain brings him up to a whopping twenty-three pounds.

➤ If you're gay and hear your presumably straight roommate's bed squeaking in the middle of the night, don't presume that's a chance to make your move. You are not the star of a porn flick, and his or her potentially negative reactions may make even the worst porn dialogue look prize-winning by comparison.

➤ Anti-gay street preachers love colleges. Treat them like that one 8 a.m. crip class that never takes attendance: only acknowledge their existence when directly tested.

➤ Straight ladies, if a guy says lesbians turn him on, don't make out with another girl in order to impress him. Instead, invite him to a lesbian separatist commune to make tempeh nuggets for the next Michigan Womyn's Music Festival. If you set him to the tune of Ani DiFranco and he returns, then both he and genuine lesbian street cred are yours.

➤ Voting is not the most exciting thing in the world. Neither is standing out in the cold, protesting the right that was just rolled back at the hands of anti-equality majority tyranny/pro-equality voter apathy. Show up at the polls = not having to freeze your ass off at the "we lost and we're pissed" rallies!

➢ If you want to do spring break in Cancun, then go for it. But go because *you* want to go, not because some drunken flunky who you'll never see again in three years thinks you're totally "gay" if you sit out this body shot bonanza.

➢ Gay life doesn't end at thirty—though you might have to join the AARP (Abercrombie Apparel Retirement Plan)

14) START SPREADING THE NEWS (BECAUSE THE BUTTER'S TOO DAMN PRICEY)

"It can destroy an individual, or it can fulfill him, depending a good deal on luck. No one should come to New York to live unless he is willing to be lucky."
—E.B. White[13]

It was somewhat fitting that my move to NYC would come within that first year following the tragic events of 9/11/01. That was a year when everything the world knew and thought about New York forever changed. Time to rebuild.

Clichéd writers will describe the tone that hung over the skyline as being melancholic. Having experienced it during that first year, I'd certainly accept that description to be as true as it is trite. While I had no pre-9/11 years to compare with that first year of residence, I know from both my own experiences and shared anecdotes from longtime locals whom I now called neighbors that the city was in an undeniable time of struggle, worry, and pain.

At the same time, it was also a period when every hope we'd ever had about old New York's endurance remained undauntedly strong. People who'd never so much as watched a Yankees game were now donning "I heart NY" t-shirts and planning their family vacations around a trip

---

13 E.B. White, "Here in New York," *Holiday*, 1949.

that they never even knew they wanted to take. The city had to find its bearings, and it wasn't going to be easy. It would take time, but it was going to do it, come hell or high Hudson waters. That was another feeling one could glean from the energy of that time: that giving up was not an option.

Same with Jeremy. Everything about the post-college move to Manhattan was personally tough. Literally, from the moment I arrived in the city and began the insane ballet of trying to park, unload, and return a U-Haul in an overcrowded borough with parking rules that were as foreign to me as the bialys being advertised at the corner deli, the NY face-slaps began. I never realized how much the counter people at just about any Tennessee business coddled the customer with niceties until I encountered employees who'd seemingly shredded their "customer is always right" memos. That was a big, initial shock about New York: the way a simple request like "Where should I return the keys?" might be met with an implicit (if not directly expressed) "Why don't you shove 'em up your ass?" Even from a manager.

Just the act of acquiring basic necessities, once so boring yet basically unchallenging, was now suddenly a feat. A simple trip could mean a bus and two subways. Not that I really minded the travel part itself, as I was more than eager to explore every inch of my new turf. It was just that it all required so much more effort than I expected, in a summer sun that'd leave me sweatier than I wanted. The movies don't tell you that part.

Sticker shock was a big one, too. I'd long been warned about the high cost of living, told that everything was going to be just a little bit higher. But loaves of bread even?! And by a little bit higher you mean a full two dollars more than I used to pay?! How am I going to take a bite out of the Big Apple when I can't even afford its smaller relative? I certainly learned to utilize the phrase "oy vey" even if I couldn't afford the knish!

Then there were the clothes. The elements were ten times harsher in this pedestrian culture, with my thrift store fashions ten times more inadequate for this city's rough outdoor climate (to say nothing of the city clubs' socially strict door policies). Suddenly I needed shoes, coats, sweaters, and outerwear galore. For me, however, there would be no Bloomingdales and certainly no SoHo direct-from-designer shops. Hell, discount chain Daffy's was even out of my less-than-beer-bottle pockets' paltry reach. I couldn't even think about fashion, only the hope of acquiring the most basic of needs. I had to hope that my mouth and physical attributes would elevate my threads.

Plain and simple, I wasn't prepared to be in NYC, even if I was more than ready to be there. Unlike the city itself, I didn't have much of a cheering section, beyond a few college friends and the guy with whom I was sharing both an apartment and a rapidly waning relationship. That alienation was pretty scary, since even some of my wealthier friends, who moved to the city with their parents' assistance and blessings, still found themselves unable or at least unwilling to make a go of it. And then you had me, here, virtually alone? Again—oy!

But like the city, I am an adapter. Test my mettle and my stubborn ass will test you right back. So over that first year, I listened. I observed. I made use of my time and resources and wits, charting forth on a new phase in life, one in which I'd figure out this puzzle of a city the way I'd spent so many years figuring out myself. In short time, I started picking up on some truisms about how to live in New York City with extremely meager means.

Here now, in no particular order: **Jeremy's nuggets o' advice for making an NYC - ANY¢ situation =** ☺

(1) Should you see a delivery person ring a neighbor's bell, not receive an answer, and then trash the bag of food in an act of frustration, it is perfectly okay to dig said meal out of the bin to feed your own hollow belly. But only if the bag remains at least one-quarter sealed shut. Oh, and only after the food messenger is out of your sight lines. One must retain standards.

(2) Bars and clubs are for the rubes playing out some *Sex and the City* fantasy. The truly hip New Yorkers know that a lack of sleep will ably mimic the effects of drunken inhibition dropping, blinking one's eyes really fast while walking through Times Square will mimic club lighting, and subway cars are more rocking than any of the five boroughs' toniest dance floors. All of the spectacle, none of the cover charge.

(3) The first acts of Broadway shows are waaaaay overrated. Spoiler alert: Fantine croaks, Maureen gets people to "moo," Christine displays a fetish for masked Phantoms, and a completely boring subplot about animals hardly makes *Defying Gravity* worth it. If you wait outside during intermission and then sneak in to volunteer your services as an unsolicited

seat-filler for Act Two, you get all of the plot wrap-up without all that needless exposition.

(4) All those square feet that you got for a song back from where you came? The excessive space made you weak. A truly round human must literally shit mere inches from where he or she eats in order to feel real. Oh, and who needs closets, especially when you spent so many years living in one?

(5) Window shopping is just as satisfying as actual purchases. Just go in, get ideas, and then head down to the thrift store for some raw materials to make your own knock-offs. A pair of scissors and some safety pins, and you can craft a get-up that's more than ready for the runway. If not Fashion Week's, then perhaps Newark Airport's.

(6) Who needs a gym and a cab when your capable feet will take care of both cardio and carting? Plus if you need to push some weights, the sidewalks are filled with stray *Village Voice* news box you can bench press (at least if you're reading this before print's inevitable extinction).

(7) TV? For what? There's no reality star more entertaining than the eccentric, possibly substance-motivated female who yells "fountains of feces" every time someone dares to share her section of the sidewalk. Those candy asses on *Survivor* have nothing on this 2nd Avenue senorita.

(8) Those aluminum can redemption centers that your college self had mocked? Yeah, well, there's no time like the present to embrace environmental activism.

(9) Jeans that haven't been washed in three weeks might not be the best potential mate bait. However, should the you that's within those funky trousers manage to both stimulate and retain a potential love's own below-the-belt goods, then at least you can take comfort in knowing it's not your money he's after.

(10) Don't drool when you walk by a townhouse window, no matter how shiny the appliances or family within. It's uncouth. Plus, saliva is the one part of you that's still liquid. You can't afford to waste it.

(11) No, that person did not leave his or her Mega Millions ticket on the street because the taxes on the unclaimed riches would've been too high. Stop picking up the littered stub and checking it—it's sad.

(12) People leave crazy good furniture on the street. Flea spray might be an investment, but what's five bucks of Itch-B-Gone for a slightly used brown ottoman?

Or wait—is it grey? Or maybe it was once actually white? Oh, and what's that on the bottom corner—*ketchup*? Yeah, let's go with ketchup.

(13) You've greatly neglected the public library, which means you're also neglecting free Internet, hours of undisturbed peace, and reliable air conditioning. It all seemed so dull back when the cash register at Barnes & Noble seemed like a near-fetched locale. But now? Now it's like a comforting grandma—musty but cozy, knowledgeable but scattered, filled with memories that'd take another lifetime to fully absorb. Stop and smell the wisdom.

(14) No, you're not an evil person just because you secretly hope that the cocky young trust funder who's rushing to board the Hamptons Jitney will trip and fall into that muddy puddle, sullying his crisp white pants and baby blue polo. Sure the sought-after Schadenfreude is petty. So is your ability to buy comfort in comparison to his. Trust me, the beach he'll be on in an hour will more than salve his wound.

(15) If a director offers to make you the star of a film he's shooting on Fire Island that given weekend and his concern for your training has everything to do with your power glutes and nothing to do with your summer stock performance as Laertes, then the role is not the only -ole that he's looking to fill on film. Carefully gauge your interest in being spit-roasted on camera before proceeding.

(16) Some salons will give you a free cut if you sign up to be a student's guinea pig. Should you go this route, a red Mohawk is not an unreasonable expectation. Whatever, you can always claim this 'do as an interesting character choice. That dirty unkempt mane that you were wearing before wasn't going to get you anything other than a callback for a lice shampoo ad, in the role of "before."

(17) Most of the snotty store clerks can't afford that $7,500 desk chair either. Don't take the condescension personally.

(18) When your friends back home ask what celebrities you've seen—and they *will* ask—resist the temptation to embellish. If your biggest sighting is the lesbian fitness trainer from *Big Brother* three seasons prior, then don't turn the story into a dinner party at Madonna's townhouse. Your pals will either want an autograph or a couch to crash on for their just-planned visits, neither of which you can provide.

(19) No, service employees are not required to follow a "service with a smile" edict here. It's a bit jarring at first to have your "pleases" and

"thank-yous" met with silence. But after a bit, you start to respect the efficiency.

(20) No amount of money can replace your freedom. Freedom to be true to yourself; freedom to live and love openly without fear; freedom to seize your life on the basis of your own terms, no matter how insanely difficult the transition period may be.

There in costly NYC, I finally felt free.

15) THE MAN, THE MYTH, THE KREPLACH

Jeremy's somewhat tragic love story, June 2000–May 2003:

BF #1 was totally wrong for me. Like whoa, wrong. But hey, I was only halfway out of the closet when we met. At that point, I just wanted to be in a relationship, even if it was with someone who treated me like regurgitated dog caca. Who knows, maybe he treated the ex that he was secretly seeing on the side better than he treated me?

BF #2 was as sweet as the first one was assholish. A gentle soul with a personality to match, he was the first guy to whom I ever said "I love you." I really did mean it, too. There was genuine love there. Love can't turn a sweet college fling into a perfect match.

BF #3 was a roller coaster. He was an actor, as I was too at the time. This was the first guy with whom I ever lived, but that grown up step didn't mask the childish offstage drama for which we were both at fault. We loved passionately, we argued passionately, we laughed passionately, and we cried passionately. After a year and change where the arguing and crying ended up surpassing the rest, we broke up dispassionately.

BF #4 and #5 were the yin and yang brothers. Both of these quickie-ationships only lasted for two weeks or so, within the same month as one another; both, however, stamped a mark on my life. I group them together not only because of time and space, but also because if I could have put them together into one person, combining one's dreams and aspirations with the other's pure desire to wake up and make me scrambled eggs on an early morning, then we might have worked. Alas, they were two people. I was therefore going to be a single.

BF #6 happened promisingly enough. Both of us were destined for New York via Knoxville, which seemed fateful. This one really seemed serious. He was a smart guy with a fun personality, two qualities I valued highly. This one was going to be my future, I thought. But after less than a year together both trying to make it in New York as individuals, we both admitted that we'd left the shared love in our shared Knoxville past.

The above half dozen happened in the span of not even three years. Plus there were some ancillary guys in between, so even the gaps between the six were filled with attempts. I think it's more than understandable why, by the summer of '03, I'd given up on finding love. Or I'd at least put other priorities before that particular quest.

Elsewhere my life was actually taking off. After some struggles on the personal and professional fronts, my noble attempt at adjusting to New York life was finally progressing toward the "might just make it after all" side of things. I had moved into a new Hell's Kitchen apartment with a total stranger, which had exactly what I needed: no baggage, no attraction, no emotional connection, and one closeable bedroom door. I had an entry-level Broadway PR job that both fit and held my interest, something that's not always so easy. Yes, the apartment may have been small, but whose wasn't at twenty-two? And sure, that job may have been affording me more connections than cash, but I had great coworkers, tons of perks, and there was a seeming promise that the purse strings would eventually loosen. I was carving out my own slice of the apple they call big in some semblance of the way that I had dreamed—there was every reason to be optimistic.

So in my second year in Manhattan, with so many failed relationships in such a relatively short time, I pretty much decided to embrace the eternally single life that has been romanticized in so many NYC-based films and TV shows. Who needed true love? Professional success was the one true goal. To my romance-weary heart, career accomplishments seemed more attainable and more desirable than matters of monogamy. A bachelor it seemed destiny had intended me to be, and I was perfectly okay with that. Thankfully, kismet was not.

Where, when, and how we met is not all that important. In fact, I don't even look back on Andrew's entry into my life with specific time and place details, but rather I *feel* the memory of those early days in every fiber of my being. For example, I can't tell you what color shirt he was wearing on the night we first shared a laugh, coming only seconds after we'd first shared oxygen. I instead remember the sense of ease I felt in his presence and the desire I had to tell him each and every one of my hopes and needs and grumps and quirks. I didn't want to stop talking.

He was just so real. So New York-y, even if he'd been reared in New Jersey. We had such similar views and goals and senses of humor, but filtered through a mostly different lens. As kids we laughed at *Seinfeld* on different levels, mine based more on broad comedy and Andrew's more on the level of exaggerated familiarity. Most importantly, we had both laughed. Because of our differences, we could be each other's teachers on the things we didn't know. Because of our common ground, we'd never have to question whether or not the other would be open to the new knowledge and growth.

I don't think I'd ever met anyone up to that point who was so straight-forward with his thoughts and feelings. In fact, in the early days I was actually suspicious of Andrew's forthrightness, thinking his willingness to lay everything on the table might be cover for behind-the-scenes shadiness. After some past relationships that were later found to have been rife with deception, I was just too jaded to assume sincerity as a norm. But I soon learned that Andrew just wasn't into the games. He really was authentic. Once I put my fears to rest, it didn't take long for me to determine that I wanted to know this person—*deeply*. I wanted to feel his kiss—*passionately*. I wanted to be in his embrace—*always*.

With Andrew as weary of heartbreak as I, we both fought the feeling at first. We kept it hot but non-committal. Loving but friendly. We wanted to deny the writing on the wall out of fear that our hearts and brains had once again misread the message. "We're just having fun," was the common refrain of our first summer together, in order to put some verbal distance on the thing. During those first few months, our fears even led us to physically separate for a very short period of time. The craving remained constant. That time apart—which I think was maybe ten days, tops—only made us want each other more. As summer turned to fall, we fell; by winter we might have just gone ahead and put a pair of rings on the deal, had we been legally able to do so at that point.

Gag if you want, but it's totally true: Andrew and I fell in love quickly, madly, deeply, and undeniably. I fell in love with his family at the same pace.

A brilliant, large family that was worlds away from what I'd ever known, the Shulmans accepted me into their clan without batting an eye. This may have been even more shocking to me than was the fact that I'd finally found such a good guy in Andrew. Not only was my own family all too unwilling to accept my homosexuality, but also I don't think I had ever, up to that point, met *any* gay people whose families fully accepted them. I, at the time, simply thought strained relations with your biological unit came with the queer territory. The best I'd really known prior to that point was the "my family knows, but we just don't talk about it" form of getting through holiday get-togethers. This being so, I was understandably caught off guard when Andrew told me that his mother and father wanted to meet me, as if it was the most normal thing in the world. I thought I'd left the getting-to-know-the-parents date back in the land where broken bra straps and explorations into the commonality of teen impotency were the date's only takeaways.

But meet we did, almost six months to the day after Andrew and I first came into each other's arms. We first met for brunch, which was shockingly easy. Fun, even. Then a few days later, I found myself in a cozy New Jersey home for Andrew's bar mitzvah videos and some type of cheese, I'm sure (the cracker kind, not the spectacle coming forth from the VHS). From that point forward, the parent/suitor meetings weren't one-shots that I could even measure in any piecemeal way. I was naturally incorporated into the flow of things—into this party or that function, that brunch or this play, their wedding or her colonoscopy—with nothing but ease. At least for me, if not the colon in question.

Long before I moved to the halls of Annie, I was a big fan of the Woody Allen canon. *Brighton Beach Memoirs* was another Hollywood fave. Entering into Andrew's Brooklyn-born family unit with deep, rich family ties made me feel like I'd stepped onto one of those colorful sets, with just as interesting plots. Everyone was so real. So alive. So outspoken. This is a family that hugs upon entering and exiting. I wasn't used to that. I didn't know if I'd even *like* that. It turns out that I really did. It's a sign that everyone involved knows just how important the other members are to each other. From day one, their embraces, both physical and emotional, made me feel loved, wanted—a part of something bigger than myself.

Independence and I had been colleagues for so long, that it was jarring at first to give myself over to the communal spirit of a thoroughly examined family that is in no way shy about dishing out advice, opinions, or even rebukes. Plus, the early exposure to this kind of family conversation was plain confusing to me, since the rapid fire Northeastern style seemed more like a competition than a dialogue, with everyone struggling to squeeze in his or her words edgewise. It wasn't off-putting, though. This new world was as exciting as it was foreign.

I remember the first Passover of 2004, taking place only a few months after I'd first met the elder Shulmans. It was just so adorable watching Andrew's parents explain to me what tzimmes or charoses was, or how to pronounce the word "dayenu." Not because they did anything particularly comical beyond the basic Seder facts, but because their desire to share this information was just so pure: one part nervous, one part eager, one part explanatory in the way that only two teachers can be. They were also a *major* part thankful that their son had found someone. All of the parts were completely loving.

Another interesting avenue was in the way they'd introduce me to new people. When in the company of a predominantly heterosexual crowd with possibly even a few conservatives tossed in, I'd come to expect introductions involving my partner and me to be coupled with some weirdness or, at the very least, qualifiers. But not only was there no weirdness or negativity attached to the way the Shulmans would introduce me, there was the completely contrarian concept of eagerness. They genuinely seemed eager, like I was their son's intended, and the pressure to register for a toaster oven had already begun. The possibility of thrilled in-laws wasn't even like whipped cream or a game show's bonus round to me, as it was far too exotic to even seem like a possible frill. However, once it went past unexpected excess and into the realm of commonplace, I found that I really liked the doting!

Though the prevailing desire to help and teach and debut me that first year also came accompanied with the one persistent question: *"Could we possibly help your parents come around?"* Not because we sat around gossiping or talking about my family, mind you—there was not even a hint of spite. It was just that they knew inviting my mom and dad to the next family function was off-limits, or that taking Andrew home for the same kinds of meetings that I was enjoying was an out of the question concept. That made them both confused and sad. My mensches of would-be in-laws were convinced that with a few phone calls, a warm dinner, and some homemade rugelach, the other Hoopers would see what they saw: the joy and love that Andrew and I share. That was understandable, since it was just so easy for them to see. What they couldn't understand was that easy acceptance of an openly gay child was as foreign to my parents as the Haggadah had been to me.

It wasn't even just the Mother and Father Shulman who wanted to help. Every brother, sister, cousin, and former roommate's co-worker's aunt in the tri-state area was a potential therapist. For them, the acceptance thing was just so damn easy. Everyone was convinced they had the keys to affect change in a previously unwelcoming heart.

First and foremost were Lawrence and Dina, Andrew's brother and sister-in-law. Both socially progressive, both parts of families with LGBT members, and both deeply committed to the bonds in their lives, neither of them could fathom being estranged from their parents, their kids, or their siblings. Since they were around the same age as my own brother and sister, I couldn't help but draw comparisons between them and my biological kin. They quickly became new models of heterosexuals who were brought up in the '70s and '80s with just as much affection for Rick Springfield and the J. Geils Band, yet with a deep respect for the kinds of Jesses who didn't want girls (I'll let you make up your own "Come on Eileen" jokes).

In fact, neither Lawrence nor Dina had even given much thought to a world where LGBT people were still struggling in such deep ways. When it comes to gay rights, Long Island, where they live, is almost as much of a bubble as Manhattan. There is bias to be found, just as there is everywhere (including NYC), but not so much of the kind where simply being gay can lead to estrangement. That wasn't what they had experienced in their own world, so my own family plight was as fundamentally unknown to them as their unconditional acceptance was to me. Of course, unlike theirs, my familiarity was not something that I hoped to impart. Not even accept as okay, in fact—not anymore.

When I first met Lawrence and Dina, they had one son. The next year they had two. A few years later came the third boy. I have never been anything other than Uncle Jeremy, and my reason for being in their family picture has never been chalked up to anything other than my love for and shared life with their father's brother. There's nothing I could say here that would present a stronger, more needed, more grateful statement than that.

Then there were the Mandels. To be honest, the first memories I have of Andrew's aunt and uncle on the maternal side, Ellen and David Mandel, revolved mostly around Southern food and my affection for it. Biscuits and gravy were as intriguing to them as bialys and hammataschen had been to me. So that was our first unifier: culinary inquisitiveness. But once we got past the pantry, I found an even deeper common thread involving social justice and truly "pro-family" values. Ellen is a lover, through and through, who's never met a stranger. Her embrace of me was immediate. Her wants for me were hopeful from the get-go.

David is the more analytical of the two. A psychologist by trade, he wanted to get into the mindset that had caused the division within my family. Whereas some were looking for ways to make me happy in the now, David was looking for the keys to unlock the past. Not in an invasive way, I should say; he did so with sincerity. I thank him for many of those early conversations, as they really did help me hash out some stuff. In fact, I probably owe him some grits or something similarly Mason-Dixon Line–crossing.

Filling out the maternal side of the family was a whole host of cousins and second cousins and eighteenth cousins. The numbers never seemed to stop. With a family that sizable, experience told me to expect at least someone who'd come across in an accepting-challenged manner. But no— *unbelievably*, no! Everyone I'd meet at this function or that mitzvah was just as arms-wide-opened as the next. If there was any discomfort, it was certainly tucked away.

On the paternal side of the family, there were the two brothers Shulman, each of whom had families of their own. These families are made up of New Yorkers, through and through, with even the ones who'd moved elsewhere retaining the spirit of the area. In their own way, each and every one of them helped me feel more connected to the family, to my geography, and to life in general. The paternal side was less sizable than the maternal side, but it was still a healthy garden filled with diverse characters and ideas. With every new first meeting, I'd plant a new root.

There was also homosexuality on that side of the family, coming in the form of Andrew's cousin Susanne, her partner Carolyn, and their two adorable boys, Henry and Leo. They have created a family unit that is strong and healthy—a family that works. Controversy? What contro-versy? Maybe when it comes to who's bringing what to Thanksgiving or whether a certain gift is age and space appropriate. But for being lesbians? If there was ever any familial strife or weirdness there, it was sorted out long before I came into the picture.

All around me was joy. Family values. Acceptance. I learned early on that braised pork shoulder is not kosher. From best I could tell, neither was a cold human one.

One of the first takeaways I drew from Andrew's mom and dad is how clearly they focus on being a team. Theirs is a union free of carefully cast roles based on gender. They realize their strengths and their weaknesses, and they work together to make it all work. Should life deal an unknown, a duo, not a single, conduct the hunt for information, and the quest for knowledge is rarely overshadowed by embarrassment or pride. If there's baking to get done, one or both will do it. If there's clothing to be bought, then man will pick up a pump and woman will size up a sport coat. If there's yard work to be done, then they'll—oh, who am I kidding? They'll outsource the yard work, what with allergies and all. But they'll place the phone call together.

A team they are, through and through. I remember back to the very first time we met, there at that Manhattan brunch spot du jour. Of course I'd heard of couples whose two halves finish each other's sentences, but this might have been my first time seeing it firsthand. For me, a comedy buff with an interest beyond my years, it was like watching a carefully rehearsed Nichols and May routine. He'd pull back so she could shine. She'd set up so he could deliver. Anyone will tell you that she talks more, but he's not sitting in silence while she does. He's an active listener, keeping an ear open for the gaps that she forgets to fill or the comic opportunities that she forgets to hit. And when spotlight dims on her side, he picks up the shine.

At the first anniversary of theirs that I was lucky enough to toast, my now-sister-in-law, Dina, said that they give us all something to which to aspire. At that moment, I felt like she was sending out a message not only to the table but also to the world. Her toast was just so honest and oh, so needed in this distrusting society, with Dina so richly realizing what we in the younger generation were so lucky to get to see and experience. The reason why they form such a relational goalpost is because Susan and Marty Shulman are themselves so aspirational, both as individuals and as a pair—determined to make a difference while remaining far too humble to ever acknowledge that they even could.

Nowhere does their ability to make a positive impact come more fully front and center than in the place that directly impacts me most: their unbreakable bond with Andrew. Not only did this man teach me to love both him and myself in new ways, but he and his parents also taught me a new sort of parent-child bond. Theirs is a world in which both kid and adult know the special role they hold in each others' hearts, and one where they seize every opportunity to show off that bond. There is nothing cynical about it, either. Andrew claims his mother and father among his best friends, something he had been proudly saying since before high school. They had never known alienation or disconnect, not really. Not anything close to what I had known.

Back in Tennessee, I could count on half a hand how many LGBT people I knew who had easy, non-controversial relationships with their parents. Among my college friends, avoidance was the measure of a healthy child-parent bond, the heights to which most of my pals only hoped to reach. Upon moving to NYC, I started to get bits of healthy childrearing tales from the gay friends and coworkers that I made in the city. Seeing Andrew and his family interact took it to a whole new level.

When Andrew came out to them, his parents didn't greet him with a negative reaction. It was more of the "thank God, I thought you were going to tell me you had cancer!" kind of situation. In fact, the biggest story from Andrew's coming out process involves a miscommunication in which Andrew thoroughly confused his dear old mom and dad when he told them that he was going out to a "tapas bar," which they, in the most *Three's Company* of fashions, misheard as a "topless bar." That's it—that's the big story I know about Andrew's revelation that he is a gay man: that his parents thought he was going to a strip club rather than going for fancy Spanish appetizers! Upon hearing this and similar stories, I began to realize that my expectations of the parent-child bond were what were skewed. This realization meant the death knell for my belief that mediocre was the only goal when it comes to gay kid-straight parents relations.

It was quite sad for me to see that my newly adopted, quite PFLAG-y family would have given absolutely anything to help my biological family share in the love fest. Making it so much more frustrating was the fact that they genuinely *could* have made a difference, if not for the vast differences in backgrounds and life experiences. The Shulmans were people who had grown up almost exclusively in the northeastern United States, most of them identified as progressive (or at the very least moderate), and virtually all had gay and lesbian people in their lives in some capacity. My bio family wasn't any of those things. The Hoopers were proudly red state, were reliably to the right of moderate, and the only openly LGBT person I remember entering our Tennessee living room came from *Philadelphia*, not Philadelphia. It was apples and oranges. Or more fittingly: biscuits and lox.

That last point segues nicely into the next: the Jewish factor, which I mean more in terms of culture than religion. When you are raised in a world that is only a generation or two removed from unfathomably extreme discrimination, and not at all removed from the kind of anti-ness that leads others to cause worldwide bloodshed, your heart tends to be more sensitive to the plight of others who have historically been placed in the "different" box. This was certainly the case with the Shulmans, as well as many of the family friends who entered into my life at the same time. They knew from bias.

Then there was the difference in treatment of the outside world. I had grown up thinking that family was important and that taking care of oneself was a chief mortal concern. At the same time, I also always felt a need to please the outside world, almost like one's opinion of me was to be considered before my own self-reflection. No matter how wrong the other person's boat might be, I always felt that rocking it was off-limits. No matter how strongly I felt about my righteousness, challenging my adversary felt rude. My tongue was sore from self-biting.

The Shulmans, like many in the Northeast, took an opposite approach to what I had known. Family and thyself were still of importance. However, if other people didn't like or respect either of those two things? Well okay, you should be as respectful as possible. Certainly try not to be rude; definitely process constructive criticism, learning what you can, where you can, when you should. But don't for a second consider changing yourself just because someone else feels you should. After all, the problem is not on your side of the fence, just because your neighbor's bitter about the view!

I liked this new portrait. More importantly, I loved how accepted I felt within it.

That being said, I also very much wanted to remain within my biological family's scrapbook. I'm not gonna lie: I *do* like grits. I *do* have fond memories of Nashville's laidback downtown scene. I *do* still think Tennessee is one of the most thoroughly gorgeous of America's states. I was the only one, from either family, who had the dual insight, knowing all-too-fully what both sides were missing. Sure the feeling of rejection was painful and even felt hostile on some days. But realizing how much time and joie de vivre was being wasted through that rejection, as well as muddling through the routine, go-nowhere conversations that sized up the never-changing situation? Well that was just plain heartbreaking and oh-so-unnecessary.

For most of my teens and twenties, I'd thought of myself as tough. As cool. I saw myself as a sort of a rebel with a cause that was solely confined within the sphere of me. It turned out that these characteristics were just the bandages I used to temporarily piece together my wounded heart. Andrew wasn't afraid to take them off and find the real me—to help me *be* the real me, at long last.

When it comes to restoring the broken bonds in my life, I will never lose hope. I refuse to. At the same time, I will never let the other sources of pain overshadow the great joys. I simply can't. And while he's obviously at the fore, it's really not only Andrew who has led to this turnaround. All of the Shulmans, Krumholzes, Krausses, Mandels, Cohens, Rivlins, and WhatHaveYas brought about this intense sense of belonging. In doing so, they healed my wounds and built up my mettle even stronger than it ever was before.

16) DUBYA.T.F?!

*M*ean Girls* had just hit the theaters, and Lindsey Lohan had suddenly become the hottest thing on two stilletoed legs. A party with a Lindsey cameo was not only the in-demand ticket in New York, it was the in-demand ticket in *the world*—especially if said party was being thrown by some little indie artiste known as Sean "P. Diddy" Combs.

In April of 2004, Andrew and I had a ticket to just such a bash. My office was handling the press for Mr. Diddy's Broadway debut in *A Raisin in the Sun*, and, as with any show, the opening night party was both a perk and duty of the PR job. Attending/working that bash was a requirement, so I happily did so with Andrew as my plus one. And it was all totally fine. Cocktails here, coordinate an interview with BroadwayWorld.com there —whatever.

However the *real* soiree, the Lohan one, was *after* the "official" party. The first was the one with all the press and the interviews and the work— somewhat stuffy, somewhat staid. This next one was to be a star-studded affair at the latest Meatpacking District hotspot, which promised pure revelry with none of the minutiae. The invitation read like so:

THE FRIENDS AND FAMILY OF

SEAN COMBS

WOULD LIKE YOU TO JOIN US AS WE CELEBRATE
HIS BROADWAY DEBUT IN A RAISIN IN THE SUN

PLEASE HELP US CELEBRATE
THIS PROUD MOMENT IN BLACK HISTORY

AT MARQUEE 289 10TH AVENUE BETWEEN 26TH & 27TH
MONDAY APRIL 26, 2004
IMMEDIATELY FOLLOWING GUASTAVINO'S

FORMAL ATTIRE REQUIRED · PLEASE RSVP TO 212-381-1577

BROUGHT TO YOU BY
ANHEUSER
World Select

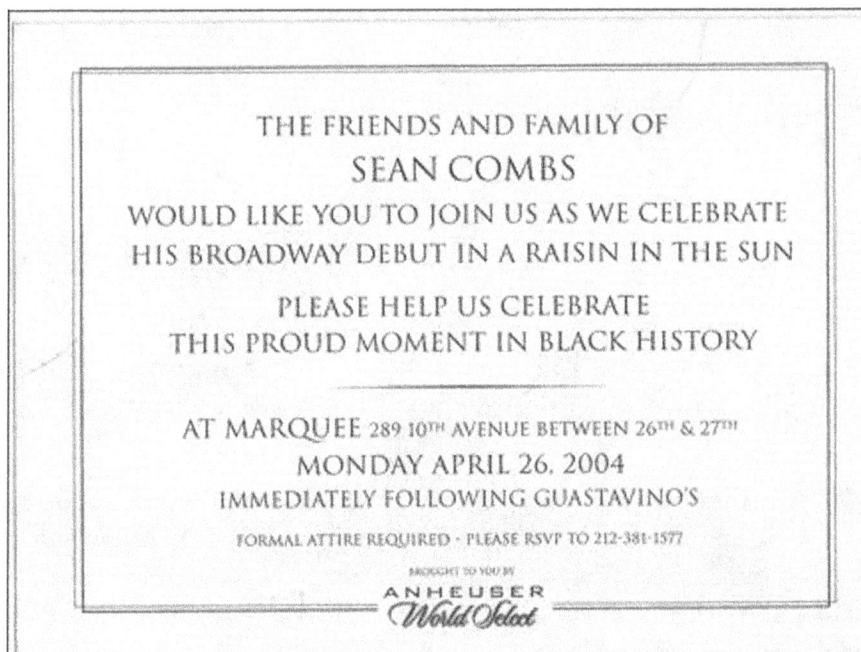

A humble invite, for sure.

Andrew and I wasted absolutely no time in making our decision. I mean there wasn't anything to consider, really. Two young guys faced with what was undoubtedly the Page Six party of the night? Where's the need for hesitation?

Oh yes, we were going, all right. We were going *home* to walk our dog instead!

Why the sit out? One could surmise this choice was indicative of sleepiness, profound canine love, or the fact that our walk home from the first party was a mere four blocks. While a combination of those things certainly played a part, a year earlier, there would've been nothing that could have made me miss this kind of a bash. I had always been a see-and-be-seen kind of guy, whose shoulders were raw from the constant rubbing. Yet I was the one who was the deciding vote on this, and I quickly chose to bag and toss dog crap instead? Really? I just did that? *Really?!*

I knew this change in focus and priority was indicative of a fundamental change within me. The party no-show didn't just mean a hangover-free tomorrow; it represented a turning point. Or if not the no-show itself, the turning point at least spun off the fact that I felt no sort of regret or guilt about the decision. There was a shift going on—a shift to a time when "everybody's gonna be there" would no longer be a compelling enough reason to get me somewhere. To a time when I would stop automatically placing unbalanced value on where I could be and start celebrating the good vibes of my current location.

It's no coincidence that this was around the same time the most powerful person in the free world was going on the airwaves to say things like this:

> If we are to prevent the meaning of marriage from being changed forever, our nation must enact a constitutional amendment to protect marriage in America . . . Today I call on Congress to promptly pass and to send to the states for ratification an amendment to our Constitution defining and protecting marriage as a union of a man and a woman, as husband and wife.[14]

My growing love for Andrew contrasted so strongly with the growing insistency that this love was some sort of terrorist act that it awakened my political sensibilities in ways that nothing prior ever had. I had been politically aware since Clinton '92 and pledged my support to the Democratic Party long before I even knew the full breadth of social conservatism that was making LGBT people feel so hurt, vulnerable, and disenfranchised. But as big as a fan of Fleetwood Mac as I was and am, William Jefferson didn't move my young political sensibilities in enough of a way to cause me to dedicate my late teen/early twenties days to progressive causes. In fact, the Whitewater and Lewinsky circuses, coupled with the intense partisanship that accompanied those years, threatened to derail my interest for all time. Then of course that was followed by Bush v. Gore and loss of faith in our political system as a whole, a series of dangerous and eye-opening boondoggles, 9/11, unjust war, and even worse partisanship than we'd seen before. Who could blame any modern American for becoming apolitical?

Having my life directly attacked by Clinton's successor *did* rock me from my sleep with the ferocity of a particularly folksy alarm clock that couldn't pronounce the word "nuclear." How dare he so unabashedly bash me? Could he not understand the power that his words possessed and not realize the danger he was inflicting on psyches and souls? Or, even more

---

[14] President George W. Bush press conference, 25 February 2004.

dishearteningly, was fostering malevolence the true Bush/Rove goal? Even if it wasn't, the mere fact that this sort of question was up for logical consideration was enough to consternate this apathetic gay's soul.

For the first time in my life, I knew that I had to do something for the greater good and not just for my own fame, wallet, or various self-interests. I was someone who had previously wanted to be a celebrity much more than I ever wanted to be an actor. Back when I considered broadcast journalism for a career, my focus was more on becoming an *Entertainment Tonight* correspondent than a *60 Minutes* one. Now I felt a new fire stirring in my belly and it had nothing to do with starring in Broadway shows, much less promoting them. I looked inward and realized that while I did enjoy and was lucky to have my job, it wasn't a role that was using my skills to tackle the world in the way I felt I could. I looked outward and saw a political reality that was truly threatening and just as frightening.

Maybe I was too carried away with *Wicked*, another show that my PR office was working on at the time, becoming one of America's first of many gay boys to take Miss Elphaba's most famous lyric to dramatic heart.

"Something has changed within me
Something is not the same
I'm through with playing by the rules
Of someone else's game"[15]

What I do know is that in a "Eureka"-like flash, I found both my conscience and my consciousness. I left job security in hopes that I might ensure the security of my own home.

Now I was determined to find some way to help others find their own voices, places, and ways forward. But how?

---

[15] Stephen Schwartz (lyrics), "Defying Gravity," *Wicked*.

17) GLORY TO THE NEWBORN STING

I had the true love. I would have the golden ring as soon as my state would allow. What my Andrew could not give me in December of 2004 was the ability to spend another Christmas in the same exact latitude and longitude where I had spent twenty-five others.

But actually we need to back up, since the nonsense really started even before the gluttonous, tryptophan-filled holiday that precedes the Gap ad–laden one. It was the week before the November '04 elections, to be exact. John Kerry making a go for the White House. Actual war abroad and faux wars against gays' ring fingers here at home. That's when I, after years of hinting and dodging and suspicions and intercepted journal entries, decided to fully confirm to my family what they had already known for years: that I was, in fact, a gay man. I could not and would not return home for another Christmas holiday without my life's co-star in tow. Andrew and I had already spent Christmas of '03 apart, since I was too chicken shit to even press the issue of bringing him home. But not this time. I refused to go another day without getting all of my kin on the same easy page on which I'd unexpectedly, yet amazingly, found myself. There was no way I could even wrap my head around going home for another Christmas sans the man without whom I'd rarely even go to the grocery store.

Now, keep in mind that at this point, I had already moved to New York, had already fallen in and out of lust with a number of the wrong men, had already pledged a life commitment to the right man, had already obtained and left my first post-collegiate job, and had already been directly confronted about my sexuality by at least three of my four family members. To me, this final confirmation was merely a formality. It was little more than an attempt to lay the cards fully on the table without hiding my personal king, in hopes that maybe I could put the silliness behind me so I could begin the process of bringing them, my biological family, into the glorious new one that I had started with Andrew and his. It was in no way a "coming out" in terms of my sexual orientation, since (a) I really didn't think there was any ambiguity left in that area, and (b) I was a grown man who didn't owe anyone an explanation about my truth. This was instead a clarion call from an East 62nd Street rooftop, letting any and everyone know that Jeremy Hooper and his intended had found their benign peace. Through my glasses, which had become increasingly rose-colored over the year and a half since Andrew and I started dating, I genuinely saw the possibility of familial peace in the forecast. At long last. True love would do the trick.

I would tell you now that I was wrong in my predictions, but that would be like saying the wise men slightly low-balled the possibility that anyone would ever notice, care, or talk about it if they re-gifted a couple of "My Camel Spits for Virgins" t-shirts rather than wrapped up some nice, new gold, frankincense, and myrrh for a certain kid's inaugural day. In reality, my story, so easy and peaceful to me, was far from it to my genetically linked parents and siblings. Oh boy, so far. What my mind had staged as a moment of musical theatre exposition instead played out like a Greek tragedy.

In the interest of time, space, and stories that are only one-fifth of mine to tell, I'll spare all of the nuances and details that followed for the rest of November and into December. Let's just say that by the holiday season, it was clear that my Jewish intended husband would be getting a lesson in Southern Santa-ocity from me and me alone. There would be no trip to Nashville for the first December 25 since 1979.

It's at times of tradition when a gay person's supposed lack of "traditional values" becomes most absurd. At that first Christmas season detached, I wanted nothing more than to indulge in my family's traditions. I wanted to see that one incredibly gaudy ornament that had been passed down through my mother's family for generations. I needed to flip the switch on that damn tinny silver bell, setting off the most ironically loud and high-pitched version of "Silent Night" one's ears had ever beheld. I craved to taste my mom's uniquely own brands of snickerdoodles and fudge, even to bicker with my brother and sister about religion or politics or the name of the Italian restaurant that the Keaton family frequented on *Family Ties* (Guido's, to be sure). All of these things that I'd taken for granted were now taking my mind for one hell of an emotional ride. Sleigh bells ring—why won't they listen?

I needed a little Christmas, right this very minute—but I was never going to get it unless I planned to haul out a girlfriend named Holly (or Joy, or Carol, or even a Vixen, just as long as it wasn't a Rudolph that I was blitzen'). The mood was frosty. The feeling was blue. This yuletide was shaping up to be anything but gay.

You wanna talk tradition? Try driving to every supermarket in NYC's five boroughs, scouring the aisles for the Christmas Crunch cereal that filled your mid-'80s bowls, not so you could quench your hunger, but so you could quell your nostalgic desperation. So that you can hold on to a past that you know will never again be your present. So that something, *anything* feels familiar.

Or maybe some of you "pro-family" readers have some thoughts about that old "family values" chestnut? Well what a coincidence—so do I. My thoughts involve a young man whose every bone is aching to do nothing more than eat a mediocre store-bought pumpkin pie with his blood relatives, yet who can't do so unless he promises to hide his chosen mate. Mine involve a family whose individuals valued their own collective discomfort over their youngest member's personal happiness.

Care to hear about an "agenda"? Well, what about the fight to hold back the tears that rush up whenever "Have Yourself a Merry Little Christmas" hits the local oldies station that has suddenly converted to all-Christmas format? Ironic that the word "gay" is actually in those lyrics, since those three little letters were the one reason my yuletide was going to be less-than-so!

In fact, it wasn't just that one song. *Every* song, *every* hokey TV special, *every* memory during the run-up to 12/25—all were sentimental samurais slicing at my heart. Charlie Brown's sad tree looked extra bare, and the Hallmark ad that had looked so syrupy and fictional now struck me as sentimental and poignant. The land mines may have been made of shiny tinsel, but they were no less explosive. Nor were my reactions to them.

At times I'd beat myself up, thinking I'd somehow failed. Had I not done enough? Not contributed enough? Had I waited too long? Were my "like a light bulb" asides during Rudolph's eponymous ditty somewhat off-key? What? What the hell did I do wrong?

The questions would inevitably turn to anger. Even if my family *was* uncomfortable with my sexuality, hadn't I given enough to earn my place at the table? After all, there were many things I didn't like about various other members' views or ideologies or whatever. And quite frankly, I'd have rather eaten my own eggnog vomit than envision my siblings having heterosexual relations with their straight mates. Yet I had to overlook whatever made me uneasy, whereas everyone else was free to veto my life and love? I was being told that I'm barred from bringing my beloved, lest one of my nieces or nephews be scarred by the 'moness in their midst? I was supposed to make the trip home just so that I could follow a different and wildly dissimilar set of rules? I was the one in the wrong simply because I was outnumbered? That's not a family—that's a dicky dictatorship!

At the polls that November, eleven states had cast ballots against gay people's unions. Tennessee would not join in those reprehensible reindeer games until 2006, but in my biological family, the referendum took place two years premature. Needless to say, I lost the popular vote.

By now you're probably telling me to get the hell over it. "Boo hoo," you're probably thinking, "you didn't get to watch *A Very Brady Christmas* with your own siblings. You were forced to spend a holiday with the man you love—Waaaaaah. You had to open your presents on the Upper East Side of Manhattan rather than in a suburb of Nashville, TN—let me shed a tear for the poor baby."

I get that, I do. But to understand why this particular exclusion was so much bigger than just one missed holiday, you have to understand how big of a deal Christmas was (and presumably still is) on my family's calendar. Out of the 365 days, the ones that immediately surrounded Santa's arrival were always the sweetest. All of us Hoopers, regardless of age or interest, seemed to work as a team toward that one brief period of the year when miracles seemed within the ballpark of possibility and 99¢ boxes of drugstore icicles could somehow look priceless. It was never just a holiday in my family—it was an annual respite on which we had placed one hell of a premium. It was an awesome time that had always delivered on its calming promises.

Even at my youngest, when I'd cut out catalog pages of items on my wish list and stare at them for a month or more until they were inevitably in my possession, the gifts were never the point. In fact, sometimes I'd feel a little gauche after I'd finally opened them. Once the wrapping-removal period rolled around and the spirit of it all consumed me, I'd kind of feel like I owed my parents an apology for having focused on the presents so intensely. I mean don't get me wrong—I loved and embraced the swag. But on Christmas Day, the culmination of the love and devotion that put those pricey objects under the tree was what made the memories. The unwrapping process was a peaceful payout, not a lurid lottery. Every gift had a resonance attached to it, even the shitty ones that I was *totally* planning to return.

I knew that everyone else felt the power of the day too, which is why I so fully knew that my exclusion from Xmas '04 was an ending. It was holiday hardball, the first time that I genuinely felt that my family would never accept me as gay. If they were willing to bust up the band on this day—*THIS* day—then I knew they meant business: business that wanted nothing to do with the one that Andrew and I had started with our hearts.

I wasn't just thinking of myself, my relatives, and our shared nostalgia, either. The whole thing also made me hurt for Andrew, who genuinely wanted to know the world from whence I came. It's important to have a window into your partner's past, to see the things that make him or her, well—him or her. I had watched both my brother and my sister bring their respective spouses into the mix, with everyone incorporating their wants, needs, and stockings into the dynamic. That first Christmas with a new member was always a little weird, since it did change the balance. It was at the same time exciting, both for the newbie and veterans. After having gone through so many such shifts with my bio fam, by virtue of not only my siblings' spouses but also their children, I felt it was my turn to shake things up. I deeply wanted Andrew to experience all this, the way I'd already gone through so many similar rites of passage with his side of the family. He both deserved and craved it.

Sadly, I knew this was a tale of never-would-be. If they weren't going to accept my mate at the event that was my family's version of a debutante ball, then I knew they would never accept him anywhere. It was not only a ghost to haunt my Christmas Present, but also one that I instinctively knew was to become the new normal for all Christmases Future. It wasn't going to be confined to this one holiday, of course, but instead extended to anything having to do with family togetherness. Right then it became obvious that the guest list to my and Andrew's someday wedding was going to be halved. This news might have been good for my wallet; my heart, however, was less than thrilled.

The only way to get through this kind of thing is to say, "their loss, not ours." That was certainly something Andrew and I tried to tell ourselves. But it was a lie. Such a big fat lie (that shook like a bowl full of jelly). We knew that we were all losing out. Me. Him. Both families.

What made it so much harder was (and is) the sheer absurdity of it all. It's one thing to have family strife because of a drug addiction or a criminal act or because of one's insistence on wearing a really tacky Christmas sweater that has more bells than cloth. But by 2004, my only problem in terms of drugs was that I'd sometimes have a beer that wasn't an organic microbrew or a wine that hadn't been allowed to breathe long enough before consumption. My criminal record was limited to a ticket for running a stoplight, and my personal record was besmirched only by some credit cards that I had defaulted on in college. Oh, and my wardrobe was stereotypically up to snuff: no jingling bells on my knitted garments. It was simply my crippling case of da gay that was bringing about all of this nonsense!

I had to compartmentalize. In my brain, there developed this separate realm where I would put my family problems. It was a reverent quarantine; I did respect that my family's lack of acceptance was largely due to culture, geography, upbringing, and even their own family situations (for instance, both of my siblings married more religious partners). Also, since I did (and do) hold out hope for reconciliation, I didn't want to move this new cranium compartment to some far off land where diplomacy was out of the question. By birthright, I had a responsibility to be more reverential than that, to my parents, in particular. They had given me much, regardless of what they were denying me now. I tried to never lose sight of that very important fact.

At the same time, I also had to be sure that this complete and utter nonsense didn't pervade into the other nine-tenths of my mind, where I was lucky enough to have found true community with a man, city, and friends with whom I shared mutual, easy affection. No matter how considerate I wanted to be to the fam, by this point I had to most fully consider the ones who were *proud* to be in my day-to-day life, and whose relationships were free from homo-shunning demands or qualifiers. It would've been unfair to everyone in my kingdom, foremost me, to let this outside situation weaken any current passions.

There was a balance to be struck, one where deserved respect and disrespect had to be willfully granted in appropriate measure. What's wrong is wrong, and it must be called out for exactly what it is; what's fair is fair, and it must be embrace for exactly what *it* is. For me to go through the rest of my days with sanity, I had to leave the door to this absurd portion of my mind unlocked, if not fully opened. I had to let my family know that while I was deeply hurt, incredibly angry, and quite realistically heartbroken, I was standing on my "side" of this emotional fence with a wish in my mind and a passion in my heart, not a stone in my hand. I had to leave milk and cookies out on a plate, in hopes that the present might deliver in the way that the past always had.

In the years since the mostly mirthless yuletide season of '04, my holidays have turned considerably brighter. Andrew and I have developed new traditions, which encompass everyone's views and upbringings, creating a wonderfully multicultural late fall/early winter season. From the time the first autumn leaf meets the ground, we both start thinking about when we should remind our loved ones that "yes, we're still vegetarian and yes, chicken stock is still meat"; begin wondering where the never-on-time Chanukah falls on the calendar (Is it early? Is it late?); and ask ourselves where to put both the menorah and the tree. That last discussion also contains a real versus artificial element, though the season itself is nothing if not authentic.

Even so, there is still not a Thanksgiving, Chanukah, Christmas, or solstice that goes by where I don't think of the countless families that have been rocked by unnecessary dissension. In fact, the easy mirth and merriment that I've managed to achieve in my own life can sometimes highlight the melancholy, since I see how obtainable the familial peace could be. It's obtainable for me, for my biological kin—for us jointly. The peace is in reach of everyone who has ever triumphed over the lumps in their throats and told their families that they are L,G,B, or T people, as well as those who greeted them with lumps of coal in return.

I challenge everyone to think about those needlessly empty chairs at countless holiday celebrations. Those who proudly decorate houses where not a creature is stirring, not even a lesbian mouse? Well, they can bury their heads in their kerchiefs if they so choose. While willfully blinded, they must also own up to the one removed bulb that's keeping their strand from glowing like it should.

18) THE EYE OF THE TIGER'S PACIFIST COUSIN

If there's a negative to LGBT media visibility, it has to come from the false sense of comfort that it has given many who believe that the fight is over. It's certainly something I felt in my own life. My generational peers and I experienced teen years with more positive gay imagery than any that came before. We knew that, if nowhere else, we could at least count on seeing gay life on *The Real World* every season. We had tangible role models and portraits of queer life playing out before our very eyes.

Ellen was out on national television before I even graduated from high school. *Will & Grace* was "must see TV" by the time I entered college. My early adulthood was filled with the promise, or at least good possibility, that gay equality might be just around the bend. Even if many of us, out of fear of ourselves or how our realities might be received, didn't acknowledge what was going on, there was still the ambient awareness of what was happening. Progress seemed to be winning, even if slowly.

So when the days turned so jarringly conservative in the Bush era, there was a whole generation of LGBT people who were particularly vulnerable to the onslaught because of little more than their birth date. To give a somewhat reduced version of twentieth-century LGBT history: Stonewall ushered in the '70s, where Anita Bryant galvanized queer populations, (Harvey-)milking the community's power for all it was worth. AIDS and the Reagan-era hostilities brought about a shared survival instinct, with the affected communities finding strengths that they may not have even realized were within themselves. But by the time both this writer and the Bush v. Gore election night results came out in 2000, even the Don't Ask

Don't Tell and Defense Of Marriage Act battles that left the gay community feeling a sense of betrayal at the hands of Clinton's '90s triangulation
were largely dormant topics in the mainstream media, and therefore in
the national conversation. Those of us who were in our late teens through
our twenties during this time couldn't really be blamed for feeling something of a sense of calm on the gay rights front. The most major storms
truly felt like they were part of history.

When my own sense of awareness was so fully rocked in 2004, both
on the political and personal fronts, I was stunned by how blind I had
been to the problems that were still in full play. I instinctively knew that
there were so many just like me who needed to be convinced of the crucial
call to step up and give a damn. There was no way that I was alone in pain,
and I definitely felt that there were many who sensed a growing need to
rally against the all-too-common LGBT acrimony that was far too par
for far too many courses. But how to do this? Where's the problem and
what's the cure? What can I, one person with a primarily communications
background, do to make a difference, both in my own family life and in
the bigger picture?

With wrapping paper cuts still fresh on my heart, I knew I had to
find a way to turn pain into pragmatism. In January of 2005, I began the
imperfect yet impassioned process.

Education was my logical starting point. I began crash coursing in all
that was "culture war" politics, and in doing so, grew ever more astounded
by how truly messed up the organized opposition's rhetoric truly was.
Sure, almost anyone who's lived in modern America has a generic impression of what the anti-gay movement, or at least the religious right, is all
about. This socio-political movement and its archetypes have been teased
and referenced in pop culture for decades. Of course I thought I knew
what the parted hair, buttoned up, conservative white men were all about.
Heck, I had seen them spoofed on *Saturday Night Live* just last weekend.

Turns out I didn't know the full breadth, or even half of it. Here
now, just a few examples of what I found in the days after beginning my
research. There were more than a few Nazi comparisons:

Americans should understand that their attitudes about homosexuality have been deliberately and deceitfully changed by a masterful
propaganda/marketing campaign that rivals that of Adolf Hitler. In

fact, many of the strategies used by homosexuals to bring about cultural change in America are taken from Hitler's writings and propaganda welfare manuals.[16]

There were nasty kid claims galore:

As Homosexuals continue to make inroads into public schools, more children will be molested and indoctrinated into the world of homosexuality. Many of them will die in that world.[17]

Some took a shotgun approach, seemingly hoping to set a world record for most hyperbole in a single commentator slot:

For more than 30 years, homosexual activists have been demanding that our Judeo-Christian culture capitulate and embrace their view of human sexuality, marriage and family. If Americans ever accept these demands, they can expect to live in a culture that will be turned upside down—literally unhinged from the sane moorings instituted by the God of heaven.

[Linda] Harvey's prediction is of a grotesque culture that includes: "Lesbian bride dolls. Fourth grade 'gay' clubs. A king and king at the high school prom. Dating tips for same-sex teens. Bathroom ogling—and sometimes quick encounters—in the middle school boys' restroom."

Fortunately, while the groundwork for these changes has been laid, it is not yet a done deal. But Americans who believe there is something inherently abnormal, unnatural and immoral about homosexuality had better stand up right now.[18]

---

[16] Louis Sheldon, "Homosexual Propaganda Campaign Based on Hitler's Big Lie Technique," Traditional Values Coalition Special Report, Vol. 18, No. 10, 1-2.
[17] Louis Sheldon, "Homosexuals Recruit Public School Children," Traditional Values Coalition Special Report, Vol. 18 No. 11, 2.
[18] Ed Vitagliano, "School's Out—Will the Rainbow Bus Take Our Kids to the Land of Diversity?" American Family Association Journal, October 2004, http://www.afajournal.org/2004/october/1004schoolsout.asp (accessed 6 June 2011).

Others used a steamroller:

> Truly, the homosexual movement has become a steamroller in nations around the world[19]

Many positioned homosexuality as a dead end:

> Homosexuality is a lonely and disillusioning way of life. There is a reason why this behavior has been considered morally wrong through-out most of human history[20]

Most all of it built around a common theme—one that pits "real" American values against the supposedly inauthentic and undeserving gays:

> [C]reating counterfeit marriage will damage the real thing and put more children at risk. Only a callous, self-absorbed culture would cre-ate legal incentives to engage in immoral, destructive behavior with children as the guinea pigs. America must be better than that.[21]

Some speakers were more obscure, sure; others were quite connected, with comments like these seeming to build rather than lower profiles. Like, for instance, check out this one, from someone who has gone on to become a major national figure within the Republican Party:

> I am not here bashing people who are homosexuals, who are lesbians, who are bisexual, who are transgendered. We need to have profound compassion for the people who are dealing with the very real issue of sexual dysfunction in their life, and sexual identity disorders. This is a very real issue. It's not funny, it's sad. Any of you who have mem-bers of your family that are in the lifestyle—we have a member of our family that is. This is not funny. It's a very sad life. It's part of Satan, I think, to say this is gay. It's anything but gay.

---

[19] Dr. James Dobson, "The Christian Response to the Homosexual Agenda," FocusontheFamily.com, June 1998 (yanked from site in 2010).

[20] John Paulk, "What happened When Love Won Out," FocusontheFamily.com, July 2000 (yanked from site in 2010).

[21] "CWA Calls on Massachusetts to End Faux Marriage Farce," Concerned Women For America press release (Washington, D.C., 17 May 2004).

—*U.S. Congresswoman and 2012 presidential candidate, Michele Bachmann*[22]

The absurdity would've been laugh-out-loud funny if it weren't so deadly serious. It would have been gloriously under the radar if the socio-political missiles attached were not so personally targeted. It would've been right to ignore had ignorance not been the reason why we were so vulnerable in the first place.

What was even more frightening to learn was how fully connected to the Bush White House some of these groups were. Some of them literally had an open door into the Oval. According to a 2009 report from the Citizens for Responsibility and Ethics in Washington, a number of prominent anti-gay evangelicals were granted major access to the President best known by his middle consonant, including some who were quoted above.

- For the period April 2001 through June 2006, Focus on the Family Founder and Chairman Emeritus James Dobson visited the White House 24 times; 10 of those visits were to President Bush.

- Andrea Lafferty, Executive Director of the Traditional Values Coalition, made an astonishing 50 visits to the White House starting on February 1, 2001, and continuing through March 16, 2008. Six of those visits were to President Bush.

- Tony Perkins, President of Family Research Council, visited the White House 14 times between February 2001 and June 2006, including two visits to President Bush.

- Wendy Wright, President of Concerned Women for America, made 43 visits to the White House between May 2001 and August 2006. Four of those visits were to President Bush.[23]

---

[22] Michele Bachmann, remarks to EdWatch National Education Conference, Minneapolis, MN, 6. Nov. 2004.

[23] "Bush-Era White House Visitor Records Show Multiple Visits by Top Christian Religious Leaders," CREW report, 4 Sept. 2009, http://www.citizensforethics.org/press/

We didn't know these above stats in 2004. We absolutely *did* know that "faith-based initiatives" were on Bush's tongue and that all of our most overheated foes were positively glowing over the George W. agenda. With our own two eyes we could see that whenever there was a queer-decrying press conference to be had, the audience was an anti-gay who's who. It didn't take a rocket scientist's uninsured domestic partner to realize that many of these peeps were on the presidential speed dial. We assumed as much.

With this knowledge unshakably on my mind, my first guiding belief as a nascent activist was formed. Quite simply, I determined that we had to challenge these groups and players as forcefully as they challenge us. This might sound obvious to some, but the truth is that we had long limited ourselves by writing off these folks as fringe. We had neglected to steadfastly put forth a counterpoint to their every misguided point and had therefore let them describe gays and gay rights for large swaths of the population. While they issued missive after missive railing off a list of whom and what we supposedly are, and where and when we do all the dastardly things we allegedly do, the most common response from our side had been to shake our heads and call them cuckoo. Understandable. But in doing so, we had broken the first rule of politics: we had let the opposition define the stakes. They had quite loudly defined us—defined us as a militant, agenda-laden enemy. Worse yet, they had done so behind a Bible and a smile. Just calling them "fringe" wasn't going to make them irrelevant.

The beauty of the situation was that because of the Internet, all of the misinformation that they'd been transmitting against us for decades was now readily available. Church bulletins and organizational newsletters that were once limited to physical mailing lists were now willingly placed online. Pro-equality activists were getting a hold of more unseemly documents and scanning those in for posterity's sake. Plus, those of us who wished to challenge the homo-hostile pitch letters and promotional items as they came could quite easily find our way onto their e-lists. The world was turning more transparent, and that was a *very* good thing for our side.

---

entry/bush-era-white-records-show-multiple-visits-by-top-christian-leaders   (accessed 30 Dec. 2011).

My mind was made up. I knew we had to start directly challenging the opposition movement.

Guiding principle number two was also born out of all the misinformation I saw, especially when it came to the myriad of false labels that the organized opposition places upon us.

"Militant."

"Aggressive."

"Immoral."

"Child-threatening."

"Society-weakening."

"Geared towards intrinsic moral evil."

"Halitosis-havers."

Okay, so that last one I made up. Although I'm sure if they thought bad breath would win them just a few more votes, our opposing forces would immediately morph into neo–Al Gores, convincing America that it is gay people's satanic exhalations that have caused this nation's climate change!

But we really don't even have to create silly fictions about this, as the actual labels for the LGBT community (and the first six *are* among the most common, with the sixth coming directly from the current Pope[24]) are all light years away from what I, like all LGBT people, know to be reality. Hell, these labels are light years away from what the organized anti-gays know to be reality! But they are labels that have stuck because they have worked, and they are labels that have worked because of their ability to stick. Truth doesn't matter to the other side—that these labels are effective is the working concern.

It didn't take much time for me to realize that it's because the pro-equality movement is so principled and is so fundamentally right that the anti-gay side *has* to recast the script if it wants to be viable. Discrimination

---

[24] Cardinal Joseph Ratzinger, *Letter To The Bishops of the Catholic Church on the Pastoral Care of Homosexual Persons*, 1 Oct. 1986, http://www.vatican.va/roman_curia/congregations/cfaith/documents/rc_con_cfaith_doc_19861001_homosexual-persons_en.html (accessed 18 Dec 2011).

and bias are ugly things. If those who foster it are to get away with it, they need to call themselves "pro-family"/"pro-values"/"pro-marriage"/"pro-[*insert good thing*]" so as to make their opposition look like the opposite. It's not just linguistics; it's a carefully workshopped strategy—born in the boardroom and reared in the mire of dirty "culture war" games.

Let's look at just one fight, marriage equality. As they attempt to justify their discriminatory push for gay marriage bans, the organized anti-gays continually present these measures as if they're morally-sanctified halos that they're placing on heterosexual marriage in order to codify it as a holier-than-thou, sacred institution. This, even though it's obvious that their fight is not to "protect marriage from attack"—it's them protecting marriage from Joe and Zack. What's almost as enraging as the attacks themselves is the fact that the attacking groups and their figureheads don't have enough courage to actually admit their true convictions!

I don't even need one half of a hand to count the number of times I've heard the organized opposition refer to anti–marriage equality measures as marriage bans. Despite the fact that even a three-year-old can see that bans are in fact what they truly are, the word "ban" is as rare in social conservative circles as "disarm" is at an NRA rally. And why don't they just take the more truthful route of saying *"We just want to ban gays from marrying"*? Well, because that would make them look mean-spirited, natch. By instead falsifying the goal posts and saying that the objective is merely the protection of marriage's sanctity, they can convince millions that their actions are operating independent of bias. Many of those who are not gay and not directly affected by the bans can go along with this line of thought, as they are not losing anything tangible either way.

And don't even think this is all just one man's opinion, either. On the National Organization for Marriage's website, the notorious and very well-financed anti-equality group reveals the following:

Extensive and repeated polling agrees that the single most effective message is:
"Gays and Lesbians have a right to live as they choose, they don't have the right to redefine marriage for all of us."
This allows people to express support for tolerance while opposing gay marriage. Some modify it to "People have a right to live as they choose, they don't have the right to redefine marriage for all of us."

Language to avoid at all costs: "Ban same-sex marriage." Our base loves this wording. So do supporters of SSM. They know it causes us to lose about ten percentage points in polls. Don't use it. Say we're against "redefining marriage" or in favor or "marriage as the union of husband and wife" NEVER "banning same-sex marriage."[25]

They seriously say this. Publicly. They tell their followers how to speak so as to not be too revelatory! It's indicative of a lack of trust in their own base, a lack of belief in their own cause, and a lack of fundamental truth in their every (mis)step. It's kind of like a doctor saying, *"This won't hurt a bit,"* as he's coming at you with a foot-long needle. If you're a mere observer of the situation or if you have a high pain tolerance, then the doctor's claim may sound reasonable. On the other hand, if you're one of the millions who find these pricks hurtful, then you can't even begin to wrap your mind around the idea that this skin-piercing violation is painless. Just like those whose arms are *not* throbbing can accept the doctor's predictions at face value, those whose spirits are not wounded by the offensive nature of marriage bans can accept the "pro-family" leader's lines with unanalyzed ease. The organized anti-gays know this. They also know that very few people are analyzing and calling them out for what they are.

In this reality, I saw opportunity. First and foremost, I felt a strong impulse to challenge the code wording as loudly and often as possible. If they wanted to make a mockery of the English language by aggressively misapplying terms, then we on the pro-equality side could highlight the clear differences between our two movements. Whereas we can talk like human beings, guided by any number of words or facts or emotions or diverging mindsets to make our cases, the organized opposition must steadfastly rely on these agreed-upon talking points in order to get anywhere with their supporters. They have to stand together with one carefully workshopped and code-worded message, to create the illusion of a strong force that's organically on the same page. There's no way any fair-minded, socially aware person can look at this patent reality without seeing the clear strategy in play. We just needed more people to start looking. I was determined to both look myself and find others willing to do the same.

---

[25] "Same Sex Marriage: Answering The Toughest Questions," NationForMarriage.org.

My third guiding principle was to try with all of my might to keep the debate on the anti-gay message, not the personality behind it.

Look, I did high school. I did the college gay club scene. I dished and dashed with the best of them, talking about who did what to whom and where they did it. That ship had sailed. My dramas were now confined to shitty reality TV. I simply didn't care about getting in personal back-and-forths with any one member of the anti-LGBT force. My life was both too short and too great to go there. When it comes to debates and heated disagreements about the work? Sure. But when it comes to petty dramas and dustups, I thought it best to entrust those to the Big Brothers, Top Models, and Kardashians who have nineteen pageant-loving kids and run a cake shop on the Jersey Shore where they hoard Trump-emblazoned runway projects. Even if someone attacked my own worth as a human, it didn't mean that I had to stoop to a counterattack based on characterization rather than the Constitution.

One with a knack for queer discrimination doesn't have to be labeled a "homophobic bigot" to be put in his place. In fact, I would argue that jumping to words like "bigot" can be a turn off to many potential allies, since some human beings hear even minor tinges of harshness as a conversational third rail. The last thing we want to do is shut down ears or close any more minds, since receptive warm beings are what will pave our path to victory.

Plus, personal labels are not always even accurate. Not a one of us has grown up in a world where LGBT people have been free, and some of us have grown up in quite the opposite. There are many factors that can lead people to embrace bias. Geography, upbringing, far-right misinformation, finding out that your opposite-sex prom date was making out with the same-sex sports star under the bleachers—all and more can contribute to anti-gayness. But often this embrace of the wrong view can be almost absentminded, as if it chose the person, not the other way around. So while it's sometimes difficult, I try my best to find possibility in anyone and everyone whose mindsets or teachings I challenge. I leave room for the possibility of growth, possibility of change—possibility of peace.

The fight for civil equality and decent treatment is largely a game of numbers, in which we pro-equality folks have no choice but to move swaths of that much-desired middle to the only acceptable side. To keep a sense of focus on that need to move minds, I vowed early on to take on the actions and messages that the organized opposition was cultivating. Exclusively. It might not work for everyone, but it certainly works for me.

The fourth belief involved laughter. I saw a great need and place for it in the equality conversation.

When faced with vitriolic sentiment and harsh rhetoric, one can react in a number of ways. Anger is a common response. Depression is another. Randomly taking up a hobby such as stamp collecting is a less prevalent, yet still viable, option. As for me, I much prefer exposing the folly of the attack with a tone good-natured enough to leave even the most stonehearted of aggressors fighting to suppress a smile. A message need not be fuming to be firm. Sometimes a tongue in a cheek can be more effective than a hand in a fist.

I use this outlook in approaching most of life's situations, so it's only natural that it's also the tone with which I approach the fight. If nothing else, it's self-protection. If I'm going to go through all of this anti-gay nonsense on a daily basis, then I have to have an outlet for detoxification. Silliness is my salve.

It's also another way to keep focus. Similar to how taking on the message rather than the messenger keeps the debate focused on the fight, the attempt to keep up a smile helps to position the fight onto a plane where our side's positive energy will not be lessened by the other side's aggression. If we keep up our spirits in the face of brute injustice, we become the casting directors of the discourse. There is no logical way that we will be seen as the ones playing the bully role.

Admittedly, it's not an easy task, this smile thing. Considering the vitriol or the personal stakes attached, who can be faulted for turning to anger? Humor also has to be kept in check, so as to not be disrespectful. For instance, you're hopefully not going to greet a brutal hate crime with a smile. Gay teen suicide ain't funny. So no, straight satire isn't always going to cut it.

Yet despite these caveats, I knew there was a place for irreverence in the movement. I was going to try my damndest to fill the lulls with as many LOLs as possible.

The fifth fundamental was the most obvious to me: casting the widest net possible. I've never viewed the goal as "gay rights" or "LGBT rights," per se, even though limitations in language make me rely on these terms. For me it's always been an equality fight—one that's far reaching and all-consuming. When thinking of approach, I felt a great opportunity to help demystify the gay experience and to explain why the controversy regarding LGBT equality is much ado about nothing. It is not a fair fight between two equally principled teams, and should not be a polarized matter in which both the gay and the anti-gay positions are given equal merit. What we have is a one-sided attack against certain kinds of humans, plain and simple. Acceptance is a matter of human decency, and the anti-gay side is clearly in the wrong! Everyone who cares for better must step up and counter the detrimental push.

The simple fact is that nobody in this world is guaranteed a queer-free life. You may not be L, G, B, or T, and you may not know anyone who is. The operative word there is *know*. As long as there are human beings in your immediate purview, there is the very real potential that you will someday have to think about where non-hetero/non–gender-conforming humans fit into this spectrum that we call normalcy. Could be a sibling, could be a child. Could be your favorite coworker who you thought just liked the bachelor/ette life. But if one lives long enough, the chances of firsthand LGBT knowledge are nearly guaranteed. Blessedly so.

But okay, for the sake of argument, say you as a heterosexual person plan to go through life somehow avoiding any and all LGBT contact. Fine. Your loss, but fine. The issues here still run much deeper and might still affect your life. Constitutional fairness, equal protection, non-discrimination, separation of church and state—these are matters that involve the stewardship of our constitutional representative democracy/federal republic. The implications could be applied to a host of other groups and situations. Majority tyranny is being used against LGBT people now, but don't kid yourself into believing that LGBT people are the only group that holds the religious right's focus. PUH-LEEZE! Reproductive freedom, school prayer, health care matters, immigration—all of these debates (and many more) come with reasons for religious right interference!

How can anyone say, in good conscience, that this fight is of no personal consequence? That's like saying there's no reason to pay any mind to the ill treatment of farm animals if you yourself are a vegetarian or like saying that you have no reason to care about the safety of NASA astronauts if you have a fear of flying. We are in this realm of existence together. It doesn't even matter how personally responsible or respectful you may be towards LGBT people (or pigs or would-be Buzz Aldrins). If you are not helping to combat the threats or suffering that you perceive, then you are not part of the solution.

If we as a people had turned blind eyes throughout history, then large swaths of minority citizens would have had to fight longer and harder in the needless wars that were forcing them to take pause during their respective days. This is no different. We in the LGBT community cannot do this alone. Period. We are *all* living through a modern civil rights battle, the likes of which will be looked back upon with great interest and shame. I can't help but think that one of the primary questions asked by future generations will be, "How and why did so many of you do so little?" These future historians will certainly, and rightly, wonder why the gay community was considered one of the most vibrant and creative groups on the planet, yet little of this ingenuity was used to challenge the oppressive politicos of the day. They will ask why we had a robust gay media presence, a twenty-four-hour LGBT cable network, and multiple political advocacy groups, yet were unable to rally our troops in a manner even halfway as effective as that of our opposition. Although LGBT people won't get all of the burden, since future students of civil rights history will surely ask why so many would-be and should-be heterosexual allies also turned blind eyes to the injustices of their shared days. They will hold each and every one of us accountable for our inactivity.

People are forgotten. Our legacies are what live on forever.

So to recap:
- Directly challenge the opposition
- Point out the blatant misinformation campaigns
- Focus on the message rather than the person
- Remember to laugh
- Expand the sphere

Bye bye, apathy. Hello, Jeremy Hooper: Overdue Activist.

19) JUST CALL ME LARRY TAMER

I started a website.
I took a new approach.
I made a few jokes in the process.
I got attention from both 'mo friend and 'mo foe alike.
This piece, originally printed in *The Advocate* on May 6, 2008, gives a primer on my work, my approach, and the reception to both, three years in.

Bees To Honey
by Jeremy Hooper
MOST OF US ARE AWARE of the intensely antigay Westboro Baptist Church, which has staged public demonstrations for nearly two decades, claiming everything from hurricanes to AIDS to the Iraq war is divine retribution for our country's tolerance of homosexuality (Check out its subtly named website, GodHatesFags.com). But who among us can say he's given church leader Shirley Phelps-Roper a primer on bagels and lox?

Over the 3 1/2 years that I've been writing the blog Good as You (www.goodasyou.org), I've had the opportunity to engage in e-conversations with so many antigay activists my in-box is starting to look like it was transplanted from Mike Huckabee's computer. And while heated discussions with these "profamily" types about our theological differences (and their predictions of my future residency in hell) have certainly occurred, they have also surprised me with their kindness, genuine concern for my well-being, and sincerity.

I've had higher-ups at Focus on the Family eagerly offer me a tour of their Colorado Springs compound. A prominent "ex-gay" advocate invited my partner and me to a family dinner. Other times, someone who has publicly denounced gay life and gay love will write to tell me they found a quip I wrote about them to be witty and spot-on. The common message seems to be: "We hate everything you have to say, but we enjoy the tone with which you say it."

That's why these folks, whose work I challenge on a daily basis, are so willing to be my friendly acquaintances. When penning an unapologetic condemnation of homophobic, heterosexist rhetoric, I never attack my adversaries' character but rather their chosen positions. The terms bigot and hatemonger are not in my arsenal. Instead of being a flamethrower, I prefer to toss the antigays' flames aside and take a piss on them.

It's one part strategy, one part sincerity. While it's true I made a deliberate choice to take a more pacifist approach, it honestly feels more like that tactic chose me. When I entered into this "culture war" debate, the stones just felt wrong in my hand. The more I studied the fight, the more I began to feel that victory would come by highlighting the slings and arrows that are directed toward our community, not by regifting those weapons in a pro-gay fashion.

Those on the antigay side want to dislike us. They need to believe our minds are "reprobate," so as to justify within themselves the all-out war they wage against our "chosen lifestyles." The robber to their cop, the Joker to their Batman, the replacement Dreamgirl to their Effie—we've been cast as the hurdles on their path toward happily ever after. But by refusing to let them get away with their polarized portrait of good versus evil, I force them instead to address my refutation of their logic. They can write off other confrontations as an exchange between the wicked and the righteous, but I don't give them such an easy opportunity to trivialize my words.

This may sound like capitulation to some. However, I think it's exactly the opposite: By engaging them human to human, I've gained a unique entrance into the hearts and minds of our most vehement foes. It may be presumptuous and self-adulatory to say so, but I can't help but believe that when they lie down to sleep at night, all quiet in the world around them, some of them might question their views because of me. They might not completely come around to my way of thinking, but they sure as hell aren't going to write me off as a demon-possessed heathen whose words they'll simply relegate to the "hater" file.

When you have truth on your side, there's no strategic need for defensive aggression. So I don't yell at my gay-unfriendly pen pals. I tell them in a fair but firm voice: "You have no way of winning because you've chosen a losing position. Wanna go have some coffee and discuss your inevitable defeat?"

20) SUFFERING THE INSUFFERABLE SUFFRAGE

I think what infuriates me the most about the gay community's most heated organized opponents is that they will never realize, admit, or take responsibility for the gut-wrenching dehumanization they inflict upon us. When it comes to the anti-equality social conservatives' messaging, playing the victim is the only thing that rivals their constant shirking of responsibility.

If one of their fallacious campaigns to roll back LGBT equality loses, every one of the folks invested in that campaign will still go about their next days, perhaps a little bummed, but otherwise unaltered. They will have lost nothing, as the cherished values and freedoms that they typically claim are at stake are nothing more than fear-mongering rhetoric. Regardless of how great the LGBT rights gain, those who opposed will not be truly threatened in any tangible, citable way, and they will not be forced to have any kind of difficult conversation with their young ones about how and why their family was just assaulted as part of the democratic process. Rather than hold them responsible for the untruths of the one particular campaign, we on the pro-equality side would always be far more inclined to briefly celebrate our triumph as the victor and then get on with our lives as human beings, not harp on the unfair victimization for months on end. Our goal is peace.

Ironically, for the same "us" that seek a live-and-let-live calmness, peace is far from the common, post-electoral experience. We LGBT people walk through so many post-election days feeling, to some degree, hated. We suffer the losses both in terms of our abilities and within our emotional cores. It doesn't matter what we might individually feel about something like marriage or whether or not our state currently allows us that or any other debated freedom. The simple fact remains that for far too many election cycles, gobs of cash and even bigger piles of targeted attacks have been wasted for the sole purpose—THE SOLE PURPOSE!— of keeping certain kinds of tax-paying citizens on a lower rung.

2008: California gets marriage equality because of a principled court ruling, only to have it rolled back a few months later in the highest profile vote yet. Ouch.

2009: Maine gets marriage equality because of a principled legislative action, only to have it taken away a few months later in a "People's Veto." Fucking ouch.

2004–2011: Thirty-one states in total go against marriage equality at the polls, with several other state legislatures also stifling basic fairness in various votes. Holy mother of ass-crazy ouch!

2012: Marriage goes back on the ballot in another handful of states, continuing the indignity of public voting on minority civil rights. Just when we thought we were getting numb to it all—*ouch*!

How can LGBT people regain their collective calm when that sense has been (and continues to be) so disgustingly rocked? How can we walk with springs in our steps when we are inflicted with a newfound instinct to look over our shoulders to make sure that we're not being denigrated via a public mocking on par with the slighting we just received via secret ballot? How do we regain our trust in the principles of a nation when those principles have been so alarmingly tested and received such a failing grade? How do we forget? Forgive?

The professional anti-LGBTs will never know this feeling. Despite their constant claims of how wrong and terrible and immoral and misguided we are as a movement and people, the reality is that the pro-equality community has no desire to inflict the same kind of pain on them or their families. That little fact doesn't matter to the opposition movement and apparently didn't matter to the majorities of citizens who turned out to vote against us in all of these states. In this society, it's still okay to inflict unprovoked strife on certain kinds of people, just as long as you say "God" and "family" and "sanctity" enough. It's okay to force a rich, vibrant population and their allies to suffer humiliating character attacks, just as long as the attacker refers to his or her chosen implement as a "weapon of marriage protection." It's okay to ratchet up familial shame, as long as the sexes are the same. It's okay to deny basic civil fairness with religious justifications, just as long as a bare majority of public polling provides your movement the cover to do so.

Ah, America: the land of the far-from-free, the home of the unwarranted attacks that must still be braved.

21) YOU ARE STILL CORDIALLY INVITED

As the guide led Andrew and me around the gorgeous property, I felt something change within both of us. Our eyes, which had been weighted down by a month of fought-back tears, had new vitality. Our voices, muted by an election in which promises came wrapped in paradoxical packaging, had restored lilts. The frosted ground crunched under our feet, but rather than make us fear a slip or a fall, it was instead giving us a new spring.

It was a cold, mid-December '08 morning in Morris, Connecticut, with a detectable fog in the air. Within our minds, however, there was newfound clarity. The tiny town couldn't have been more foreign, with neither of us Gothamites having family or even friends within a radius that one could reasonably call close. Yet finally, here in this nonnative countryside, it seemed that we had found the proper home to host our love. Even though our unrealized California dream might have to be relocated 3,000 miles away, it was this moment when we first saw that our every wish would still be fulfilled.

But to get to this moment, I need to now bring you back a few months. August 2008, to be precise. It was three months after (a) the California Supreme Court ruled in favor of marriage equality and (b) New York Governor David Paterson solidified the idea that out-of-state same-sex unions would be fully recognized when local couples returned to their Empire State homes. Andrew and I could finally marry and have that marriage recognized at home—we just had to go somewhere else to have the legal union performed. It was an absurd scenario, yes; it was an open window, regardless.

The stars seemed aligned for two Upper East Side gay boys to finally solidify their bond, and the decision was quickly made: we were headed west to the great Golden State to seal the deal. And not just to city hall, either. The Hooper-Shulman wedding was going to be the same sort of production that our hetero friends had enjoyed, minus the dress and non-pluralized bachelor party. Now we just had to plan!

Before we left for CA for the first of what we presumed to be many trips, Andrew, the meticulous planner to my more spontaneous free spirit, mapped out an impressive itinerary of places in the San Francisco Bay and surrounding areas that he winnowed down as potential locales, vendors, and whatnots for a proper destination wedding. With our gay agenda in hand and our plane tickets booked, we used a few late summer days to put it all together.

Being TV junkies, we had seen more episodes of *Bridezillas* than we would admit in certain company. Naturally, the trash TV exposure put in the backs of both of our minds the fear that if not careful, this whole wedding planning thing could catch us in its neurotic grips. Yet much to our surprise, the planning started falling in place almost as soon as we stepped off the tarmac at San Francisco International. The venue, located in nearby Los Gatos, CA, was as beautiful as it had looked on the web; the green tea with vanilla bean frosting wedding cake, from the first bakery that we sampled, seemed to have been whipped together exclusively for our palates; the reception caterer was able to put together a vegetarian menu that would leave even the most cow-eating among us to forget about mammalian-based nourishment for at least one evening; through the guidance of a serendipitously like-minded florist, I discovered that not only did I have strong feelings about floral arrangements and surface textures, but that I actually had a bit of a knack for it; DJs, photographers, guest accommodations, and the whole lot of could-be annoyances were proving to be laid-back, and even enjoyable, experiences. Oh, and this impressive slate of planning all came together in just two days' time!

We had rented an Infiniti, but we were navigating our California adventure on the back of a cloud. It was easy. Fun. Exciting. We couldn't wait to regale our friends and family back home with the details of what was to be our spring '09 fantasy soiree.

Once back home in NYC, the good luck kept on coming. From save-the-date cards to a mother-in-law dress, our elements were falling into place with the same gentle ease that the leaves were now using to descend from Central Park trees. "What is so hard about all this?" Andrew and I would frequently ask each other. "Why the drama?" While other "I do"–bound couples might have been fretting, we were propping up our feet and enjoying a nice Pinot.

Even though my professional life is built around slaying the anti-gay dragons that guard the moat of peace, the joy of all of these special, easy moments led me to completely forget that any sort of socially conservative fire was breathing down my wedding's neck. I had been covering the Proposition 8 battle with a fine-toothed comb, so I knew polls were tight, that donations on both sides were coming in at insane levels, and that the proposed stoppage of California's same-sex marriages could theoretically prevail. But *no way* was this thing going to pass, I thought. After the Bush/Rove marriage ban years, this was to be *our* time. This election was different. Barack Obama's "hope" mantra seemed to apply to all, especially in a reliably blue state like California.

We stayed on our cloud and made it to our October '08 engagement party with little to no scathing. It was unseasonably warm, the night of this pre-wedding bash. The delayed cold annoyed me a little, since my long-planned outfit skewed autumnal. However, it was actually a fitting temp, since the climate inside our SoHo party was defined by an equal amount of human coziness. This was our moment to be feted, and our loved ones gladly sucked up the good vibes. The stage was set for a mild winter.

There are some simple facts in life, certain inevitabilities. Chilly temperatures might be delayed, but they will eventually come to be. One must be prepared for the bitter frost, so as to not be left out in the cold.

I wasn't prepared on November 4th, 2008. Neither was Andrew.

In our Manhattan voting district, Andrew and I were literally the first two people to pull a lever for President Obama. On the other shining sea, 52.24 percent of voting Californians sent us a statement that we were among the last two people they would ever want to see swapping golden bands in their Golden State. The loss that seemed so unimaginable had become reality. The wedding crasher that I had considered too hurtful to acknowledge had actually shown up, uninvited and ready to ruin it all.

It hurt. A lot. As much as Andrew and I held each other, and as much as we huddled close at the protest rallies that filled our next few nights and weeks, our bones remained chilled.

The irony of being an activist for something like LGBT rights is that with great strife comes heightened attention. In the days and weeks following Prop 8's passage, I dealt with my heartache by diving into my now-more-exposed work headfirst. I was on a hunt for something— some misstep, mistake, or miscalculation that would change the result. It all just seemed so wrong. With persistence, there had to be some way I could change the tone back to jubilation. If my heart poured out through my fingers and onto the web, my postmortems could somehow rewrite the game. Right? Maybe? *Please?*

But by Tofurky day, it was clear that my polemics, poetry, and prose pieces—no matter how ably articulated, purposely punned, or appropriately enraged—were not going to cause an immediate change. While semi-reasonable hope rested within the court system, Andrew and I knew that we weren't going to be able to keep our April '09 vow exchange. Not if we wanted it to be legally binding. Not in California.

If the vendor contracts had been easy to sign, then giving those same vendors the okay to utilize the Prop 8 clauses that we had specifically placed into our agreements was ease's antithetical cousin. If the save-the-date cards were easy to create, then the "release the date" email was its polar opposite. Publicly, Andrew and I feigned an indefatigable spirit, as best we could. Privately, we were defeated.

I can't say if Andrew cried alone as much as I did, but I suspect the answer is no. We wear our emotions in different ways, and closed-door tears would seem much more my jurisdiction than his. I can, however, say with certainty that he began *Googling* alone in ways in which I was incapable.

SEARCH: "Gay-friendly Massachusetts or Connecticut wedding."
SEARCH: "Connecticut and Massachusetts wedding planners."
SEARCH: "Eco-friendly CT or MA reception."
SEARCH: "Please let my baby smile again."

While I was beginning the yearly hunt for Amazon.com holiday bargains, Andrew was finding within himself the determination to plan wedding 2.0 in the 2.0 states that, at the time, would still afford us equality. He was determined to transplant our plans.

I'm sure the first time he mentioned his Connecticut and Massachusetts findings to me, I met him with a sigh and possibly an eye roll. It wasn't that I was willing to put off our marriage—I was going to wed this man in 2009 no matter what! However, my desire for a lavish party had dissipated. I was more than ready to put on my best wedding jeans and find the nearest JP, CT or MA, who would civilly bind us. But Andrew knew better. He knew I wanted more. With persistence, he eventually got me in a car for what he promised would be some light wedding hunting—just to put out some feelers.

The first few attempts were as unfulfilling as I'd imagined they would be. The initial couple of venues we tried on for size fit us about as well as a three-fingered glove. Some of them were so uninspiring that even after making an almost two-hour trek, we didn't even bother to get out of the car. Others, where we did make it inside, were so cookie-cutter boring (e.g., *"for an extra $10 a person, we can put a nice sash on the chairs"*) that it felt like being in a bad romantic comedy. Nothing felt like us.

These experiences weren't coming from a place of pessimism. We were sad but we were trying—we really were. Trying to get into it. Trying to like something. Trying to envision the photos that we knew we'd be looking at until death parted us. Trying, if I'm honest, to replant our California plans. Yet for the first time in our shared time of planning our big day, we were failing.

The turning point came on like a song. Quite literally. It turns out that our planned California wedding performer, the soulful Jacqui Naylor, had family ties in Connecticut. Quite out of nowhere, she told us that if we were to need her services in the Constitution State, she would gladly traverse the country to perform at our reception, as we had intended in CA. Jacqui was as annoyed with and embarrassed by Prop 8 as we were, and she was determined to facilitate our day in any way she could.

For me, that was a huge spark. If someone who knew virtually nothing about us could pick up and move her and her band's plans from one coast to another, then couldn't I find the strength to rise above the funk of one unjust vote? Through the whole Prop 8 mess, I never doubted that someday it, like all anti-gay bans, would be overturned. The hostile agenda's demise is inevitable—I never lost sight of that. If I could look the historical pockmark in its face and laugh, here when laughter was far from the easiest impulse, wouldn't that be a step in the right direction, both in terms of personal sanity and professional activism?

With a semi-restored gusto, I agreed with Andrew that an intense weekend dedicated solely to our wedding, hitting up many and varied potential venues, might get us in the right frame of mind. So that's what we did. We packed our bags, cancelled work plans for the following Friday, and set out to find the easy beauty that had been crushed under the weight of majority tyranny. No distractions, no dark clouds. We already knew who'd be serenading our sweet dances—how hard could it be to find an appropriate stage?

Was I convinced that we'd find it? Honestly no, not 100 percent. But if there was a perfect "it" to be found, I had nothing but faith in my and my fiancé's ability to know it when we saw it. To just know—ya know?

And that takes us back to that literally foggy December morning when the figurative fog began to lift from our eyes. Our very first stop was Winvian, an artful resort in Morris, CT that Andrew had found and loved at first digital sight. From my first *literal* sight, I became equally enchanted. It had all of the elements we were seeking and more: rustic like our CA locale, yet with a sophisticated style to rival the most chi chi hotel. It was quiet yet passionate. Incidentally enough, that is exactly the tone through which Andrew and I, via our exchanged glances and non-verbal hand squeezes, told each other that we'd found our Connecticut calling.

Love it. Done. Book it!

The extra planning meant pushing the date back to June. However, the lack of looming ballot initiative meant that no group, no matter how deep their financing or willingness to create duplicitous ads, would have the power to hurt us this time. In fact, there was almost zero organized pushback in Connecticut, with marriage equality seeming more like a non-controversy than it had in any state prior. That was reason alone to reward the state with our dollars and reward our hearts with the peace. For the sense of comfort, we could handle a delay.

So there we were. We began anew, GPS-ing our way through a second state so that we could obtain our legal rights and take them back home to state number three. A planner here, a bakery there. After a while, we even stopped comparing every new vendor with our old CA ones, freeing us to judge and plan based on a new set of merits and realities rather than to bring up old shit that was apparently never meant to be. It wasn't a delicate ballet, that's for sure. We remained a little bruised. However, we knew that the first dance would be all the sweeter having survived the Prop 8 mosh pit.

On June 13, 2009, Andrew and I finally had our dream wedding. Words cannot describe the joy. Hopefully a few pictures will give some semblance of insight:

DESPITE WHAT YOU MIGHT'VE HEARD . . . #4

➢ Rights activists actually *don't* want to destroy all that is holy in the world. We want to destroy all that is hole-y in this world's equal protection policies.

➢ Republican and Democratic politicians will both sell the LGBT community down the river. A wise politico will invest in floaties.

➢ The more a group uses the words "family," "traditional," and "values" in its organizational name, the less likely that group is to actually support the same. Scientists are stumped as to why. Although it doesn't even matter what the pros think, since these groups would just ignore the science anyway.

➢ The LGBT community doesn't wish to "hijack" any prior civil rights movement. Socio-political fights exist on many different planes, and we are quite capable of peacefully piloting our own, while at the same time learning landing lessons from our forepersons in flight. No hijack necessary.

Now that that's out of the way, I'm hoping you might help me on a speech I'm working on. I call it: "I Have A Civil Rights Yearning During REM Sleep" . . .

➤ Gay pride parades represent gay revelry, not gay life itself. Just like most heteros aren't daily standing on Bourbon Street showing their tits for beads or littering the NYC streets with green-hued puke on days other than St. Paddy's, LGBT people aren't typically going to the grocery store in assless chaps.

➤ Most LGBT people don't hate God or religion. Though some TGLB dyslexics *do* hate dogs and men named Neil Igor.

➤ "God created Adam and Eve, not Adam and Steve" is such a dumb quip. Gay folk need not have been *first* on Eden's bus to have eventually found their seat on it (which is not at the back, incidentally, despite how many try to force us there).

➤ Not all gay men can dress, design, cook, party plan, or do hair. Plenty of straight men *can* do those things. While there are stronger propensities for certain things in certain populations, refinement comes from learning to utilize multiple tools, not specific affection for one that hangs below the belt.

➤ The more a person cries about supposed "gay indoctrination" in public schools, the more likely he or she is to force his or her children into a certain faith, to home school with books that deny dinosaurs and fossils, and to demand government buildings feature Ten Commandments monuments. Frankly, the kettle and the pot are sick of dealing with it.

➤ Civil marriage and religious ceremony are actually two different things. If you wish to use the latter to deny gays the former amid claims that "eyes of God" marriage is what really matters, then we best not see you at city hall signing up for the state license.

➤ Gay people should not argue with a thrice-married politician who uses the phrase "sanctity of marriage." They should unapologetically laugh in his or her face for at least ten minutes (the approximate time that his or her first marriage lasted).

➢ A comically sizable number of anti–gay rights personalities themselves have LGBT children. While the apple may not fall far from the tree, clearly it does sometimes look back at said tree and say, "Screw this!"

➢ The homosexual agenda is not a bound book that we LGBT folk are all granted on our eighteenth birthdays. Being nothing if not trendy, we gays have naturally now moved it over to an e-book format.

➢ It's not okay to ask your gay kid to have a "don't ask don't tell" policy on life, unless you ask the same of his or her straight siblings. You're a family, not a talent booker for *The 700 Club*.

➢ The old joke about lesbians bringing a U-Haul to a second date is so not true. Everyone knows that by their second date, the couple has already returned the moving van, gone on three morning jogs, brunched at Sue's Tofu Emporium, screamed at the TV during not one but two sporting events, and played a few rounds of pool with both of their exes (with whom they remain oddly, yet admirably, friendly).

➢ When you call someone a "fag," the British cigarette manufacturers win.

➢ Lady Liberty? Never married. Relentlessly mum. Athletically built. I'm just saying . . .

➢ It's fine if you want to go to a drag show for your heterosexual bachelorette party. That is unless you plan on voting against faux-Beyoncé's right to be a real fiancé.

➢ LGBT people are not single-issue voters. It's just that gay rights opponents keep making an issue out of keeping us single!

➢ Having grown up in the same unequal world as everyone else, same-sex marriage is just as unfamiliar to many LGBT people as it is to conservative heterosexuals. But unknown does not equal bad.

➤ "Are you the man or the woman in the relationship?" is not a cute question to ask of a couple. Unless it's Mother's Day and you're looking to buy me something nice—in which case, come to mama.

➤ One hint, straight pals: if every time you see a gay person the only thing you can think to talk about is something even tangentially queer, then you're still seeing the world as divided. These attempts to relate might be incredibly well intentioned. They probably are, even. But full lives are built with well-rounded curves, not one-track minds.

➤ Separate is not equal. Divided is not united. It's "we the people," not "wee on some of the people."

22) THE SANCTITY
OF MARTHA

She practically owns Connecticut, so the fact that our wedding was set in that great state certainly worked in our favor. Also our photographer, Jacklyn Greenberg, is as talented as she is talkative, so the editorial quality of our images was surely a key component. Plus we're a pretty rad couple, if I do say so myself.

Despite all these factors, it was still completely shocking to both my husband and myself to learn that *Martha Stewart Weddings* magazine was going to feature us in the Winter 2010 issue. Who would ever expect such a thing? It's like a wedding fairy tale for countless "traditional marriage" supporters. Yet here we were, two guys who have been painted as a threat to tradition and all that is holy about ring fingers, earning a blessing from the America's top-selling wedding magazine? Get out!

As a proud person who'd put my gorgeous wedding on the Times Square JumboTron if they'd let me, I was thrilled to get to share my special day with an even larger audience. As an activist who dedicates a big portion of my fight to marriage equality, I was even more astounded to learn that Andrew and I would be the FIRST same-sex couple to ever make the publication. THE FIRST. *Ever*! The happiness was going in my scrapbook—the history in my bio.

Neither Andrew nor I can fully remember how the selection came to be. As a freelance writer, I'm constantly pitching myself here, there, and everywhere, looking for the various ways that I can adapt my passion, wordplay, and affection for a good dick joke to new and uncharted literary

waters. I know I submitted our wedding photos, along with some associated words on the topic, to a few publications. But when the *Martha*
editor contacted us, it was difficult to piece together how it all happened.
Partly because of the aforementioned prolific pitching on my part, but
also because Andrew and I were too busy "Oh My God"-ing each other to
accurately process the whole thing. The choice felt less like an effort and
more like kismet, and we were ready to move on to visions of our family members walking out of various tri-state supermarkets with stacks of
mags bigger than themselves.

As exciting as it all was on a superficial level, the coolest prospect for
me was the opportunity to effect change via something that was already
such a joy. Much of my activism is enjoyable, in terms of soul satisfaction,
yet undeniably laborious in terms of defending myself against targeted
attacks, researching the minutiae of various state and federal laws, and
coming up with ways to fight against pure and unadulterated nastiness
without losing my cool. Yet here was a chance to change hearts and minds
vis-à-vis the happiest day of Andrew's and my shared life, and I wouldn't
even have to lift a gloriously gold-ringed finger to do it. This wasn't
even armchair activism—this easy advocacy could be done in my sleep!
Plus the people who would see this wouldn't have to know their ENDAs
from their DOMAs, their cloture votes from their filibusters, or their
asses from their holes in the ground. The only prerequisites were eyes, a
heart, and a mind, with all three possessing something of a willingness
to remain open.

Through my work, I'm always trying to expand my sphere of influence, little by little. Preaching to the choir, while effective for those who
like their praises crooned solely by folks who already sing the tune, is not
the most effective way to turn a civil rights message into a mainstream
hit. When dealing with attacks from the religious right, I don't just seek
out like-minded gays, but also atheists, progressives, fair-minded folks of
faith, Republicans who are sick of the way their party has been expropri-
ated by so-called "values voters," and others who might understand the
implications of using a Bible as a weapon. When talking about voting on
minority rights, there are any number of other vulnerable communities to
turn to, using both history and current threat to highlight how and why
the intolerance could eventually target others. From animal rights activists who understand the concept of cruelty as it applies to every living
thing, to labor activists who understand the economic benefit of support-

ing our unions along with their own—the idea is to expand the base as fully and widely as possible. I'm always on the hunt for new and unique ways to do this.

If pro-equality voices are going to get anywhere, we can't only take on the outrageous homophobia that leads to protests, anti-gay votes, and hate crimes. Sure, that's the big enchilada that rightfully gets the media attention, but below the surface is the arguably more pervasive problem of casual heterosexism. You know what I'm talking about. We talked about it in chapter one: that subtle idea that while gays are fine and dandy, they are still "different," and/or the belief, even among lay supporters, that gay issues are for "those people" to handle. It's this blasé, almost imperceptible way of thinking that leads to apathy—apathy that will never match the hyper-motivated far-right, what with all their religious fervor.

With this *Martha* development, I'd be looking to engage a new group. Namely, heterosexual brides- and grooms-to-be who are with us in heart and spirit but who have not, for whatever reason, gotten off their booties to help us fight this battle. Who better understands the reasons, wants, and desires of marriage than those who are deep enough in the process to actually purchase a magazine on the subject? When the marriage machine is churning at its fullest force, those around the intended can barely even fart without the fiancé/ée considering whether or not the proffered sound might translate to trumpet so as to become part of a possible processional tune. So when these same, betrothed, deep-in-the-machine duos see two gay dudes who've gone through the process they're currently in, I can't help but think their consciousnesses might be raised in new and unexplored ways. "Aha! They're like us!" The dots of connection could finally force a new sort of awareness. Through this awareness, peace?

After a few months of struggling to keep it somewhat quiet, the day finally came. December 18, 2009. In a Blockbuster video of all places, we see it: our issue. It was a week earlier than the publishers told us to expect it, so who knows if its early unveiling was an accident or what? Who the hell even knew that Blockbuster carried wedding mags? But they did and there it was, wedged in between movie-sized boxes of candy and pre-rented copies of *Milk*: our *Martha* awaiting our eager paws.

Andrew and I grabbed the copy and tore it open with ferocity. There we saw it, on page 98:

REAL WEDDINGS

JEREMY HOOPER &
ANDREW SHULMAN

June 13, 2009, Litchfield Hills, Connecticut

"SOMETHING OLD" is nothing new at a wedding. But when two design buffs recycle found objects for their nuptials in fresh and incandescent ways, well, that's something altogether different. The pair, who met through friends in 2003, wanted their day to "be pure joy, not stuffy — but without sacrificing luxury, says Jeremy. The result, an every-detail-counts affair that blended haute elements (gourmet food) with down-home whimsy (a *Dukes of Hazzard*-themed table), was just that.

Clockwise from top: Beside a sun-dappled pond at the sublime Winvian Resort in Connecticut, Andrew (left) and Jeremy break the glass, one of several Jewish traditions they incorporated into the otherwise secular ceremony. Every table had a different theme; perched atop the "music" table's orange shag carpet is a rack of 8-tracks and a Woodstock LP tucked into a Fisher-Price record player (florist Candi Millard rooted succulents in a retro cork planter and used craspedia to playfully suggest a disco ball). Andrew's family flanks the jubilant couple. The pair couldn't resist campy golden cocktail napkins from Mk-Wright, "we tend to seek a balance between the high and low" says Jeremy. "Pooch of honor" Bosley sports a custom seersucker suit. The "photo" table holds vintage View-Master discs, slide carousels, wooden frames, and a classic camera; larkspur, peach roses, scabiosa seed heads, and craspedia shoot out of the centerpiece's wheat-grass base.

ONE THING I LEARNED
"Don't feel like you have to follow anyone else's plan. And don't stifle your creativity because your idea isn't 'traditional.'"

SOURCES
LOCATION AND CATERING
EVENT PLANNING Erica Krusel Ambiance Chic Wedding
FLOWERS Candi's Floral Cre
CAKE Sweet Maria's
WEDDING PHOTOGRAPHY Jacklyn Greenberg and Chris Brown of JAGstudios

MORE IN OUR GO-TO GUIDE

KELVEN BOOK
Caterer, CANARD

"Hats off to you and your team. *Martha Stewart Weddings* has been our inspiration, our source, and our partner. Congratulations on 15 years, and here's to 15 more. Thanks for your continued dedication and endless creativity over the years."

26

We were thrilled. For our family, for our love, for our napkin vendor—we were honored to be part of this. We were included right alongside two other opposite-gender "Real Weddings," as if the *Martha* folks had been periodically featuring same-sex couples for

---

[26] *Martha Stewart Weddings*, Winter 2010 edition, pg. 98.

years. Andrew's and my wedding was not separated in a "gay" section. Our sexuality was not noted in any way. Our wedding was simply part of the mix. The way it should be.

And the kiss? That was an editorial choice that should not be overlooked. The folks behind the piece had several other images to choose from, yet they made the conscious choice to include the lip lock. That's not a minor footnote—it's a major advancement in the area of easy, casual acceptance!

In fact, I see the whole thing as a tipping point. On the mainstream news outlets, potential allies see debates, protests, and whatever stock footage the editor and his or her associated agenda wants them to see. In the pages of *Martha*, however, they see nothing short of love. Commitment. Honor. They see the same kind of principles that any of these other loving couples are hopefully gearing up to exchange. Once we get to the point to where we are showing gay people's peace for exactly what it is, there is no turning back.

That's where the *Martha* editors already are. Andrew and I are not a one-shot. We're not an anomaly. We're not a commemorative issue. We are a changing wind, one of many wedding portraits that will blow the book of history to its next page.

I'm not a big fan of the term "gay marriage" because it describes some sort of "other" thing. Gay couples are not fighting for an "other"—we're fighting for entrance into the same civil institution that our heterosexual brothers and sisters enjoy. The fight is for equality: in law, in practice, in rights—in mass-market magazines. Federal government and a majority share of U.S. states may still have a ways to go, but the doyenne of American domesticity has dished up a heaping serving of marriage equality. Andrew and I are as humbled as any of Ms. Stewart's pies to serve in this role.

23) ADOPTING A NEW SET OF PLANS

She is part of every last one of our life decisions, and we've never even met her. We don't know her name. Hell, she's likely not even born yet. But despite the unborn and unknown status, she's as real as a 4 a.m. feeding, and as omnipresent as the bags under any new parent's eyes.

Or *him.* I guess it could be a him. We always say we want a girl, but we've certainly placed no true limits on the gender. Either way, the child we will adopt already has a palpable presence in the life of my husband and myself. Our minds are constantly thinking through the list:

- We'll get a bigger city apartment within two years.
- A country house will hopefully happen within the next five (since we do want the child to know green grass and a backyard swing set).
- Do we get a second dog now or wait until after the child joins our fam?
- Public school or private? Let the research and debate begin!
- How do I train my comatose sleeper of a husband to arise at the sound of a baby cry when it takes full-blown Alarm-ageddon to wake him now?

There's not a children's section in a Manhattan boutique that we pass by without stopping to discuss our views on appropriate style of dress for the toddling set. There's not a car we look at without also considering a car seat. We're mapping out not only our own destinies but also that of a third human life. And you know what? It is the most soul-satisfyingly joyous set of plans we've ever had to make!

Had you told this writer back at the turn of the millennium that his next-decade-self would be considering whether to use cloth or disposable diapers, I would have told you to "shut up and get me a Smirnoff Ice, for that new show *Queer as Folk* is about to come on," before making some joke about a "hanging chad." At that time, the thought of fatherhood was simply inconceivable (pun absolutely intended).

Then I met Andrew. One of the first things he made known to me when we first met was that he *absolutely* wanted kids. To which I reacted— well, I didn't know *how* to react. It was an idea that had simply never crossed this then–entertainment industry professional's celeb and "fabulous party"–absorbed life! However, as it became apparent that Andrew was the one who would be in my life for all of our allotted time on this spinning orb, it became clear that joint fatherhood a concept with which I was going to be forced to contend.

Now don't get me wrong—I've always adored children. I worked in my mother's day cares as a teen and have always been able to relate to and form a bond with those under legal driving age. All of the kids in my life have always been my good buddies. I deeply appreciate the pure innocence that comes with youth, even when the unencumbered freeness leads to uncomfortable questions or comments. Plus I look much less silly dressing up like a pirate and/or fulfilling my Legos addiction when a kid is within a reasonable "Can you believe they're making me do this?" range.

But *my own?* Someone calling *me* dad? That was a thought I crossed out of my mind on the day that I finally admitted to myself that this whole dude-attraction thing was not, in fact, a phase. I had so much else to work through during the years that followed—from college to relationships to work to New York to pondering the new breed of "famous for being famous" celebutantes—that somehow child rearing had gotten lost in the shuffle. But now? Now was somewhat stable. Was this really a possibility?

I sat down to think about it. I thought of the love Andrew and I share and of the dedication we have to making the world a better place. We're a team that is decidedly working toward peace. We strive for the good. We recycle, even when a bottle is particularly dirty and therefore needs scrubbing. There are so many children who need this kind of calm, loving home in their lives (and we could use an extra set of bottle-scrubbing hands).

I thought of our ability to provide. Andrew and I have managed to carve out a nice life with a fair number of spoils. Were we selfless, willing, and ready enough to turn over the larger portions of our wallets to the rearing of a new love? Our clothes budget runs pretty high, and I've seen some children's threads in neighborhood storefronts that transcend fashion and move into the realm of art. Very pricey art. Could we afford it? Were we mature enough to sacrifice cross commerce?

I thought of Manhattan, the other love in both of our lives, which will also be part of us as long as we're still breathing. There are undeniable perks and joys that come with raising a child in the urban wilderness. There are also undeniable hardships. Will that balance tilt in our family's favor?

I thought of my own strained family bond, as well the amazing relationship we have with Andrew's family. Do I have baggage that I need to more fully work through before becoming a dad? Will the tight knits on one side be enough to answer the inevitable questions that he or she will have about the broken seams on the other?

I thought of a Snickers bar, as all the thinking started to make me hungry. But then, after silencing the stomach rumblings, I thought again of all of the kids in the world who deserve a good home with parents who will willingly put their own interests aside to be there for every one of the little one's needs. Warmth. Shelter. Candy bars that are packed with peanuts (which I hear are a big allergen for kids under three). Were we ready?

After weighing the pros and cons (yes, complete with that annoying scales thing that people do with their hands), it didn't take long for it to become clear: *I was going to be a parent!* We were going to be parents. No timeline was set, but the choice was made.

It also didn't take so long for the earlier apprehension to disappear and for sheer excitement to set in. In fact, if I now have any regret about the decision, it is only that I spent so long denying myself the possibility when I could have instead been researching homemade baby food recipes. Oh, and industrial strength, Andrew-rocking alarm clocks.

We decided on adoption, for the aforementioned reason that there are just so many kids worldwide who need good homes. Some sort of fateful wind brought Andrew and I together, and while it sounds hippy-dippy, we put stock in the idea that the same fate will bring us to the child we were meant to love and raise. Our timeline for the process is loose but defined, with efforts to step up when a few more concrete realities shape up. We are as nervous, excited, apprehensive, and happy as any pregnant woman during her own gestation period, except we will have to press forward with these feelings for far more than nine months. That's okay— we can use the extra time to learn and plan, so that by the time we are fortunate enough to be blessed with a new addition, we will be flawless daddies who will never make any errors, never be saddled with worries, and never ...

Oh, who am I kidding? Extra time or not, we'll surely still make loads and loads of mistakes, just like every other parent in the world. But that's okay. We will learn and grow from them as a family.

All the time, we hear social conservatives lambasting gay parents, suggesting that adult activists are putting selfish interests before child welfare. Of all of the attacks they launch against our lives and loves, I truly feel that this is one of the most heartless. Whereas they may find legal or religious reasons to oppose things like marriage, their refusal to wrap their minds around the idea of two same-sex parents taking in and bringing up a new life in the way that they personally see fit is a short-sighted view that's glaringly detrimental to the greater good. Who are the social conservatives to define "normal" families by the method of conception, not parental fitness and *actual* child welfare? Where do they get off seeing the world not through the lens of actuality— wherein heterosexuals sometimes cannot raise their biological children, where LGBT folks do have the ability and desire to conceive, and where LGBT-headed families have existed for eons—but rather through a more convenient looking glass in which only fertile male/female pairings matter, where all of the overpopulated world's kids will magically find homes, and where claims of gay parental corruption are true simply because they want them to be? Why are we told to accept that they are "thinking of the children" simply because they've exalted myopia to the level of "family value"?

The organized opposition's refusal to see the truth and failure to accept ideas that don't jibe with their worldviews is the root problem of all of their antipathy for the LGBT community. It's just that when it comes to parenting, their attacks hurt far more human beings than just adult gays. These particular stones also hurt the children that they claim to be so desperate to "protect."

While I'm clearly biased, I often find gay-headed homes to be the most loving, happy, and peaceful around, with the kids as adjusted as any others. It is my great hope that Andrew and I will soon get to realize our dream of becoming one of those joyous homes—not only for ourselves but also for our future valedictorian, cancer-curing scientist, award-winning actress, and eventual leader of the free world. Yes, we've gone ahead and made those plans too.

Now seriously, parents, tell me: cloth diapers are better for a number of reasons, right? Help me out on this one, as Andrew is quite against the idea at this point!

24) MASTERING PEACE

Imagine, if you will, that you've just bought a new piece of artwork from one of those online auction sites. For the last many months you've been looking for the exact picture that you want to hang above your mantle, and you think you've finally found one that fits that mental image to a T. You're beyond excited for the new addition to your world, and you can't wait to begin your journey together.

As the days pass, you start to imagine how great life will be once it's in your possession. You tell your friends and family that you're expecting something grand and glorious. In fact, they're all getting a little sick of your incessant chatter. But whatever, you don't care. You're glowing too much for any dark clouds. The anticipation is like nothing you've ever felt before—so pure, so true, and so honest. You're sure your friends will understand once they graduate from dorm room posters to grownup reproductions.

After what seems simultaneously like forever and a day, the big moment finally arrives: delivery day. A box that looks like a million other boxes, but this one belongs to you and only you. This is a moment that's meant to forever change your view in ways that you can't predict. The package alone is almost enough to satisfy, but you know that there's much more than just the exterior shell.

You pry open the box to see what's below the surface and SURPRISE— *It looks nothing like what you'd had in mind*. All of the details are the complete opposite of what you'd always envisioned. The lines that you'd thought were straight are actually bent. The colors you'd thought were muted instead stick out like a rainbow. Its frame, which you've expected to be sturdy, is instead slight.

You're completely speechless. Everything you'd imagined for yourself and your new baby are immediately thrown out the door. *This* couldn't possibly ever match *your* life! It doesn't go with anything else in your world! Heck, you've never even seen this kind of painting in the real world, only in movies. Plus you've heard so many bad things about these kinds of creations: that they were made shoddily and could never hope to fit into a traditional world. In fact, aren't they capable of destroying households? That's what you've always been told.

You instinctively know there's no return policy. There never is on something like this. Commitments of this kind are for life—shipping it back is not an option. And despite your despair, you aren't thoughtless enough to put it out on the street, left to fend for itself against the elements. You're stuck with it.

You begin to cry. Bawl, even. This is certainly not the role you were expecting to play on this, the first night with your presumed new bundle of joy.

Those tears then turn to anger. You start to blame yourself, wondering what you did to "cause" this. The rage then turns to the creator, who you seem to think owes you something better than this. Whenever there's a lull or a lack of other targets of your indignation, you choose to wallow in your own self-pity, unabashedly embracing your self-absorbed ego the way you'd hoped to be embracing your new creation.

Until suddenly, a streak of determination comes over you. You know what you'll do: you'll just "fix" the situation. Somehow, some way, you are going to convert this abomination into the sort of item you can show off to friends. You are going to reform it into something you can be proud of. Something that may even be worthy of further reproduction. Something fit for mantles, not dark closets.

Your newfound determination remaining strong, you head to your computer to research any and all available options, when almost immediately, you see something that strikes your fancy: Artistic Reparative Therapy. The sleek website, with lots of formerly-unhappy-but-now-smiling customers, says that through hard work, faith, and determination, one can change a painting from a worthless piece of junk to a priceless masterpiece. They say they can make all of the darkness go away, leaving only light inside the frame. The promise is a total restoration, with the canvas reworked into a more heterogeneous display.

"Sounds good!" you say. You don't even feel the need to consult your painting one more time to see if this is something that seems like a need or possibility. Why bother? Your selfish desire to obtain the picture that was always in your head trumps any further debate. The all-knowing man upstairs—the benevolent sculptor who lives in 2B, or is it 2E?—might say he's the ultimate judge, but for the moment you've appointed yourself the almighty art critic.

But then, just as you're about to sign up and buy the expensive books, videos, CDs, and classes required for the conversion program, you stop yourself. You've already been fooled once, and you just want to do one last bit of research before moving forward with this "ex-junk" program. So you do another search, this time for any available scientific support for the therapy. After all, if they're going to be bold enough to make these almost unbelievable claims, then they better be able to back them up with something concrete. *Right?*

Well, what you find this time is a very different side to the tale. On one site you learn that this sort of process doesn't have the backing of even ONE credible body of science or art. Then you stumble upon an online support group whose members tell you that, many times, those paintings that have gone through the treatment come out the other side in horrible shape. Then from an art lobbying organization, you learn that the vast majority of the artistic community considers this movement to be a dangerous fraud. In about as much time as it took you to find what you had thought was a possibility, you've managed to round up three times as much evidence essentially proving that this supposedly restorative movement is nothing more than a crooked sham. Even in your desperation you retain your logic, and you can't ignore the truth. What you'd hoped was a new beginning has ended before it started.

"It's over," you moan to no one in particular. Your determination has now left you and you collapse in full-blown despair. You turn to the heavens and plead, "WHY? WHY DID YOU GIVE ME THIS? WHY CAN'T I JUST HAVE A NORMAL PIECE OF WORK LIKE MY SISTER? WHAT DID I DO TO DESERVE THIS?

Me, me, me, me, me, me, me!

After several hours, you eventually pry yourself off the floor and wipe away your tears. "Maybe there are other options," you feebly whimper. Like perhaps if you put the right items around it—in the right colors, shaped in the right molds, and constructed in the right fabrics—then maybe your piece will adapt to its surroundings. Its nature may be unattractive to you now, but perhaps you can nurture it into social acceptability?

Or there's always the game of pretend. You think back to your mother's friend, at whose house you used to play as a kid. She had one of these kinds of works of art. Everyone knew it. Everyone could see it. But no one—NO ONE!—dared talk about it. Maybe you too could play the "don't ask, don't tell" game? It might be harder at holidays, when everyone's over with his or her own creations, though if you stand firm in your convictions, it just might work. Maybe?

Oh, who you are kidding? You know this is never going to be an acceptable style for your life. It's an abomination—that's what you're always hearing on TV, quips courtesy of self-appointed artisans who build careers around keeping society's picture looking one certain way. "So just give it up," you tell yourself.

Defeated, you head over to the painting, which has been sitting there through your entire emotional breakdown without so much as a personal consultation. And though you had approached the painting in a mix of sadness and anger, you are stopped in your tracks when you see something on its canvas that captures your eye. Something you'd never noticed before. A speck of yellow that is the most beautiful shade you've ever seen. It is truly like the artist has captured a ray of sunshine and dabbed it on precisely at the heart of the picture.

From that yellow, you start to see the beauty in the other colors as well. The blues begin to pop. The reds become more vibrant. All of the shades, in fact—they're *all* so rich and complex. The colors are rarer than some others, sure. "But wait," you ask with mouth open and eyes wide in surprise "since when is the worth of a creation defined by the majority?"

This is the first time you are looking at the work for what it truly is. And you know what? *It's gorgeous!*

Then it fully hits you. An artistic force has created this painting to be exactly what it is. It's not junk. It's not wrong. It's just not what you'd originally thought. But who the hell are you anyway? What gives you the right to set the parameters of acceptability? How could you have been so blind?

Art is not perfection. Art is not cast into one set pattern. The beauty comes in the differences. Even in the flaws. Now that you've actually looked at it and considered it as a viable option to grace your plane of existence, you realize this work of art will go perfectly with your surroundings. You realize that you can quite proudly show it off to your friends. You're embarrassed to admit it, but it's easy to see that *you* were the one in the wrong, not it. You see now that even though society has sent you certain unfortunate messages, you are not a victim of your surroundings. In fact, it is your duty to find beauty in the full spectrum, not limit the same.

This special creation doesn't need any converting or fixing. It's perfect just the way it was made. *We all are.*

25) SPOILER ALERT: WE WIN

LGBT people have been victimized. However, the LGBT population is not a community of victims. This distinction matters.

Yes, my kindergarten crushes had to be closeted. That demand could not and did not weaken my heart or mind. In fact, in some ways the forced perseverance gave me a sense of passion that might otherwise have been more muted, or at the very least understated. Attraction, and the eventual love associated with it, was not something I would ever take for granted. How could I? Every step required doggedness that was driven by passion, even when society was telling me to put a lid on it.

Yes, I've paused some of my professional goals to take on a fight that neither my fellows nor I ever provoked. Yet in doing so, I've gained knowledge about government and political process that I likely wouldn't have ever taken the time to explore otherwise. There are related social injustices towards which I'd definitely have a lowered consciousness (and conscience), had I not taken on this work. There are people whose intensely inspiring words would remain anonymous to my brain. Some say all politics is local, and in my life, the nature of the game was certainly localized on a core set of issues. It still awakened me on global scale.

Yes, I had to take the wrong gender to prom. Score one for me, since while the rest of my friends were busy making out at the post-prom after party, I took the last Zima. Yeah that's right, Nikki: *I drank it.* 'Twas I. And it was good, too. That's what you get for letting your lust for smooches trump your affection for mid-'90s malt beverages. Deal with it.

Yes, when I married, two years before New York granted in-state same-sex unions, I had to take extraordinary leaps to get hitched, whereas my heterosexual friends can literally roll out of bed and pay a few bucks and find themselves married to an opposite-sex stranger whom they picked up at the security desk on their way in. But marriage is not something that should be taken for granted, and I *certainly* haven't had the opportunity to do so. The meaning of that "I do" was ten times more powerful than it might've been under easier circumstances. The so-called "sanctity" was not lost on me in any way.

Yes, I've sometimes felt like the piece whose jagged edges keep it from fully fitting into my biological family's puzzle. That's true and unfortunate, though the arguments, discomforts, or exclusions have never dimmed my trust in family bonds. I remain eternally open to the possibility of restoring easy kinship with my parents and my siblings. With a few deserved apologies, all will be forgiven. If that's not to be, I will never let that sore spot weaken my truly pro-family outlook.

Yes, in bad situations, I've felt pain. I've cried. I've bitched. I've moaned. I've raised an angry fist. I've marched. I've farted. I've wafted that away and gone back to marching. I've blogged. I've lobbied. I've voted. I've fundraised. I've pontificated. I've farted again and blamed it on the stench of discrimination that still pollutes this world.

Through it all, I've eventually found some semblance of a silver lining. I've always found a way to smile. I've ultimately come to hope.

In the beginning of this book, I defined the LGBT community as being bound by the shared feeling of exclusion. I said we are connected by the difference that almost every non-heterosexual or gender non-conforming person feels, to some degree, at some point in life. This is true, however many chapters later. This forced differentiation is the tape that spans across our ragtag band of consonants, L, G, B, and T.

That said, there's also a more wistful concept that you will find in abundance within the LGBT community—the one that became a cliché during President Obama's historic election, but one that has been piloting the downtrodden for eons pre-Barry. That guiding notion: the concept of hope.

We hope for our own chance at love.

We hope for a world where our existences are no longer political footballs.

We hope for the ability to be as benign and non-controversial as our siblings.

We hope for an end to HIV/AIDS.

We hope for an end to the false belief that we all love pink, since many of our skin tones are much more suited to the autumn palette.

We hope for an unwavering majority of citizens who are willing to stand on principle.

We hope for peace.

We hope. Because really, what choice have we? We can give up and in, or we can look up and out. To give in is to passively allow unfair rules to police this shared experience that we call life. The only active choice is to aspire beyond the negatives; to rise above the bias; to move beyond the barriers, be they emotional, geographic, or physical. We must aim to make a difference, not only in one's personal story but also in the shared human tale.

It's not even that this hope is the yang to differentiation's yin. Rather it's *because* of the ostracisms and barriers that so many LGBT people have cultivated their keen senses of hopefulness. This is actually one positive by-product of the pain. When robbed of certain dreams in the real world, one will often turn inward and dream even more fully and colorfully within one's fantasy life. Those fantasies become tangible visions. These visions become goals. These goals become a plan. And the plan? Well, the plan becomes an aspirational script for a reclaimed life.

It's easy to find this hope in some places. Polling data, for instance. On issues like marriage equality, there's no debating the national trends, the forward momentum, or the age patterns attached to the same. The world is headed in one clear direction. A tipping point has already been reached. Even if the change feels slow in some sense, the polling is undoubtedly with us, not the opposition. We should all draw confidence from this prospective perspective.

We should also find a silver lining in mass media portrayals. The simple truth is that the very same ideas that the organized gay rights opponents use against us in politics would never earn mainstream acceptance in film or television. Or think about the overheated "pro-family" pundits who decry gay people. These folks could never be the sympathetic heads of non-agenda-driven programming because their tales, at least as they have presented them, would never remain sympathetic when given such a treatment. There could never be a homo-shunning equivalent to *Will & Grace* or *Modern Family*, where a mass audience is asked to laugh with and not *at* those who protest gays for sport. That's because even if the population still has some ways to go in terms of acceptance, the public has largely pinpointed what homo-hostility looks like—and the consensus has largely cast our opposition's position as the foible, not the goal. When fleshed out in a script or on a screen and therefore subjected to the noise of mainstream criticism, it's in some ways easier to see that the arguments that have fostered non-acceptance are almost exclusively built around lies and misinformation. A certain movement can say that "gays harm children" and still sometimes use this abstract fallacy to earn the bare majority needed at referendum—but that movement can't negate the certainty of our continued and increased media presence or slap down the patent upper hand that we have in this arena. In this presence, which will itself change even more hearts and minds, we should see a changing channel.

Sticking with our organized opposition, there's also hope in their overwrought logic, which continually fails. One of the most common questions I get from readers: "How can you constantly deal with the anti-gay attacks without getting depressed?" The simple answer can be found in the attacks themselves, which are, quite frankly, about as meritless and waterlogged as sponge-covered umbrellas. If there ever was any resonance, I might stop myself and go, "hmm, maybe they're on to something." Guess what? There isn't any validity. Ever. Not even once in awhile. Instead, I get a constant chain of half-truths, untruths, and insane claims. I'm routinely shocked by the willingness of my political challengers to swim up to the pool of actuality, only to take a steaming dump in those clear waters. In their desperation, I find my inspiration.

Art is another well of expectation, be it music, theatre, visual, or something more twenty-first century. I don't think it's any coincidence that LGBT people have been among our civilization's greatest visionaries or that so much beauty has come from our guiding hands. I truly believe that there is a link there. Whether it's that the stifled desires have led to more of a need for a heightened imagination or if there's something more genetic going on—that is up for debate. Not up for debate is the fact that drive, vision, and aptitude for innovation are all in abundance among LGBTs. Through the creative process, I find a continuing dream that cannot and will not go unfulfilled.

There's also an important area of promise in the little ones who've never known bias. In their unqualified embrace, there is peace. In the non-issue way that the younger crowd views the gay adults in their lives, there is promise. We modern pushers of principled fairness have made something of a faith pact with the enlightened generations who we expect to finally get us to a "culture war" truce. In time's march, I see a sweet dance.

Sticking with the topic of generational shift, we have to look to the growing number of young people who feel safe enough to be true to who they are. Through my work, I get to meet and chat with loads of gay teens and young adults. The most common question they pose to me: "How did you get so stunningly gorgeous?" Then, after I wax poetic about the benefits of moisturizer and good grooming for a good hour or so, the second most common question they throw my way is: "Hey egotistical weirdo—should I come out?" My response to that one is always the same: You should be as out as your situation will allow. For your own mental sake, you must be true to yourself when you first feel comfortable doing so. For your own physical sake, however, you must gauge how coming out might threaten your survival. Most people, including this writer, describe coming out as like having a great weight lifted off of your shoulders. However, if that freedom comes with the price tag of intense ostracism, familial abandonment, inescapable financial hardship, or any major obstacle, then that newfound openness might just come with a whole new set of weights whose burdens may be even heavier. The balance between ability to surmount obstacles versus ability to be free is both personal and unique, and it's up to each individual to determine the formula for his or her self.

Those caveats out of the way, it's hopeful to know that as time marches forward, the balance is tipping ever more towards truth, with the Big Closet lobby feeling the pinch. Through this shuttering, we should all find a promising new light shining through a vastly more ajar door.

Personally, I have to talk about the respite I find in my husband. A heart so pure in a vessel so adorable, this man has made me such a better me. I know you probably have to go clean yourself, since that's such a nauseatingly clichéd bout of romantic sentiment. However, it happens to be true that my baby is a gem among men. In his love I find solace. But it's not just a personal gain, since in that solace I find even more wind for my sails, boosting my push forward on behalf of anyone and everyone who seeks the freedom to experience and enjoy the same.

Then there's technology. Some think it'll destroy us in the end, but I take a decidedly different view. I firmly believe that the equality movement has everything to gain from transparency, while the 'mo foes have everything to lose. We LGBT people have long known that our visibility is key, since a nameless, faceless enemy is much easier to hate than a living, breathing human being. Thanks to the past few decades' rapid explosion and convergence of technology, that visibility is at an all-time high. Because of the ever-expanding social media landscape, fewer and fewer people can genuinely say that they've never known an LGBT person. Conversely, fewer LGBT people are speaking only to their own choirs. In this ability to connect with new and more diverse audiences, I find rich opportunity.

What about law? There's a reason why the organized anti-LGBT crowd has so fully cultivated the "judicial activism" meme. Quite simply, it's because they know that the odds are stacked against them in the court of law. Fair-minded justice bends our way, obviously and ultimately. This is something we're seeing more and more, as even Republican-appointed justices in places like Iowa side with the gay community's equal rights. This is also why the religious right wants issues like marriage to be decided at the ballot box rather than in the chambers of justice: because they *need* places where their skewed views and religious motivations aren't subject to such strict scrutiny. They need a decision that is beholden to people's personal whims, fallacious ads, or mysticisms, rather than one based on equal protection. But since courts *do* traffic in equal protection, providing a fundamentally American safeguard that has historically defended so many minority rights in the past, the professionally anti-LGBT voices know that they need to turn "the people" into the ultimate arbiters of justice and turn the robe-wearers into phantom menaces. In witnessing their obvious fear of this crucial branch of government, I find a great sense of repose.

Then there's the LGBT rights movement itself. Few scrappy bands of fighters have had to put up with so much, coming from so many different sides. Through it all, the commitment and compassion have remained firm. Throw us a bomb, we'll toss it aside. Vote against us, we'll only grow stronger. We've met seemingly insurmountable obstacles with an even more indefatigable spine. In this enduring spirit, I find my own resilience.

But even with all of our strengths and gains, it's still true that the LGBT community will not get much further without the vast and growing community of straight allies who are seeing why this whole thing matters. It's noble to care about a cause that directly affects your day-today life, but it's uniquely honorable to realize that *any* biases against *any* group of people affect us all as a human collective. The dots of connection have become more indelible, and broader swaths are starting to see the clear line between this modern civil rights fight and their own lives. In the LGBT community's ethical allies, I find reason to be optimistic about the essential goodness of the human race.

There are oases of hope all around. No population is more eager to drink from them than those who have long been pushed into the desert. The undeniable reality is that hope is the commodity of the wronged. The professional anti-gay proponents know this, which is why they have worked so hard to flip the script so that it makes them look like the "victims" (of religious persecution, militant agendas, indoctrination, skinny jeans, etc.). However, their false setups will only get them so far. In fact, by wronging us even further via their denials of any wrongdoing, they are giving us another area of hope: the hope that this, like every other prior time in history, is an instance when the side that strives to mask its campaigns of hurt will turn into the side that *needs* to mask its past role in fomenting bias, since prevailing opinion will have evolved enough to grant favor to the unifiers rather than the dividers.

Our driving passion is upwardly mobile. Theirs is regressive. We are standing on a hill, trying to pull everyone up so that we can finally know our collective strength. The organized anti-gays are not only pulling us down; they are telling people that our peak is really crafted out of Pandora's and Satan's dandruff and pubic lice, and that our upwardly mobile efforts only come if we stand on the backs of religious freedom. That is, of course, when they're not otherwise occupied cutting off our ring fingers to spite humanity's face, painting our homes as innately incapable of childproofing, or envisioning our eternal futures as the guests of honor at Beelzebub's backyard BBQ.

It's time for our organized opposition to stop. Done. Finished. Out of business. The biased bullcaca must end, and it must end now. We as a people will one day look back on this wave of discrimination justification with the same disdain we view each and every inequality encouragement that's come before. Even if each civil rights battle has its own defining characteristics and uniqueness, they are all linked, in real and undeniable ways, by the assertion that one certain kind of person is in some way better for having been born a certain way. That outlook has always been based on flawed logic, and this time is no different.

To break free of the marginalized role into which we—decent folks of all sexual persuasions—have been placed, we must first admit there is a historical pockmark currently being lived. The crumbs of this casual acceptance are on the hands of anyone who isn't challenging the same-sex-stigmatizing status quo. While it may not seem at face value that helping gays hop on the marriage caboose or adopt tykes affects the heterosexual realm of existence one iota, the very concept of allowing brothers and sisters to suffer at the hand of prejudice weakens humanity, period. We are all in this game of life together. However, unlike the super-fun board game that shares its name with the concept, a noisy spinner doesn't control our destiny. This one's controlled by each of us, the masters of both our sole and collective futures. Unless those of us who give a damn about the future of our world focus our energies and dedicate a little bit of time to the cause, the opposition not only will win more battles—they *DESERVE* to win them.

So what do we do?

We must take the proverbial step up and let our voices be heard. We must shout our convictions from the rooftops and rage against the machines that crank out the vitriol.

We must be as fearless as they, willing to stand by our beliefs to an almost religious-like degree and to challenge even faith-based claims with a staunch spine.

We must show them the misguided nature of their notions and help them to see the error of that sort of thinking, remembering that it's not really *them* we oppose, but rather their discriminatory actions that we resist.

We must clear up the lies, myths, and misinformation that have been propagated for years, decades, and even centuries.

We must think—really, deeply THINK—beyond media-crafted sound bites and encourage others to do the same.

We must not forget to laugh when someone farts. After all, no matter how old one gets, inopportune gas expulsions remain funny.

We must keep smiling.

We are brothers, sisters, cousins, doctors, hairdressers, friends, and roommates. We are people. We are not second-rate. We are all on the same team; it's time we stand together against true societal ills.

I never forget that I am one of the lucky ones. My course has been bumpy and imperfect, but I write to you, here in my fourth decade of life, feeling nothing short of blessed for having made it to a place of harmony. I see this privilege not as a license to rest, since I realize that none of us will truly be free until we are all free. I see my advantages as a fortuitous set of circumstances that come with a certain responsibility. I am always aware that not everyone has gotten to the place of acceptance that I've been able to reach. I am always cognizant of how differently life could have turned out for me, had I let the senseless controversy rock my senses.

My hope for the world is that we'll one day come to a place where everyone can accept everyone else for who they are, in turn eliminating the need for the anti-gay-challenging work of folks like myself. I not only want to put the anti-gay industry out of business but also to take my own personal pro-gay machine out of commission! It is for those who are still oppressed that I write and fight. It is for my future irrelevancy that I seek gay rights relevancy now.

Am I special? No.
Am I equal? Yes, but not yet in law.
Am I committed to victory? As committed as the Pope is to calling me immoral.
Am I going to prevail? As long as calendars continue to run forward.
Am I good? Eh, **good** as you.

ABOUT THE AUTHOR:

Since founding Good As You (www.goodasyou.org) in 2005, Jeremy Hooper has garnered a reputation as a fresh voice in both the worlds of Internet publishing and gay activism. With a background in theatrical arts and communications, Jeremy approaches LGBT issues with a show-man's spirit, pointing out perceived wrongdoings and folly with the clever exuberance of a seasoned entertainer. Every weekday, Jeremy delves into the rhetoric being spewed by the 'mo foes, as he attempts to diffuse their verbal landmines with truth and wit.

It's a dirty job, but somebody's gotta do it. Or, well, on second thought—nobody *has* or should even *have* to do it. Unfortunately they *do* still have to do it, so Jeremy does.

Jeremy and the Good As You website have been profiled in the gay and lesbian newsmagazine *The Advocate*, featured on the PBS program *In the Life*, on the Logo network, on Sirius radio, and across every corner of the web. As a sought-after consultant, strategist, and speaker, he has worked with leading national organizations like the Human Rights Campaign and GLAAD.

Originally from Nashville, TN, Jeremy now lives on the West Side of Manhattan with his husband, Andrew, and their unbelievably adorable dog, Bosley. Andrew & Jeremy LEGALLY tied the knot in the spring of 2009.

www.ingramcontent.com/pod-product-compliance
Lightning Source LLC
Chambersburg PA
CBHW022104280326
41933CB00007B/251